FRONTIERS OF PSYCHOLOGY

FRONTIERS

OF PSYCHOLOGY

BY JOHN MANN

THE MACMILLAN COMPANY, NEW YORK
COLLIER-MACMILLAN LIMITED, LONDON

© JOHN MANN 1963

Printed in the United States of America

The Macmillan Company, New York
Collier-Macmillan Canada, Ltd., Toronto, Ontario

Library of Congress catalogue card number: 63–15276

DESIGNED BY CHRISTIAN OHSER

Contents

FRONTIERS OF PSYCHOLOGY

Introduction

The Nature of
Modern Psychology

Modern psychology might be described as a schizophrenic octopus: it is split in the middle and extends in all directions. The basic division in this discipline is between the search for knowledge and its application. The tentacles are the various subdisciplines within psychology that grow ever farther away from one another as they reach out from the creature's center.

There are many ways in which psychology can be subdivided. Psychologists in this country use the following distinctions in order to organize themselves within the larger body of the American Psychological Association:

1. General Psychology
2. Teaching of Psychology
3. Experimental Psychology
4. Evaluation and Measurement
5. Developmental Psychology
6. Personality and Social Psychology
7. The Psychological Study of Social Issues
8. Esthetics
9. Clinical Psychology
10. Consulting Psychology

3

11. Industrial and Business Psychology
12. Educational Psychology
13. School Psychology
14. Counseling Psychology
15. Public-Service Psychology
16. Military Psychology
17. Maturity and Old-Age Psychology
18. Engineering Psychology
19. Psychological Aspects of Disability
20. Consumer Psychology

These categories are not necessarily the most logical that could be formed, but they have served psychologists who wished to make such distinctions.

In order to clarify the nature of modern psychology by using the terms formulated by psychologists and prepare the ground for a description of the frontiers of the field, it will be helpful to discuss briefly each of the above divisions. Such a description can take two forms. First, reasonable distinctions can be drawn between any given category and all others. Second, one can describe the actual work that is carried on by psychologists in each of these areas, thus providing an operational definition. Since each approach enriches the observer's perception of the complex total field of psychology, both will be used.

The first division, *general psychology,* is a catch-all field to which all psychologists belong but to which few owe their primary allegiance. Individuals in this area consider such problems as "the general psychology of knowledge," "the social psychology of the psychological experiment," or "the current status of Soviet psychology."

All these topics are broad in scope and involve many subtopics within some general framework. General psychology therefore appears to include the philosophy of psychology and other topics within the field that do not fall naturally into the other more specific divisions.

The *teaching of psychology* is a relatively specialized area within the broader field of educational psychology. All psychologists who teach in universities may contribute logically to this area by their evaluation of their experience in the teaching of psychology to students. Persons in this area study such topics as "student reactions to student-centered teaching," "IBM punchboard construction item (automated) self teaching," or "the shortage of psychology professors in liberal arts colleges." Thus this division is concerned both with the effects of specific teaching devices and the more general problem of supplying the demand for competent teachers of psychology at the university level.

Experimental psychology refers strictly to scientific psychology in the most limited sense. Experimental psychologists are, as one would expect, usually found in laboratories, conducting carefully formulated and precisely executed experiments involving the effects of the systematic variation of one or two variables on a third. Experimental psychologists often work with animals rather than with human subjects—in particular with the rat, the ape, and the guinea pig. Animals are favored as subjects by such psychologists because physiological variations can be induced without incurring ethical or moral resistance from society at large. One can decorticate a cat with impunity, if it is for a scientific purpose, but not a human being. In addition, the use of animals allows the psychologist to control the heredity of the subjects that he studies. The family history of a rat may be recorded and directed for many generations, thus assuring a known and pure strain. While some psychologists have, on occasion, recommended rational mating procedures for human beings that would produce an equivalent result, it does not appear that human mating is likely to be subject to rational or scientific ends in the near future.

The studies conducted by experimental psychologists often have rather exotic titles. Consider the following samples: "Differential satiation effects of central self-stimulation and metabolic feedback products on hunger-drive mechanisms," "Effects of component duration on multiple schedule performance or temporal chromatic induction." However, rarefied topics such as these have their equivalent in other areas of psychology, as will be documented in the following paragraphs.

The experimental psychologist is identified more by his method than by his content area. He may study such diverse topics as motivation, sensation, perception, or concept formation, but whichever topic he investigates, the experimental psychologist typically proceeds with great care in the selection, formulation, and execution of the experimental design that he follows.

The term *evaluation and measurement* covers the methodological and statistical problems that underlie the application of scientific methods to psychological problems. Perhaps the central difficulty faced by the psychological researcher is the variability of his subject. Each human being is different from all others, and therefore the results obtained from the study of one human being or animal do not necessarily apply to others. Such a problem does not arise in the study of elements or compounds. One atom of oxygen may be considered to be identical to another, and one sample of salt tastes like another, as long as the sample itself is pure.

With human samples the only principal that can be taken for granted is variation. It is the problem of psychologists who study evaluation and measurement to evolve new instruments, methods, and mathematical statistics that utilize human variation as a means for specifying and controlling experimental error. Such procedures do not and cannot eliminate error from scientific research, but they can identify and make quantitative its extent. In this way the probability associated with any statement of fact can be specified.

Studies conducted in this area may be of an equally esoteric nature as those of experimental psychology. They may be obscure even to psychologists who specialize in other fields. Consider, for example, parts of the following titles: "Matrix reduction and approximations to principal axes," "The latent structure of the simplex," and "A graphic method for the perimetric test for association."

Developmental psychology provides us with our first clear example of basic scientific subject matter in modern psychology. The developmental psychologist studies the processes by which human beings develop from infancy to adulthood. He employs a "longitudinal approach" for the study of a variety of basic psychological processes. Thus, he may investigate a number of topics, such as intelligence, learning, and personality. However, he is not concerned with a cross-sectional account of these areas; his interest lies rather in tracing the areas' development over a period of time.

Some developmental psychologists may specialize in childhood and others in adolescence, but the longitudinal approach is common to them all. Studies by developmental psychologists are relatively accessible to the layman. They cover such topics as "achievement inducing and independence granting—synergistic parental role components," "sharing in preschool children as a function of amount and type of reinforcement," or "antecedents of personality differences in guilt responsivity." In practice the work of developmental psychologists extends into many other areas of psychology. It is the nature of their approach rather than the content of their studies that particularly distinguishes them from their colleagues.

At one time *personality* and *social psychology* were two separate psychological topics. In fact, in most universities they are taught separately. However, psychologists themselves now group them together. The main reason for this method of organization is that in any study of personality social influences on individual personality formation must be considered. In practice, however, the two areas often are studied separately. The subject of personality involves the description and explanation of individual human behavior in terms of certain general, relatively fixed responses that characterize the individual rather than the situation, such as aggressiveness, sociability, energy, and so forth. In addition to the description of the individual, the psychological study of personality involves the theoretical and experimental attempt to explain given personality formations in terms of the dynamics of individual adjustments to various intra- and inter-individual events.

Studies of personality involve such topics as "self-body recognition in schizophrenia," "threshold reduction under hypnosis," and "response to attitude similarity-dissimilarity as a function of affiliation need."

In contrast to the focus on the individual that characterizes the study of personality, social psychology studies the influence of social and group forces on individual development and behavior. Social psychology thus lies in the borderland between sociology and psychology. There are social psychologists who are trained as psychologists and others who have received a degree in sociology. In theory "sociological social psychologists" place greater emphasis than do "psychological social psychologists" on the group as the primary focus. In practice, however, it is often difficult to make a distinction between the two.

Much of the work in social psychology is organized around the concept of interaction as the basic unit of analysis. But the actual content of social-psychological studies is rather broad, since it concerns the interaction between a variety of psychological and social forces, all of which may be studied separately by other specialists. Among numerous examples of social-psychological studies are the following: "determining factors of group structure," "self-enhancement and interpersonal attraction," and "humor judgments as a function of reference groups." The increasing application of psychological findings to various applied social settings has increased the importance of social psychology in recent years.

The Society for the Psychological Study of Social Issues (SPSSI) was formed by social psychologists who, in addition to their scientific interests, sought to apply the findings of psychology to various pressing social problems ranging from delinquency and racial prejudice to problems of political action and organization. At meetings of the SPSSI topics such as the following are covered: "determinants of political behavior," "social organization, self-esteem, and mental health," and "the psychological implications of increasing population." The SPSSI is not itself an independent area in psychology so much as an expression of the need that is felt by psychologists to consider various practical issues and their relation to psychological research in progress.

Esthetics is a relatively well-defined and limited area of investigation that actively involves only a few psychologists. Esthetics is concerned with the scientific experimental investigation of various sensory and artistic phenomena, with the purpose of determining how the ordering of different stimuli are related to variations in perceptual satisfaction. In addition, psychologists in this area are concerned with the identification and measurement of the esthetic response, as well as the relation that this aspect of personality has to other facets of individual expression and development. Studies of esthetics include the following kinds of topics: "painting preferences and their justification in childhood," "dimensions and correlates of texture preferences," and "drugs and the visionary experience."

Perhaps the most widely held stereotype of psychologist is that of the *clinical psychologist*. Clinical psychology concerns the application of psychological findings to the treatment of mental disorder. The two most prominent activities of the clinical psychologist involve personality testing and psychotherapy.

The most often debated function of the clinical psychologist concerns his performance of psychotherapy. In particular, the psychiatrist, trained as a medical specialist, has claimed that psychotherapy was medicine, and, as such, should be performed by a doctor. Psychologists have countered this argument with the one that their training in the principles and applications of psychotherapy is as good or better than that of the psychiatrists, since it emphasizes the study of normal principles of behavior, which form the logical frame of reference for any study of psychopathology. Regardless of the relative merits of the various sides of this controversy, clinical psychologists are in fact performing psychotherapy in a variety of settings, including clinics, hospitals, and private offices. As practitioners their effort and attention is devoted to testing and treating persons with various types of mental illnesses. As students of abnormal behavior they perform such studies as: "some effects of brain lesions on MMPI profiles," "the intuitive formation and scientific evaluation of hypotheses in dream interpretation," and "client likability as a variable in the study of psychotherapy."

Closely related to clinical psychology is the area of *consulting psychology*. As the name implies, a psychologist in this area is concerned with the opportunities and difficulties that arise when psychologists are called in as consultants in a variety of situations. The breadth of this area is determined by the agencies requesting the consultation rather than by the psychologists themselves. These agencies include mental-health units, industry, and education systems. Consulting psychologists often are trained as clinical psychologists. It is only in as much as their activities exceed the typical clinical activities of testing and therapy that they are described as consulting psychologists. However, the definition of this area—and the persons who work in it—is still fluid.

Industrial and business psychology has constituted a clearly defined separate area of psychology for many years. The industrial psychologist is not a consultant called in from another area but a psychologist who specializes in the problems of business and industry. These problems concern such varying topics as executive selection, conditions associated with productivity, and leadership training. The limitations on the functioning of the psychologist in industry are essentially those imposed upon him by business executives, rather than those which he imposes on himself. Typical studies in industrial psychology involve "job difficulty versus job worth as criteria in job evaluation," "the effect of communicating performance appraisals to subordinates" and "organization size and member participation." While most industrial psychologists are located in specific industries, there are a number of research laboratories located in university business schools that carry on comprehensive research programs in problems relating to industrial psychology.

Educational psychology involves the study of the learning process and the evaluation of the effectiveness of alternate methods for learning different types of material. The teachers of psychology, previously described, belong, in a sense, to this broader group of learning psychologists. However, educational psychologists are not limited to a particular content area. They maintain an interest in all aspects of the learning situation, including the study of teacher-pupil characteristics, analysis of the learning process itself, and the comparison of the effects of the different methods of presenting material to be learned, including the effects of teaching machines. Typical studies in the area of educational psychology involve "relationships between divergent thinking abilities and teacher ratings of high-school students," "automation and the profession of education," and "human curiosity as a function of information input."

Closely allied to the educational psychologist is the *school psychologist*. The school psychologist is not primarily a researcher. His duties include the testing and guidance of students who have intellectual, social, and emotional difficulties in school. The school psychologist administers tests of educational achievement and provides remedial instruction and limited psychotherapy. He may also counsel teachers, individually or in groups. In general, the function of the school psychologist is determined by the educational administration, so that the job is defined differently in different school systems. However, when school psychologists perform research they act very much like educational psychologists. Some typical examples of such research involve: "the mental skills employed in solving arithmetic reasoning problems," "adjustment and acceptance of mentally superior children in regular and special fifth-grade classes in a public school system," and "relationships of children's interests to school achievement."

The area of *counseling psychology* falls midway between clinical psychology and school psychology. All three groups administer psychological tests and engage in varying degrees of therapy. In contrast to the school psychologist, the counseling psychologist advises university students and adults rather than grade-school and high-school children. In contrast to clinical psychologists, the counseling psychologist is primarily interested in vocational selection rather than personality reorganization. Counseling psychologists are almost without exception located in university clinics where they concern themselves with counseling only insofar as it is necessary because of the failure of the client to perform adequately in school or work situations. The counseling psychologist is reality oriented rather than psychodynamically oriented, differing in this manner from the clinical psychologist. It must be admitted, however, that it is often difficult to separate psychological counseling from psychotherapy. The distinction between the two is usually drawn in terms of depth of interpretation and severity of the personality problems that are studied. But these distinctions are not always followed in practice. Studies in counseling psychology are more likely to be concerned with the tests that counselors use to assess their clients rather than the therapeutic aspects of counseling, though both types of investigations occur. Examples of studies in this area are: "the California Psychological Inventory as a potential screening device in an academic setting," "parental identification in relation to vocational interest patterning," "some relationships between therapists' style of participation and measures of case outcome."

The next division contains the *public-service psychologists*. In recent years the federal government has employed great numbers of psychologists in various capacities in the civil service and governmental branches. These psychologists consider themselves to be a separate group characterized by their employment in various public services. While they form an occupational entity, their work does not appear to be conceptually very different from industrial psychologists on the one hand and school psychologists on the other, except that their employer is more complex than the school system and less dependent on business conditions than the employers of industrial psychologists. Psychologists in the public service are concerned with such topics as "attitudes toward federal employment, as measured by group interview and questionnaire," "performance on manual and electric typewriters in the United States Employment Service typing test," and "communicating mental-health information to nongovernment agencies."

A relatively new and important development in psychology is the application of psychological knowledge to military problems. *Military psychology* covers a variety of topics, ranging from the selection of officer material to the design of efficient man-machine weapons systems. Political and historical conditions have accelerated the growth of this branch of psychology. Since psychologists in the military often have direct access to funds and subjects not easily available to psychologists working in university settings, they have been able to expand the area of their interest and its applications with relative ease.

The military psychologist bears a resemblance to both the industrial psychologist and the psychologist in government or public service, but the character of his work is usually more basic than theirs. The military psychologist is one of the many indirect benefactors of the vast sums spent on the creation and development of our advanced weapons technology. The problems he must solve often are created by these new weapons, so that the growth of military psychologists include such topics as "individual differences and the teaching machine in military training," "attitude changes in small groups under prolonged isolation," and "a method of job analysis for the Air Force."

In direct contrast to the problems created by advances in military technology are the problems created by the increase in life span produced by recent medical discoveries. Problems related to *maturity and old age* have attracted a number of psychologists working in such varied settings as universities, Veterans Administration hospitals, and the National Institute of Mental Health. These psychologists are grouped together because of their common interest in the problems of the aged, rather than any similarity in their previous training. This fact is illustrated by the broad range of studies that persons interested in this area are conducting on animal as well as human subjects. Consider, for example, the following topics: "response variability, memory, and learning in young and old chimpanzees," "intellectual functioning in aged mental hospital patients," and "aging and death: the strategy of survival." While the problems that are studied by psychologists interested in maturity and old age are certainly of social significance, they represent a relatively small segment of the total area that the field of psychology encompasses.

Engineering psychologists have assumed an ever greater importance with the coming of the space age and the increasing emphasis that is being placed on the study of the relation of man to the machines that he has created. The engineering psychologist is concerned intimately with the problem of automation, the proper application of the electronic computer to problems in the behavioral sciences, and the design of machines to suit the unique capacities and limitations of the human operator. His work overlaps, in part, that of the military psychologists, but the engineering psychologist has a broader focus on problems relating men and machines though he does not extend his interest to problems of training and selection. Typical studies in engineering psychology involve such topics as: "the effects of whole-body vibrations in the three directions upon human performance," "multi-dimensional nonredundant encoding for a visual symbolic display," and "a model for predicting two-man team performance in man-machine systems." Engineering psychology is a relatively recent development that has been encouraged by a widespread demand for such services by large corporations engaged in the design of complex machinery.

A relatively small group of psychologists are concerned with the problem of *psychological aspects of disability*. These psychologists are, as one would anticipate, usually located in medical or university installations. They are not directly concerned with the medical diagnosis and treatment of the physically disabled, but rather with the effect of the disability on the personality and adjustment of the patient. While this interest is essentially clinical and therapeutic in orientation, studies of such patients do have direct implications for theories of personality. These studies are of the following character: "psychological remotivation of the chronic mental patient," "a study of the imagery of the chronic mental patient with the semantic differential," and "perceptual and perceptual-motor dissociation in cerebral palsied children."

A final, recently formed division of psychology is concerned with the lucrative question of *consumer psychology*. Psychologists interested in this area generally work for businesses or in industrial and other corporations and are therefore primarily interested in the relative effects of different advertising techniques, the psychology of the consumer, his image of corporations, and related questions. While psychologists have worked in industry for a number of years only recently has their importance been widely recognized by the business community at large. Examples of the studies conducted by psychologists in this area include: "curiosity or disbelief: a study of cognitive dissonance engendered by advertising," "factor analysis of adult male viewing behavior," and "the influence of repetition and familiarization on consumer preference." The recent excitement caused by studies of the perception of advertising stimuli without awareness of the perception also falls within the direct concern of consumer psychology.

The preceding description of the various facets and divisions of modern psychology constitutes a description of the arms of the octopus. A review of these divisions suggests a number of significant conclusions about the nature of modern psychology itself. Perhaps the most striking generalization that can be made is that most, if not all, of the distinctions between fields of modern psychology can be characterized as either basic or applied in character. A basic aspect of psychology is one in which a particular area of knowledge is studied without any direct interest in immediate practical application. From this viewpoint general psychology, experimental psychology, evaluation and measurement, developmental psychology, personality and social psychology, and esthetics can be viewed as basic aspects of the field. All other divisions are either partially or totally applied in character. Thus the school psychologist and consulting psychologist are almost wholly involved in practical problems presented by individuals in need of help. On the other hand the engineering psychologist falls somewhere in the no man's land between the basic and the applied. His interests usually are applied but his research is often basic.

The distinction between the applied and basic aspects of modern psychology is extremely important. At the beginning of this chapter psychology was described as a schizophrenic octopus. The schizophrenia that is ascribed to this field is the deep split between those persons whose primary interest is in research and those whose primary activity and aim is service. While persons in either of these general areas may have had in common the same basic graduate training, their interests, values, and technical competence vary so greatly that communication between them often proves very difficult. Officially, the basic researcher sets the standard for psychology, since the psychologist aims first at the image of a scientific psychology. Introductory college textbooks in psychology are illustrative of the strong emphasis on basic experimental psychology that is the official policy of most psychologists, whatever their area of interest. However, the fact is that most psychologists are not scientists except in a very general sense. A recent study of psychologists conducted under the auspices of the National Science Foundation showed that only 27 per cent of the psychologists specialized in basic fields of psychology. The remaining three-fourths were engaged in applied and service activities. As anyone who has engaged in activities of this kind is well aware, the knowledge supplied by basic scientific studies is always far behind the immediate needs of the practitioner, as he faces complex and ambiguous situations that require immediate action. As a result the basic and applied psychologists tend to grow away from each other. The one has little to contribute to the other at any given moment, and both tend to think that the other's interest and activity is in part misguided.

The reasons for this basic division in this field are a result of the conception of psychology that is taught in the graduate schools. In contrast to psychiatry, social work, nursing, and other service professions, the psychologist is trained both as a researcher and as a practitioner. In theory the dual training is meant to enable him to understand both of these differing viewpoints. In practice he usually chooses to emphasize one and let the other become atrophied. The average psychological practitioner working in an applied setting is not interested or involved in research efforts. He doesn't have the time, and is not always convinced of its value. On the other hand the researcher in a university or laboratory tends to view people as subjects for study rather than as clients in need of help.

However, all psychologists, in comparison to those in the other service professions, place greater emphasis on research in all areas, applied and basic, as evidenced by the kinds of studies previously described in relation to each division of psychology.

The nature of these descriptions serves to emphasize another general conclusion that can be drawn about modern psychology—namely, that each area tends to have its own concepts, instruments, and vocabulary. As each division grows, it tends to become farther removed from areas to which it was initially related. This is in part a defensive maneuver that is made in order to clarify differences between areas that are initially quite similar. In part, however, the differences are real. Metaphorically these differences may be symbolized by the outstretched tentacles of the octopus. The farther one moves along the tentacles from the center of the animal, the greater the distance between adjacent tentacles. Thus the experimental psychologist may find it difficult to understand the clinical psychologist; the military psychologist may be incomprehensible to the developmental psychologist. All these difficulties are magnified in the minds of interested laymen who lack the graduate-school background common to all professional psychologists who have received the Ph.D. degree.

As in many other fields of science, the layman is shut out from direct access to the research literature by his unfamiliarity with the technical jargon and the theoretical and methodological presuppositions that underlie it. In part this condition is unavoidable, since science spawns specialization. The difficulty in scientific communication is generally directly proportional to the progress of the science itself.

However, many of the social and behavioral sciences, including psychology, are somewhat self-conscious about their relatively recent arrival in the scientific community. They therefore employ vocabulary and theory in a more esoteric manner than is warranted by the facts, in order to reinforce the impression that they are indeed dealing with highly intricate and complex scientific matters that the layman could not possibly understand. Such a tendency is, of course, to be found throughout science. It presents a particular problem to anyone interested in learning of recent work that has not been translated by a science writer for popular consumption. Unfortunately, it also slows down scientific progress, since after a certain point even psychologists in different areas cannot really understand each other.

Many of the internal difficulties experienced by modern psychology can be attributed to growing pains. Between 1920 and 1950 the number of psychologists who belonged to the American Psychological Association increased by a factor of more than 18. Among a sampling of other professional scientific societies, this figure exceeds all other membership increases. The nearest competitor was the American Physical Society, whose size was multiplied by seven over the thirty-year period. These figures testify eloquently to the fact that whatever ethical, philosophical, semantic, and methodological problems beset psychology, the importance of psychology has been established in the society at large.

Occasionally critics are likely to question whether this growth resembles an infection rather than a normal rate of development. However, such criticism is generally allied to anti-intellectual attempts to return to prescientific, pre-hydrogen-bomb days when men knew less but could sleep more. The growth exists. Modern psychology exists. It will continue to grow along the lines that have been described, and along others that are not as yet formulated. The rate of growth depends partly on historical conditions and partly on public support.

Financial support plays a key role in the growth of all science. In psychology, the differential application of financial reward has produced a peculiar situation that tends to undercut the whole area. In general, the applied aspects of psychology are rewarded more highly than those directly involving the more basic scientific development of the subject. The inevitable result is a continuous leaking of valuable talent into the applied areas, where it is directly focused on realistic human situations, but lost to the more important long-range cumulative effort of obtaining scientific knowledge. When this situation is reversed, as in certain areas in engineering psychology, rapid scientific progress usually occurs. But in many basic areas, rewards are disproportionately low. In such cases the growth of the applied areas are accelerated while the growth of the basic scientific knowledge that is ultimately needed to support the applied areas is slowed.

In addition to this differential in rewards, the absolute amount of money spent on psychological research is extremely small in comparison to that spent by the government and other large organizations on "hard sciences" such as physics, chemistry, engineering, and so forth. For example, in 1958 the various agencies of the federal government spent six hundred and seventy-three million dollars on research in the physical sciences but only twenty-three million in psychological research. This is a ratio of approximately thirty to one.

When money is spent, as it is, in such areas as man-machines relations, or computer simulation of human behavior, results are usually quickly forthcoming.

All the behavioral and social sciences share with psychology the chronic shortage of adequate research funds. This condition is due in part to the relatively recent graduation of many of these areas from the humanities to the sciences. In addition, however, there is a deep-seated distrust on the part of many officials and a large segment of the general population with regard to the scientific study of human behavior. The average person likes to feel that he and his actions are in some sense unique. The scientist, however, looks on each person only as an example of a general tendency. That which is unique, if it exists, is ignored for the purpose of scientific generality. Such an approach is distasteful to the ordinary individual who resents being depersonalized. In addition, many people are afraid that the behavioral sciences may succeed in learning so much about man that his every action will be manipulated with scientific precision. This fear is not entirely unwarranted, as recent developments in advertising, brainwashing, and studies in hypnotism and reinforcement-conditioning suggest. On the other hand, there is really no alternative to progress if one's enemies are advancing along similar lines. The problem is rather one of coping with the advances as they occur, since it is safe to assume that they *will* occur. It is only the pace of the discoveries that is unknown.

Another indirect effect of the psychologist's growing pains, in addition to what has been outlined above, is his oversensitivity to the philosophical tradition from which psychology sprang. Until the late nineteenth century psychology and philosophy were considered to be one general area. Scientific psychology in the modern sense was unknown. The origin of modern psychology is usually related to the establishment of the first laboratory for the study of psychology by William Wundt in 1879. By this dating modern psychology is a little over eighty years old.

When a science is that close to its origin in time, it is bound to be somewhat oversensitive about its parents. It is for this reason that any tendency toward philosophical specialization in the absence of experimentation is greeted with great suspicion in psychology. The relative youth of psychology also may help to explain why certain subjects of interest and possible significance, such as extrasensory perception, are regarded as taboo, though a few hardy investigators ignore the general opinion and subject even these problems to scientific investigation.

It is one of the ironies of history that Sigmund Freud, who never performed a psychological experiment in his life, and who engaged in extremely general and broad philosophical speculations about a variety of psychological topics, is considered by psychologists as the outstanding contributor to the field, even though he ignored both the methodological techniques of scientific psychology and violated the unspoken law against philosophical speculation.

However Freud must be viewed as the exception who proves the rule. Even Freud, if he were working today, probably would find it impossible to win a wide audience among psychologists unless he submitted his theories to direct experimental tests.

It may have struck the reader that the description that has been offered of modern psychology is at variance with the popular notion of the psychologist as therapist and tester. Quantitatively both of these functions are important in accounting for the actual behavior of psychologists in the field. But qualitatively it is neither therapy alone nor testing alone that advances psychology, but programs of systematically conceived research. The general public is usually unaware either of the existence or the nature of this research until its indirect effects filter down to it. But it is this research that forms the ever-receding borderline between the known and the unknown. In the most literal sense this research is the frontier of psychology.

But, as has been abundantly shown, there really is no such animal as psychology, in the singular. Rather, there are psychologies and psychologists who share certain common principles and traditions but who differ in interest, vocabulary, and technique. Thus each area in psychology has its own frontier that may or may not overlap with other frontiers formed in other areas. Further, the rate of growth in all areas of psychology is not the same. Some areas are sedate; others are almost manic in their intensity. Therefore, while each area must have its own frontier, the relative significance of these frontiers is not equivalent.

Unfortunately any assessment of the significance of a given psychological frontier must be subjective. A psychologist in a given area always will tend to assume that his area is one of the most important in psychology (or if it isn't, it should be). Therefore any psychologist's selection of frontiers is bound to be biased and to some extent unique.

In a different sense, the differential weighing of frontiers in terms of their relative importance involves an attempt to outguess the future. It is only a supposition at any given moment as to which areas shall prosper in the reign of time and which shall not. The significance of a frontier can, however, be judged by several different criteria. The most obvious criterion is the one of present activity. Any area that is in a state of great accelerating activity is presumably an important one in which significant discoveries are likely to be made. A second criterion that can be employed is one of latent significance. A given frontier may be almost totally ignored at the present, but seem to contain within it great possibilities for future growth and exploitation. A third criterion is one of social significance. If the results obtained in a given area are likely to have immediate and important social consequences, the area itself may have an importance out of proportion to the extent of its actual contribution to general psychological knowledge.

Each of these criteria, in varying combinations, has been employed in order to select the limited number of psychology topics that are discussed in the following pages. Other selections might have been made on the basis of other criteria. Certainly the list of significant frontiers could be expanded with justification. Some psychologists reading over the list may feel rejected, while others may feel embarrassed at the amount of attention devoted to their work. It is difficult to strike a middle ground when describing the growth of a complex organism such as modern psychology. But the very difficulty of the undertaking makes the attempt worthwhile.

Any description of a frontier attempts to translate new and generally inaccessible materials into a palatable form. Such a process tends to do violence to the complexity and specificity of the actual research in progress. Clarity is obtained at the expense of truth. The reader must therefore be ready, in certain instances, to accept incompleteness as the price of accuracy, and in other cases to accept partial truth as the price of generality.

In the future rather than the present lies the answer to the question of the significance of any frontier. The best that can be done now is to make an educated guess based on an informal calculation of future probability. And in this spirit the present work is undertaken.

Chapter One

The Psychological Aspects
of Space Travel

The most literal frontier of psychology is outer space. While space has existed as a scientific concern for thousands of years, only recently have its psychological implications been drawn. As recently as 1960 the *Annual Review of Psychology,* devoted to the yearly summary of psychological research, contained no reference to space travel. This omission serves as indirect documentation for the fact that in the early days of rocket development little thought was devoted to the problem of maintaining man in space, if once he arrived there. It was natural that engineering problems were paramount in the initial stages of missile development. However, as early as 1960 physical scientists were saying that they had the information and experience to place a manned space vehicle in orbit around the earth and bring it back. Having conquered the basic ballistic problems, it was natural that greater attention had to be given to the maintenance of man in space in psychological terms. Physical scientists and project administrators who earlier had reduced man's importance as a functioning organism to that of an inconvenient passenger in an otherwise well-designed vehicle, or who had hoped to design man out of space altogether as an unnecessary inconvenience in the gathering of scientific data, were forced to change their views, both because of political conditions and because of re-evaluation of the possible contribution that man might make to a successful space mission. At the same time it became evident that man would impose upon space travel a large variety of problems that would have to be carefully considered if a manned space flight were to have a successful consummation.

The more thought that was given to these problems, the more diverse and intense they became. They were there all the time, of course, waiting to be discovered. But their diversity and character were rather awesome to those who uncovered them. In general, it can be said that almost every basic area of psychology has some direct application and implication for space travel. This topic is therefore a useful one for us to describe first, since it demonstrates the way in which many separate aspects of psychology can all be focused on a single frontier, each complementing the other. In addition this subject is helpful in illustrating the way in which psychology can be combined with other sciences in order to complete the understanding of a complex man-machine interaction system.

In the Introduction it was stated that the basic fields of psychology included experimental psychology, physiological psychology, evaluation and measurement, developmental psychology, personality and social psychology, and esthetics. All these fields except developmental psychology and esthetics are directly related to manned space projects. In addition, the applied areas of clinical psychology, military psychology, and engineering psychology are directly relevant. At the present time the contributions from each of these fields are not equally significant. In the future the ordering of importance may shift. Thus engineering and military psychology, which presently occupy a position of great importance, may be reduced in significance, whereas the importance of social and clinical psychology may be increased.

For purposes of clarity the contribution made by each field of psychology will be described separately. In actuality, of course, all approaches are being investigated simultaneously, and the findings in one area tend to interact with those of another. Thus studies of sensory deprivation in physiological psychology may lead to new kinds of investigation in the area of personality; studies of the senses may lead engineering psychologists to revise their notions of instrumentation design.

For technical and historical reasons the exploration of space has developed from a ballistical problem to a biological problem and finally into a psychological problem. Because of this ordering of development, it is natural that early interest in psychology was in the areas of physiology and the functioning of the body as a biological organism, rather than upon the implications of personality theory. This concern was realistic, since spacemen must, before anything else, be able to survive. But as survival problems are resolved, greater attention will inevitably be placed on the quality of survival rather than on its simple maintenance. While the contribution of psychology to space travel is bound to change in character as a function of general progress, it is still possible to outline the probable directions of such contributions in the various areas mentioned, though in some cases they may be in their infancy.

THE CONTRIBUTION OF MILITARY PSYCHOLOGY

While all men hope that the exploration of space will be a peaceful enterprise, it is nevertheless true that the tremendous impetus given to such exploration at this time is military and political. It is therefore natural that many of the previous studies in military psychology should be applied directly to missile and space problems.

These contributions have taken several forms. First, military psychology contains a backlog of information about the selection of men for appropriate military placement. Second, military psychologists have considerable experience with training procedures in teaching selected men new skills. Third, military psychologists have experience with complex man-machine relationships such as are found in radar stations, where a number of men are involved in the surveillance and guidance of complex radar and warning equipment. Fourth, military psychologists have conducted studies of the effects of enforced confinements on small groups of men in equipment such as the atomic submarine, and hostile environments such as the South Pole. Finally, military psychologists, particularly those connected with the Air Force, have a variety of experiences with the effects of various physical and mental stresses on the performance of airplane pilots whose task is similar in many respects to that of an astronaut. This list could be extended, but it would begin to overlap unnecessarily with other psychological areas in which such topics are described more logically.

It is not possible to summarize the contribution of military psychology in any of these areas. Findings are accumulating too rapidly. Any review is out of date by the time that it is published. All that will be attempted is the presentation of certain typical studies in this and all other areas of psychology that will be described in this chapter. In this manner some sense of the work being done may be transmitted, though its full breadth and intricate detail cannot be shown.

The selection of astronauts presents a number of problems that will change with the passage of time. At present there are relatively few rockets and many men to choose from. With the improvement of technology the situation may be reversed, but at present the selection of personnel can err on the side of caution. Thus any possible single reason for rejection can be used as cause for such rejection, simply because so many candidates are available.

In general the experience of military psychologists indicates that it is best to use seasoned pilots as astronauts, since they already have passed successfully through situations that are similar to those that the astronaut may face. Such a rather simple solution is satisfactory for the present, but in the future greater selectivity will be necessary. However, previous experience in pilot selection has shown that while candidates for pilot training can be selected by the use of appropriate tests, the actual later success of the pilot beyond training school is difficult to predict. Thus the problem of selection may be difficult to solve.

Military experience in training men for new positions has indicated strongly that, while specific drill in new skills is helpful, the more realistic the training situation, the easier will be the transfer of learning. This principle is applied in training combat troups by the use of maneuvers. It is also seen in the design of various space-age training equipment. Each of these machines is designed to reproduce some facet of the astronaut's physical experience of flight under controlled conditions, in such a way that variations can be introduced at will by the trainer.

Perhaps the most graphic of these training devices is the SAM space cabin simulator. SAM is actually a life-size model of a space cabin complete with instruments and controls. The information fed into SAM is controlled by the trainer. The astronaut is required to make appropriate responses to each problem presented by the trainer.

The third application of military psychology involves the knowledge obtained from previous experience with complex man-machine systems. While some of this work verges on the area of engineering psychology, the focus is somewhat different. The military psychologist is faced with situations in which man-machine combinations either detect sudden and lethal danger, as in a radar network, or are involved in the operation of inflicting destruction, as in modern aircraft and missile systems. The urgency of such situations and the extreme consequences of error distinguish such work from the general problems of engineering where much greater tolerance of error may be appropriate.

The study of man's interaction with various types of military equipment has been helpful particularly in matters of equipment design. Military psychologists and others in the area of aviation medicine have demonstrated, by the analysis of pilot errors, that many flight difficulties are caused by perceptual conflict engendered by poorly designed instruments. For example, during World War II a number of crashes were traced to pilot misinterpretation of instruments under high stress conditions. From further investigation it was found that these instruments were calibrated in a manner that conflicted with a pilot's natural tendencies. In the heat of battle he would forget how they were meant to be interpreted, with unfortunate or disastrous results. The design of new equipment is a problem for the engineer, but only experience with the human operator under realistic conditions can validate the engineering in human terms.

Out of practical necessity, rather than because of any theoretical concern, military psychologists have studied a number of real situations involving long-term confinement in small groups. These situations bear some resemblance to long-term space flight involving a small crew of men. In studies of submarine crews, for example, the need for substitute gratification is clearly shown. On long voyages food is found to take an ever-increasing role in the life of the crew. The cook achieves an extremely high position.

An interesting practice that has been observed among submarine crews is called the "long eye": when one member of a crew is ignored by other members in a form of social ostracism. The ostracized crew man begins to disintegrate socially. He loses interest in his appearance and his work. He finds it difficult to sleep. He spends his time increasingly staring at nothing. It is this peculiar stare that gives the condition the name of "the long eye," since the individual appears to be looking a few feet beyond the wall of the room in which he is confined.

Informative observations have been made of men confined for a period of many months in a hostile environment close to the South Pole. Under such conditions most men undergo three stages of reaction to their isolation. The first of these occurs during the early days of "getting on the ice." It is marked by heightened anxiety, and may culminate in a psychotic episode in individuals who are so predisposed. The second phase, occupying the greatest part of the time, is characterized by a generalized but diffuse depression. While the men are not happy, they are able to perform assigned tasks efficiently. Status differences are leveled under such conditions and the original formal authority structure may bear little resemblance to the group structure that evolves during this period. The third phase occurs as the men are about to leave the Antarctic. It is characterized by an increase of emotional and aggressive behavior. Tasks are ignored and many errors occur.

While these stages occur over a period of many months, the same sequence has been observed in persons placed in isolation for only three days, so that this three-phase sequence seems to have general validity as a description of human reaction to isolation.

Finally, military psychologists have studied the performance of various military personnel under a variety of stress conditions. These studies have shown clearly that every man will break down perceptually, emotionally, and intellectually if he is subject to various kinds of undue stress. These disruptions may occur under a wide variety of conditions. A sudden external emergency may interfere with the individual's normal functioning patterns. An excess of incoming information may temporarily overwhelm his nervous data-processing system, so that he can respond to almost nothing. Long periods of sustained effort and attention may induce permanent exhaustion or personality breakdown. Experiences with these various forms of stress, and their effects on performance, have led to an emphasis on emergency training for astronauts. The first step in such training is the isolation of possible emergencies that might occur in the flight of a rocket, such as motor failure, puncture of the capsule, or failure in the atmosphere control within the capsule. These emergencies are then simulated on appropriate equipment. The astronaut learns the correct solution to any given problem so presented. However, he continues to practice until he has overlearned the response. Experimental tests, as well as practical experience, have shown that in emergency situations and other stressful conditions, an overlearned response will resist disruption better than any other. In this way the solution may be applied semi-automatically because it was overlearned.

THE CONTRIBUTION OF ENGINEERING PSYCHOLOGY

The contribution of engineering psychology to space flight is hard to overestimate. In part, the work of the engineering psychologist overlaps that of the military psychologist. Both are concerned with the performance of the astronaut as an operator of the spacecraft. But the engineering psychologist has at his command a methodology and theory for the analysis of any man-machine relations in terms of which he can approach the problem, whereas the military psychologist either borrows from him or relies to a great degree on experience in the field.

The central job of engineering psychology is to adapt the human operator to the spacecraft that he operates. In order to be able to perform this function the engineering psychologist must analyze the nature of the astronaut's job into its components, relate these components to the inherent limits of the astronaut himself, and then indicate where redesign of the space vehicle may be necessary. In performing these functions the engineering psychologist usually formulates his analysis in terms of communications theory, which can, with equal facility, be applied both to man and machine. The nature of communications theory will be considered at a later point in this book, but the application of it must be described briefly at this point. In space flight it is necessary for the machine to communicate with man and for man to communicate with the machine. The machine communicates with the astronaut by means of a series of dials and signals that are designed by engineers for just this purpose. Man communicates with the machine by the use of various levers, wheels, and other methods of control, also devised by the engineer. Both man and the machine have certain inherent limitations that must be taken into account if they are to communicate successfully with each other and thus insure the efficient functioning of the complex unit of which they both form a part.

In regard to the space vehicle, the engineer must design a machine within given weight requirements, with parts that have specified limits of tolerance and reliability. These problems fall outside the province of psychology. The human operator of the machine also has very definite limits as well as certain special capabilities. It is necessary to capitalize on the latter while mitigating the former. In comparison to the machine, man is an efficient mechanism for making decisions in complex situations. In addition, man is superior in noticing unusual and unexpected events. Man is limited, however, in the amount of information he can absorb at any given instant, in his ability to interpret what he absorbs, and in his ability to act both quickly and correctly on the basis of this information. Engineering psychology has studied each of these aspects of the human performer in great detail. For example, task load has been intensively studied, resulting in a redefinition of the problem in terms of speed of signal and the complexity of the sensory load produced by the particular signal. Each of these input characteristics works independently but both must be considered in fitting the mechanical task to human capabilities.

Utilizing this information, the engineering psychologist carefully analyzes each unit and phase of the job that the astronaut will be required to perform, looking in each instance for aspects of job performance that exceed the limits of human capacities. For example, the limitations of human sensory input and the limitations of human vigilance may lead to misinterpretation of complex instrument displays or a tendency to overlook danger signals that occur within long and otherwise uneventful periods.

On finding operations in which the capacity of the human operator is unequal to the task, the psychologist draws the attention of the designing engineer to the problem, and an appropriate solution is developed. For example, the instrument display may be simplified, or other sense modalities may be employed for purposes of signaling information. A danger signal may employ not only a flashing light but also a loud bell, or even a sudden blast of heat or cold.

One of the most difficult problems in engineering research is human variability. All calculations must be based on average values, but in a given example a human operator may vary widely from the norm in capability and resistance to stress. In other cases the psychologist may fail to anticipate a problem situation, and the effect may be disastrous. In still other cases, the effect of certain situations, such as weightlessness, cannot be tested beforehand, even though they are known to exist.

All these factors complicate the job of the enineering psychologist, who has little room for error. It is for this reason that he places great stress on the study of human reliability. Studies of a variety of man-machine interactions suggest that human reliability of performance is related to at least six general factors. The first three concern the interaction of the man and the machine. They are the simplification of the task to be performed through appropriate engineering, the elimination of sensory overload connected with certain limited task functions, and the use of extensive continuous and augmented feedback constantly to alert the astronaut to the effects of his actions. The remaining three factors relate to the training of the astronaut. They involve the use of systematic overtraining so that performance of many tasks is semi-automatic and resistant to stress; specific training for various emergency situations; and, finally, the spacing of the astronaut's periods of work and rest to maximize his efficiency. Other factors, such as the use of physiological stimulation, may well play an important though limited role in the temporary improvement, or reduction of astronaut efficiency as the occasion demands. All these factors must be considered in any unified approach to the problem of maximizing human reliability in man-machine relations. With these factors in mind, the engineering psychologist seeks to anticipate all contingencies by appropriate modification of the machine design, and in this manner adapt the machine to the peculiarities of the human operator.

THE CONTRIBUTION OF CLINICAL PSYCHOLOGY

Clinical psychology has made a less immediate and less well-defined contribution to space flight, but nevertheless an important one. Clinical psychology is concerned with the diagnosis and treatment of personality disorders. It therefore can make two general contributions to space flight. First, it can aid in the selection of spacemen who can withstand the stresses associated with space flight. Second, it can aid spacemen to maintain their emotional equilibrium when in flight.

There are two contributions that the clinician can make to the selection of spacemen: the projective test and the depth, or clinical, interview. Both these procedures are used widely for diagnostic purposes and to aid in the selection of personnel. While there is some question as to their validity, there is not, at the present time, any alternative method for obtaining the type of information that these procedures provide.

The projective test consists of a standard ambiguous stimulus that the subject is asked to interpret. The stimulus may consist of inkblots, as in the Rorschach; a series of pictures, as in the TAT, or Thematic Apperception Test; photographs of various types of criminals and mental deviates, as in the Szondi Test. The principle is always the same. The subject is forced to project himself into the material presented, because the material is inherently ambiguous. The way in which he does this reveals something of his personality. For example, a man who appears otherwise normal and well adjusted may report TAT stories suggesting that he thinks persons are looking at him accusingly and suspiciously. Such tendencies may go unnoticed in normal situations but be disastrous in the isolated conditions of space flight. At best, these tests may reveal hidden features of the individual personality that might, under special conditions, cause him to collapse. On the other hand the individual may be shown to be stronger than he seems on the surface.

In testing programs involving the simulation of space trips such diagnostic problems have been uncovered. For example, one individual who had appeared to be a normal candidate was placed in SAM. He there experienced such anxiety that he had to be removed without completing the experimental simulated flight. In this instance simulation of the flight proved an effective indicator of astronaut fitness. Presumably projective testing might have uncovered these personality patterns without the necessity of bringing them to the fore through the simulated space experience.

Even more widely used than the projective test, is the clinical interview. This type of interview, when conducted by a psychologist or psychiatrist, is used for diagnostic purposes. Since clinical interviews are not standardized, their reliability and validity vary with the expertness of the clinician and the visibility of the subject's personality. In general clinical interviews of potential spacemen cover many of the following topics: general life history, including early family experience; nature of current adjustment; relation to same sex and opposite sex; general physical health; and motivation for interest in space flight. These and related topics may be investigated systematically one after the other or discussed in a free, open-ended manner, guided by the nature of the interaction itself rather than any set order of topics.

It is not the information, or specific life history, that is in itself so important as much as the subject's reaction to it, which can only be inferred by the clinician as he listens to the subject's self-description. Often the clinician may give more weight to what the subject fails to tell him than to what he talks about, or to the subject's failure to be afraid of something that it is normal to fear. In World War II, for example, candidate pilots who denied that they were afraid of heights did poorly in flight training. It is normal to be afraid of heights. If an individual denies a normal fear, it may indicate that he is unable to accept this fear in himself. Under stress such a defense may break down, with unfortunate results such as misjudgment or, in extreme cases, panic.

The second major area of potential contribution by the clinical psychologist is in the maintenance of the mental health of spacemen on long flights. At the present time the necessity for such service may seem rather vague. Nevertheless, when all engineering and biophysiological problems have been solved, the mental health of spacemen may be the paramount problem to be met. A variety of studies to be discussed at a later point indicate that various stresses connected with isolation, encapsulation, and the forced interaction with a limited number of other persons will place a great strain on the resources of any sound person. It is reasonable to assume that only persons who are exceptionally resistant to such influences will be allowed to act as spacemen. Even such men may break if they are not prepared to meet situations that accumulate so slowly that one cannot be aware of them until it is too late.

For example, it is typical that a man about to experience a psychotic episode may feel himself to be perfectly normal. What are other members of the crew to do at such a moment? How would they recognize that such a moment had arrived? Such questions would imply that some training in clinical psychology might be helpful to spacemen in recognizing symptoms of mental deterioration in themselves and other members of their team. However, it is notoriously difficult for members of the same unit to help each other. An outside expert usually is necessary, and this, by definition, is impossible, except over such partially satisfactory media as radio and possibly television.

The basic problem faced by spacemen is that many of their sources of satisfaction are eliminated for long periods of time. Their physical motion is restricted. Their diet is limited; they are removed from their wives and families; all the familiar aspects of the everyday world vanish. In addition, they are subject to long periods of boring routine, perhaps interspersed by sudden periods of emergency activity. All of these conditions threaten the inner equilibrium of the spacemen, and, collectively, they may impair it temporarily or in a permanent fashion.

Any student of personal adjustment would predict that under these conditions breakdown may occur, and, certainly, alterations of behavior will occur. Two types of corrective measures might be adopted to meet this situation. First, provision might be made in the spacecraft for the equivalent of a strongroom, in which any person temporarily out of control might be placed. This necessity is great in such a vehicle since a spaceman might, in a fit of anger, depression, or panic, destroy valuable equipment that might endanger the success of the mission and the lives of other crewmen.

A somewhat less extreme measure would involve some appropriate form of tranquillizer administered either as a pill or by injection. The use of such medication would have to be controlled by some form of external authority, since it might reduce operating efficiency if used routinely.

On a less extreme level, the most practical approach to the maintenance of psychological health in a closed social system, such as is found in space flight, might be group therapy. Presumably one of the crewmen would receive some training in the use of group therapy, so that he could initiate it and guide it successfully. As an alternative, such therapy might be instituted before take off, under an experienced therapist, who might establish the therapy group and bring it to the first stages of maturity before the men were on their own. The emphasis in such therapy would not be on deep analysis but on the ventilation of feelings and discussion of the problems occurring each day. This therapy would help to prevent more serious problems from building up and aid the men in understanding their own weaknesses and strengths so that they might have realistic expectations of one another.

Another more futuristic approach, but one that is bound to be perfected in the coming years, is the therapy machine. In essence such a machine would give a series of therapeutic responses to the statements made by the person using it. The heart of the machine would be a computer that could analyze the meaning of the words spoken or typed into it and that was programmed to make appropriate responses. As a variation the machine might respond to the various acoustical properties of the speech rather than its meaning, in order to react to the emotional overtones, such as intensity of sound, hesitation and pauses, fluency, and the like. Such machines do not actually exist, but a simple version based on nondirective supportive therapy could be constructed even at this time. With these machines every man might have his own therapist.

THE CONTRIBUTION OF PHYSIOLOGICAL
PSYCHOLOGY

It is sometimes difficult to draw a line between physiological psychology and physiology. In general, physiological psychology focuses on the way in which the functioning of the internal environment affects outer behavior, rather than studying the effects of the inner environment as an end in itself.

It is clear that the environment of space is almost totally hostile to the physiological functioning of man. It contains no air to breathe, it is either deathly cold or terribly hot, filled with undiluted radiation, and so forth.

In order for man to survive he must compensate for all such hostilities in the environment of outer space. In theory, each of man's physiological requirements can be provided for in the design of a space vehicle. In practice these requirements present tremendous problems that are entirely independent of the engineering problem of projecting and guiding the vehicle.

The physiological problems of human survival in space can be classified as either acute or chronic. The acute problems are those that have been mentioned—atmosphere, heat or cold, the need for protection from radiation. The chronic problems have to do with such nonlethal conditions as weightlessness and elimination of the cycle of day and night.

Psychology is not directly concerned with the problems created by acute physiological needs except in an analysis of the effect that partial deprivation or overexposure may have on the behavior of the individual. An interesting and dramatic illustration of the importance of such partial deprivation effects occurred during the Manhigh III balloon flight. In this instance observers on the ground noticed that the pilot's pulse was increasing at an alarming rate. A cross check of the temperature of the capsule as transmitted by radio signal indicated that it was greatly overheated and could not be controlled. While the pilot had been vaguely aware of this condition, it had not concerned him and he had not mentioned it to the ground observers. Fortunately the observers' ability to detect the conditions in the balloon capsule enabled them to alert him in time. However, it is striking that the pilot was unaware of the danger that could have threatened his life.

The easiest way to control such insidious deficiencies is by a mechanical warning system—for example, a flashing light, a bell, or a taped voice. However, such equipment may fail or, in an emergency, the deficiencies may be undetected. Only training and education in the effects of this kind of deficiency can serve as the final warning for the astronaut. He must experience various deprivations in order to understand their general effects on all people and any unique effects they may have on him.

The chronic forms of physiological disruption have been subject to careful scrutiny. For example, preliminary studies conducted in airplanes have suggested that weightlessness might present a major problem in space flight. Because the sense of balance is maintained by canals in the inner ear that are filled partially with liquid, it was felt that weightlessness would lead to disorientation, since the liquid would not be held down by gravity, and consequently strange nerve patterns would be stimulated. However, more recent experience with space flight indicates that weightlessness for periods of several days does not seem to present any particular functional problems, and does not necessarily induce nausea or a sense of disequilibrium, as had been feared.

The main problem associated with weightlessness that still exists is its long-term effect on the physiology of spacemen. It seems reasonable to suppose that men who are weightless for periods of months and even years will undergo certain physiological changes in their inner physiological rhythm. When such men re-enter the earth's gravitational field, they will in a very short period of time suddenly be subjected to the full force of gravity. Such an experience may have physiological and psychological effects that temporarily disable them. Unfortunately it is just at this time that maximum alertness is required. Thus the point of greatest stress coincides with the need for most efficient functioning. It may be that no physiological problem actually will exist. Unfortunately, there is no way to tell whether this is so until someone has been in space for several months and then returns to the earth or lands on another planet. The only safe procedure would appear to be to arrange the first such landings as entirely mechanical, so that human failure would not have disastrous effects.

Another effect of chronic physiological alteration will be produced by the elimination of the twenty-four-hour cycle of waking and sleeping. Since weight will be at a premium in a space capsule, only the fewest possible men will be sent on early space voyages. The limiting numerical factor is human endurance. Obviously one man cannot run a spaceship by himself for any length of time. Two men leave little margin for error. Regardless of the number selected, studies of around-the-clock operations in submarines, factories, or spacecraft simulators have shown definite variations in efficiency that are related to the twenty-four-hour cycle. In general, it has been found that operating efficiency increases gradually from early until late morning, and thereafter slowly decreases until bedtime. This cycle is extremely general and pervasive. Its implications for all around-the-clock operations are obvious. From the viewpoint of efficiency, it is desirable to have men working equally well at any hour of the day or night. Physiologically it appears that systematic diurnal variations occur.

Industrial engineers have been greatly interested in such shifts in efficiency, since they affect factory production. Military psychologists have attempted to study variations in the cycles of sleeping and waking in situations involving constant vigilance, such as those in radar stations and underwater submarine patrol.

Physiologists have pointed out that this cycle is found not only in man as a functioning totality, but it can be found in a variety of physiological functions, such as the rate of cell division and the amount of cortisone and various blood components, all of which vary according to the twenty-four-hour cycle. These physiological shifts have been found in mice as well as men and appear to represent an extremely general tendency throughout the animal kingdom (in the case of nocturnal animals the cycle is reversed, of course).

Some preliminary work has been done on systematic variation of these cycles both in simulated spaceships and in actual submarine missions. Studies in the SAM space cabin simulator have shown that astronauts can function effectively over a seven-day period on a four-hours-on, four-hours-off schedule, sleeping part of the off time, irrespective of day or night. A more ambitious and realistic test conducted by Air Force scientists has shown that well-motivated and well-trained crews can perform highly complex and exacting tasks in a fifteen-day continuous period, using a four-hour-on and two-hour-off schedule. Such a finding suggests the possibility of three-man crews being practical in early space missions. In such a scheduling two men would always be on active duty. It thus appears that the diurnal cycle is capable of modification and might be adopted for long-term confinement in the space vehicle.

The chronic physiological problems and virtually all the psychological problems that are involved in space flight could largely be solved if it were possible to suspend physiological activities for long periods. Such a process would be crucial for extremely long flights in which the ship itself would require little or no guidance. For many years science-fiction writers have described various schemes for suspending life in and out of spacecrafts. The most popular method is freezing, though the use of strange gases and drugs has also been suggested. Unfortunately, the suspension of physiological and behavioral activities appears to be far more difficult in practice than in fiction.

To date, freezing, or lowering body temperature, has received most of the attention as a method of reducing physiological activity. This is natural, since cooling the body has precisely the effect desired. Unfortunately, the restoration of the organism to the normal state after such exposure presents grave problems. As a warmblooded creature it is unnatural for man to hibernate by means of the lowering of body temperature.

A number of studies of body cooling have been undertaken on animals. These studies have not, to date, been encouraging. Experimental studies have been made with dogs artificially cooled below 25 degrees centigrade for twenty hours. While there is no problem in cooling or preserving the dogs at this temperature, the survival rate is relatively low. Approximately one in three dogs survives the experience. Obviously such a procedure would not be practical in space at those odds, whatever advantages it might have if the man survived. Various drugs have been used to increase the percentage of those surviving the experience with but slight success. At the present time the cooling of animals appears impractical for a long period of time, although a man and a monkey have been cooled as low as 9 degrees centigrade for a short period of time, with complete recovery.

Another approach to the same problem is the selective use of drugs, or electroshock, designed to induce sleep for relatively short periods during times of severe stress (such as take off) or to break the monotony of the long journey. The disadvantage of such sleep is that the ship remains defenseless and unmonitored. However, engineering advances may well make the major part of the voyage an automated operation, and thus make limited suspension practical and desirable.

The problem of suspension is a physiological one—but the implications are psychological. If successful suspension of activity were achieved, many problems of space travel that are produced by prolonged confinement in a hostile environment would cease to exist. In this sense the success of such experimentation has a great many implications for psychological research on the problems of space flight.

THE CONTRIBUTION OF EXPERIMENTAL
PSYCHOLOGY

In one sense physiological psychology is an aspect of experimental psychology, so that the previous section could be considered a part of the present one. Experimental psychology, however, goes beyond directly physiological factors into matters of sensation, perception, motivation, and learning. Experimental psychology fertilizes the areas of clinical, military, and engineering, as well as physiological, psychology. In addition, certain aspects of experimental psychology make certain relatively unique contributions to space flight.

Perhaps the major area of contribution is in the study of perception. The most striking aspect of space travel from the human viewpoint is in the alteration of the perceptions that it will provide. These alterations will involve all sense modalities. The general bodily sense and spatial orientation will be disrupted by weightlessness. The senses of taste and smell will receive relatively little stimulation. The sense of touch will be largely confined either by a space suit or by the limited nature of metallic materials employed in the construction of the spacecraft. The ear will be dulled by whatever constant sounds are given off by the rocket machinery. Beyond this, silence will prevail except for human voices. But it is the sense of sight that will be limited most severely, even though the spaceman will, from another viewpoint, see entirely new things. Objects outside the spaceship will be either white or black, or possibly gradations of gray. The world, except for special features of the ship itself, will be colorless, though the variations in intensity will be extreme. In addition, the sensation of space will be strange. The inside of the spaceship will be perceived as extremely limited in depth. The depth of space outside the ship will appear endless.

All these conditions considered together suggest two problems: first, sensory deprivation; and second, sensory malfunction. In general, the amount of stimulation that will be received from the physical universe will be reduced sharply in quality and, in most cases, in quantity. Thus a sensory deficit will undoubtedly be produced. Further, navigation in space will pose new perceptual problems that do not have any direct analogy to experience on the earth. Under such conditions perceptual miscalculation is likely to occur.

Sensory deprivation has been the subject of serious investigation since 1947 when the Canadian and American psychologist Donald Hebb compared the intelligence of rats blinded in infancy with that of normally sighted controls.[1] He clearly demonstrated the superiority of the sighted rats. Perhaps the classic study in this area was conducted in 1954 in the Hebb Laboratory.[2] Twenty-two college men were placed in a partially soundproofed room, wearing gloves and translucent goggles, and lying in a reclining position with their heads resting on a foam-rubber pillow. Under these conditions of sharply reduced sensory input, certain very typical phenomena were experienced by the men. At first they could not sleep. They were restless. They became emotionally upset and found concentration increasingly difficult. In a number of cases visual, auditory, and even somaesthetic hallucinations were noted. Finally, blank periods occurred for which the subjects could not account. Similar blank periods had been noted much earlier, during World War II studies of radar watches. In such studies it had been demonstrated that after an hour lapses of attention occurred even though the task being performed was of great importance.

From these relatively simple beginnings a wide variety of approaches and techniques have evolved for the study of sensory deficiency and deprivation. Individuals have been made to float in warm water, wearing masks; they have been given drugs to reduce sensory input to the central nervous system; or they have been placed in highly constricted environments with routine operations to perform over long periods.

The sophistication of the experimental designs employed has increased consistently. Recent studies examine not just the absolute effects of deprivation but systematically vary the type of interference with sensory input that is employed; the personality and character of the persons subjected to deprivation; the relationship between the experimenter and the subject.

The early experiments in the field were concerned almost exclusively with varying the kind of sensory interference that was employed. However, it soon became clear that people varied considerably in the degree of disturbance produced by a given deficit. Therefore it was necessary to consider whether these differences were due to specific personality characteristics, or simply reflected the general emotional balance of the individual. This problem is important particularly in connection with space travel, since the selection of individuals who are resistant to the effects of sensory deprivation is of prime importance in any astronaut-selection program.

Finally, the relation between the experimenter and the subject has proved to be a crucial variable in mitigating the effects of the sensory deprivation. If the subject is more or less left to his fate by an impersonal experimenter he tends to drift toward disorientation, anxiety, and highly charged emotional fantasy. However, if discomfort is reduced to a minimum and a "safety man" is used to communicate instructions to the subject, the results of the deprivation can be highly enjoyable for the subject. The safety man is a person who previously has experienced the deprivation state and therefore is aware of the heightened emotional tendencies associated with it. These studies employing safety men suggest that men can be trained to tolerate sensory deprivation. When such training has been successful they even can learn to enjoy the freedom from societal restraint that deprivation entails.

It is clear that the subject of deprivation has not been explored in any definitive sense at the present time. In some cases very negative and disturbing effects are noted as a by-product of sensory deprivation. In others, with proper precautions, the experience is positive. Research currently is proceeding along at least six fronts. First, the effects of sensory deprivation on the development of animals is being studied. These studies have fundamental implications for personality theory and developmental psychology. They provide the clearest evidence for the long-term effects of such deprivation. Second, studies are determining the effect of reducing the amount of sensory input reaching the human subject as previously described. Third, the effects of certain situationally induced reduction of stimuli are being studied in natural situations, such as the radar installations mentioned earlier. The fourth approach involves the blocking of sensory nerve connections within the body through the use of drugs and electroshock, so that stimuli do not reach the central nervous system. These studies are difficult to control since the precise action of the shock or drug usually is unknown. However, the findings that are obtained are usually similar to those produced by the reduction of outer stimuli. Particularly marked is the increase in anxiety associated with disruption of the space-time sense through the blocking of sensory channels. The fifth avenue of investigation concerns the effects of reduced stimulation on the responsiveness of the individual to stimulation, both from the outside and from within. In general, it appears that subjects become increasingly aware of internal stimuli in the absence of external stimuli and increasingly dependent on those external stimuli that may be provided. If these external stimuli fail to follow the expected pattern the subjects may become unduly anxious. The final approach to the problem of deprivation is less formal and involves the attempt to extract from written records of people who have been in shipwrecks, experienced Arctic winters, and the like certain common effects of prolonged social isolation.

It is too early to be sure how serious a problem sensory deprivation may be for space travelers. However, the factor has clearly been isolated and experimentation continues actively in the area. As these studies illuminate the various effects produced by the degree of reduction of input; the pattern of reduction employed; the anticipations and expectations of the subjects in regard to the experience of deprivations; the effect of drowsiness caused by the isolation experience, as distinguished from the experience of deprivation itself; the effect of lying still for long periods of time, regardless of sensory deprivation; and the ways in which tolerance for deprivation can be raised it becomes increasingly clear as to how serious the problem really may be for the astronaut. It may turn out to be little more serious than weightlessness. But it seems more probable that the fundamental nature of stimulation in the maintenance of the integrity of the personality will require the application of some relatively fundamental training experience if the astronaut is to survive the experience of sensory deprivation successfully and without permanent personality damage.

The other major factor in the alteration of sensation during space flight is produced by the peculiar visual conditions under which the space vehicle must be navigated. The spaceman's world is eternal night punctuated by brilliant points of light. Under such conditions depth is swallowed up into infinity. Any attempt to navigate or guide the spaceship under such circumstances would be extremely difficult. Careful navigation inevitably will be necessary for refueling at space stations, for transfer of passengers and material from other ships, and for any maneuver relating the ship to any other material body. Special training is required for such navigation and piloting in space. Any other vehicle or small object toward which the spaceship may be headed will be brilliantly illuminated by direct sunlight and partially illuminated by reflected earth light, while other parts may be completely dark. In such a strange and foreign visual field the astronaut will have to make complex three-dimensional estimates of position. Such an experience has no direct precedent in previous earthbound experience.

Another problem relating to experimental psychology concerns the attempt to fabricate gravity. At present little is known about the effects of long-term exposure to weightlessness, or to the problems that it may create in day-to-day living. One solution that has been proposed—if a solution proves to be necessary—is the creation of artificial gravity. Such a sensation can be produced in various ways, varying from the slow revolution of the spacecraft (substituting centrifugal force for gravity) to the use of magnetic shoes. Neither of these procedures appears to be successful. Shoes are effective only when in direct contact with metal. The effects of long-term slow revolution are unknown. However, at present there is no evidence to indicate that short periods of weightlessness interfere with performance. The effects of long periods must await experience with actual flights through deep space.

A final significant contribution of experimental psychology to the actualization of space flight is the use of trained animals to test the effects of space without having to risk a human pilot. Psychologists traditionally have used animals in their experiments. They have, therefore, a long and intensive experience in working with animals in the performance of relatively complex experimental tasks of one kind or another. This experience has proved of great assistance in utilizing higher animals as substitute astronauts in the early testing of complex rocket vehicles. One of the most famous of these animals is the chimpanzee Ham who preceded Alan Shepard in the trail-blazing Project Mercury flight. Ham had been trained to operate a lever whenever a light flashed before him. During various portions of the flight the light was flashed by a ground signal, and Ham's response was recorded. By this relatively simple means, the effects and stresses of flight could be tested. As long as Ham responded as he was trained, it was reasonable to presume that he had control of his mental and physical faculties. In fact, during all but a few of the most stressful moments of the flight Ham was able to respond successfully, indicating that the flight was practical and that a man might be risked in further tests.

The original suggestion with regard to the use of animals in ballistic missiles and vehicles appears to have been made by the American psychologist Burrhus Skinner, who thought that a pigeon could be trained not only to ride in the vehicle but actually to guide it.[3] If the pigeon was trained to peck according to signals given by the rocket its pecking could be used to maintain the rocket within a fixed path. Thus if the light went on at the right, the pigeon would peck to the right; if on the left, it would peck to the left. Through an appropriate mechanism the direction of the vehicle might be controlled.

By the use of animals it may even be possible to test the effects of prolonged weightlessness. Animals could be kept alive in satellites for several months and then be returned to earth, with the effects of re-entry being observed through appropriate instruments.

THE CONTRIBUTION OF EVALUATION AND
MEASUREMENT

The main contribution of psychological evaluation of measurement is in the efficient selection of spacemen. However, the advance of new statistical and methodological research techniques underlies progress in all psychological areas, since the power of research is, in the long run, determined by the availability of proper methodological and statistical tools.

In a more specific sense the selection and analysis of the behavior, personality, and abilities of spacemen depends on the availability of appropriate measuring instruments to assess these characteristics. The most difficult aspect in the development of any test designed for selection purposes is the discovery of a suitable criterion of success. In the case of space flight success is all too apparent, but unfortunately it is desirable to develop appropriate tests before the criteria for judging them exist.

At the initial stages of any new enterprise each step is a discovery, and the initial problems always seem greater than they do in retrospect, when their solution is reduced to a routine procedure. Thus many of the complex instruments and training devices that may reveal poor performance are relatively inefficient and expen-

sive tests. It is not necessary to lock up each candidate in SAM in
order to be able to judge his reaction to stress under confining
and isolating conditions. A simple paper-and-pencil test may do
as well. But in order to devise such a test it is necessary to work
backward by examining the test scores of successful and unsuccessful astronauts. Each astronaut candidate, if he is utilized as a test
subject, can provide valuable information that eventually will allow greater simplification in the selection program. In addition,
such information would be of great interest to psychologists interested in understanding the relation between personality and task
performance. At present little is known about the type of person
who would make the best astronaut, and it can only be assumed
that general competence and excellent adjustment would probably
help in this task, as well as in any other. However, many possible
types of individuals have been suggested for space flight, varying
from psychotics, creative writers, yogis, and, of course, women, who
by virtue of their sustaining power and patience might be fitted for
space as well or better than men.

THE CONTRIBUTION OF PERSONALITY PSYCHOLOGY

Many of the fruits of the study of human personality are reaped
by clinical psychology, and therefore already have been described.

The personality psychologist is interested in the problem of
space flight because it presents him with an extreme situation for
testing his understanding of the nature, organization, stability, and
strength of personal organization.

The spacemen and those involved with them do not share such
a scientific interest, but look rather for practical ways to preserve
their personal organization in the face of grave physical, physiological, and psychological threats.

Students of personality are well aware that all persons are to
some degree segmented. Invididuals insulate as well as intercon-
nect their own components so as to maintain a reasonably efficient
level of functioning. Because they are so constructed, they can be

dissociated relatively easily under certain conditions. The simplest way to produce such a dissociation is through hypnosis.

A variety of uses have been suggested for hypnotic dissociation in relation to space flight. Hypnotism may aid in the selection of personnel by reproducing space flight in the mind of the applicant without the need of expensive and time-consuming simulation equipment. Hypnotism can be used to create an added dimension of realism in the minds of trainees when they use trainer simulators. Posthypnotic suggestion can be used to reduce the fear and anxiety that may be associated with space flight. Such suggestion can also be used to reduce the boredom of the long space flight by producing any desired image or fantasy in the mind of the astronaut. For such purposes self-hypnotism would have to be taught to the astronaut. In the same way suggestions can be given to reduce physiological discomfort and to control undesirable physiological reactions, such as increased oxygen intake. Finally, hypnotism can be used to put the astronaut into lengthy trances.

All these possibilities are interesting, and some of them may prove of great value. It would be ironic if hypnotism, which has always occupied a tangential place in psychology—viewed with some misgiving and little respect—should at last come of age in the space travel of the future.

Personality shifts do not occur in a few days or weeks, except under extraordinary conditions. It is therefore premature to speculate on the effects of space travel on personality formation. Such effects, if they exist, will be revealed only by prolonged space flight or a simulated space flight of long duration. Some interesting speculations can, however, be made if one extrapolates from studies of persons in solitary confinement or who have been shipwrecked. But these situations differ from space flight. They are the result of imposed punishment or impersonal disaster, not of conscious choice on the part of the participant. In general, these experiences suggest the importance of freedom of social interaction and access to group resources. Because of the repression of sexual impulses that usually occurs in such situations, oral gratification is emphasized. As was reported earlier, in the experiments with submarine crews, the social status of the cook is enormously enhanced. On the other hand there is a general leveling of other social classes as the experience continues.

It is reasonable to expect that long-term personality changes will result from such a drastic and unique experience as space flight. The importance of such changes will be great since they will help to determine the useful life span of the spaceman as pilot, and suggest problems that may occur as a function of experience rather than the immediate stresses of flight. But studies of the effects of space flight on human personality must await future experience in space itself.

THE CONTRIBUTION OF SOCIAL PSYCHOLOGY

Social psychology deals with the impact of social forces on individual behavior. The spaceship team, regardless of its final size, will constitute a small group situation. The fields of such small groups have received intensive investigation in social psychology. While the kinds of small groups that have been studied vary widely, and often do not resemble space crews, many of the findings obtained from such research may be applicable.

For example, an issue of direct importance in the selection of a space crew is group size. Studies of small groups have shown that the size of the group, regardless of the nature of the group members, imposes certain requirements upon the members to which they must adjust. For example, in groups of three, a number of interesting findings have been obtained. In such situations a coalition is formed between two members in order to establish some order in the group. When this occurs the third member is in a difficult position. He must either agree with the other two or face social ostracism, which in isolated groups can be an extremely severe punishment. Since early space crews may consist of only three members, in order to reduce human weight to a minimum, this tendency in three-man groups may be serious. It is particularly noteworthy in this connection that the American psychologist Solomon Asch has shown that when two persons disagree with a third, the latter can be made to perceive two lines of equal length as apparently dissimilar.[4] In terms of navigation such social influence on perception could have serious consequences.

Another significant issue in the organization of space crews involves the use of authority. Should the space crew have an appointed leader with final authority, or should it function as a democratic unit, setting up its own rules and regulations within the limits imposed by the space flight itself? A number of studies of this issue have been made. The classic study in the area was conducted in the late 1940s by the German-American psychologist Kurt Lewin, and the American psychologists Ronald Lippitt and Ralph White, who compared boys' clubs run autocratically, democratically, or in a laissez-faire manner.[5] They found that the democratic condition was associated with greatest membership satisfaction and the highest quality of output but not greatest quantity. These findings have been replicated in a number of other studies. However, recent research suggests that the situation is more complex than was first believed. Apparently authoritarian persons do better under authoritarian leadership. Also the leadership effectiveness depends somewhat on the nature of the task. These studies seem to suggest that a generally democratic equal-status arrangement in space crews along with clear definition of task function and provision for handling disputes in a democratic manner may be the best general procedure. However, in specialized instances or with certain types of personnel, such an arrangement may be wasteful and even dangerous. The issue needs careful exploration in the context of space research in view of the special pressures to which such leadership would be subjected in long isolated flights.

Another problem that inevitably will arise in the course of long space flights concerns the issue of "reference groups." A reference group is one to which an individual refers in setting a standard for his own actions. Ordinarily an individual has many such groups, including his family, work group, and friends. Each of these groups lends complexity to the character of the individual and collectively helps to maintain the complex balance of forces that constitute his personality. In space flight all but one of these groups will be removed physically in space and time. Only the space crew will remain. The situation may not be unlike that pictured by Thornton Wilder in his play *Our Town*: At the end there is a scene set in a cemetery, where the dead people are shown talking to one another. Here, it appears, they wait, slowly forgetting who they were on the earth and what they did. They are depersonalized. If this occurs to spacemen, it could have unfortunate results for them and for the success of their mission. They might lose interest in the original goals of the mission and decide on new ones. They might become estranged from their families and friends, forget their country, or be seized by delusions of power, and establish plans to utilize their position in space for obtaining special concessions, treating their own country and friends as enemies. Such reversal of loyalty is observed in connection with brainwashing, though in that case the procedure is administered by an enemy, rather than by the impersonality of space. However, the isolation of the individual from his own kind and the elimination of familiar reference points in his routine does resemble brainwashing to some extent. The effects may therefore be similar, except that the goals of the crew rather than those of the enemy would tend to become paramount.

It therefore seems that everything that can be done to maintain at least a skeleton of reference-group influence on the crew should be done. Radio and television communication with family, friends, and workers on the mission should be used. The nature and the form of the records that are kept can be designed to foster an unconscious recognition of reference groups. For example, reports may require the astronaut to interpret the events of the day to various different key research, technical, military, and political groups on the earth. By completing the records, he unconsciously remains in contact with these groups, even if they do not interact directly with him. Books dealing with normal community problems, movies, and other cultural products will help maintain the spaceman's frame of reference as an earth man temporarily on a space mission. However, it is reasonable to expect that all these methods will become less effective as the voyage becomes more extensive. Eventually the earth man will tend to forget who he is, where he is going, and why he is going there. Social psychology can only delay the date of this existential confrontation.

Perhaps the primary social problem that the space crew may face is the poverty of their social environment. In spite of movies, radio, television, and so forth, in the long run they have only each other. As the days stretch on they may find one another incredibly dull. In such an instance a general social apathy may result, the equivalent of sensory deprivation on the social level. The results of this kind of deprivation are similar to those produced by reference-group dissolution. In this case the crew members may face dissolution of all social ties with a resultant drift toward indifference, dullness, and perhaps autism bordering on psychotic breakdown. Obviously such developments would severely impair the likelihood of success, and could damage the spacemen permanently. The only direct way to approach this problem is to train the spacemen to have a wider repertoire of behaviors and responses than would normally be the case, since they are each other's whole social world. The most feasible technique for accomplishing this end would probably be role playing—that is, the use of spontaneous playacting. Such a substitute for variety might work along the following lines. First, role playing could be used as a device to expand the poverty of the social environment through the enactment of roles and situations that would not normally occur in a spacecraft. Second, role playing could be used as a therapeutic vehicle for the resolution of interpersonal difficulties among crew members in a quasi-realistic setting. Finally, role playing could be used to aid in the personal adjustment of individuals who were having particular difficulty at a given time, ranging from homesickness to incipient psychotic breakdown. The effectiveness with which any of these possibilities could be realized would depend on the quality of the initial training that the crew received in the use of role playing.

Another extremely significant aspect of the social situation in determining the success of space flight is the relation of the structure of the group to its productivity. Great interest has been centered on this question in studies of work groups, but little precise knowledge is available.

Studies have been made comparing the productivity records of different combinations of personality types. Some evidence exists favoring the use of sociometric choice as a basis for the grouping of productive teams. Persons who choose to work together are able to work together more effectively. However, the composition of the group must be viewed in the frame of reference of the task to be performed. In general, there has been little study of the effect that man-to-man interactions have on man-machine interactions. The system of relationships is extremely complex and not likely to be reduced to any simple formulas.

Other topics are also relevant, particularly the phases of small-group development, decision-making processes, and the relation between different group tasks. It has been observed in studies of small groups in laboratory situations that during the first few meetings a crisis develops related to the setting up of a status hierarchy. The success of the group appears to depend on its ability to resolve this struggle in a satisfactory and permanent manner. In space crews rank may impose status, but as status is leveled it seems inevitable that some realignment would occur, creating developmental problems.

It is the common practice in military settings to look to the leader for all decisions. However, as mentioned earlier there is a large body of research that questions the use of authoritarian leadership in small-group situations. It is necessary to reconsider the distribution of the decision-making function among the space crew. Since all men die if the mission fails, should each have an equal voice in decisions? If not, how is authority to be maintained? If so, how are the decisions to be enforced? These social problems must be faced before the mission is undertaken, if severe chronic social difficulties are not to arise in flight.

Finally, it must be emphasized that the astronaut's task is complex. It can be broken down into such activities as sensing, interpreting, planning, and manipulating. However, in each specific instance the actual operations are complex. All other social, personal, and physiological factors are relative to these tasks. One set of social, psychological, and physiological conditions may apply to one type of task but not the others. Since, in the last analysis, the task is paramount, it is necessary to re-analyze the effects that different tasks have on the psychological and social aspects of crew development and interaction, in order to clarify the way in which psychology can contribute to the various task problems that the astronaut will face.

These are some of the ways in which psychology is contributing and can and will contribute to space flight. As these possibilities are expanded, it seems inevitable that the role of psychology in space flight will do much to increase the public estimate of the character and importance of psychology itself. This, in turn, should do much to improve the public image of psychology. From this development may come a greater channeling of funds for psychological research that previously might have seemed either unduly abstract or implying more threats than promises.

It seems also inevitable that the relationship between psychology and space flight will be a two-way interaction. Psychology will contribute in the ways in which we have outlined. However, the research generated by the practical interest in space flight will surely provide much of interest to basic psychology. The breadth and depth of many areas in psychology will be increased, as the limiting case of space flight casts new light on the behavior of all men in more normal situations.

Chapter Two

The Computer:
an Electronic Catalyst

THE NATURE OF COMPUTERS

The application of electronic computers to psychological research bears some interesting similarities to the application of psychology to space travel. Both areas involve technical devices that have been perfected only recently. Both areas involve the simultaneous application of a great number of sciences. Both areas involve many of the sub-areas of psychology. There is, however, one important difference between the computer and the spaceship as they relate to psychology. Psychology contributes to the design of the space vehicle, but it does not contribute to the design of computers. The computers were designed by engineers. However, once their existence was a technical fact, their application to psychology, and to most of the other sciences, was only a question of time, thought, and ingenuity. The computers' applications to psychology are in no way unique to the nature of the subject matter. The computer is being applied to problems of physics, chemistry, biology, geology, and any of the sciences in which numbers are used for purposes of description or analysis.

A final point of comparison between computers and travel in deep space involves their essential function. The space vehicle extends the range of man's spatial frontier, much as the telescope extends his visual frontier. The computer, in contrast, extends man's temporal frontier. It is able to shrink time, and thus enable man to compress more numerical events in any given time unit than had ever been possible before. More strictly, the computer is a device for increasing the density of time, if we define density as the number of distinctive actions or events that can occur per second.

In order for a computer to perform this densifying of events, any problem with which we wish to confront it must be translated into terms that the machine can understand. If this translation is possible, and the machine is properly designed to handle the problem, then the machine is able to perform the shrinkage of time as described.

This process is most easily and clearly illustrated in relation to simple arithmetic operations such as addition, division, subtraction, and multiplication. In 1952 when the Illiac computer was made available, it was possible to perform addition and subtraction at the rate of almost eleven thousand operations per second. Division and multiplication could be made at the rate of approximately thirteen hundred per second. These operations were performed on ten-place decimal numbers. Even at that relatively early time in the development of computer operations, their speed of operation was fantastic in comparison with that of their human creators.

These rates, or densities, constantly are being exceeded by new machines, or by improved versions of old ones. It is difficult to set any limits on the speeds that may be attainable. As the limits are approached for machines of a certain type, new engineering principles are introduced to establish entirely new possibilities.

Some conception of the rates with which machines have been improved can be grasped from the following figures. The IBM 7090 currently in routine use can perform two hundred fifty thousand arithmetic operations per second. The IBM 7094, which is beginning to be applied to the commercial field can process five hundred thousand mathematical operations per second. These figures are incredible. If we assume that an individual could subtract two ten-digit numbers at the relatively rapid rate of once each two seconds, then the 7094 is just one million times as fast as the human operator.

The typical high-speed computer resembles the stereotype of scientific equipment that the public has come to associate with high-powered scientific exploration. It is complex-looking, but neatly and efficiently designed. When it is in operation there is a continuous pattern of lights that shift with each machine operation. In short these machines appear, on casual inspection, to be capable of doing anything, including creating life, as in a Frankenstein movie.

In actual fact the basic principles of computer design are extremely simple. All computers have four central functions. First, a computer must communicate with its operator. It can usually do this in several ways. The operator can feed into it information either telling it what to do, or providing it with the raw data on which it will then operate. The machine also communicates with the operator at each stage of its operation by the display board, which tells the operator exactly what operation the machine is performing at each instant. Such instantaneous communication is necessary for the correction of machine malfunctions, or the detection of errors in the directions given to the machine. Finally, the machine must be able to communicate to the operator the final results of its calculations in a form that the operator can understand. This communication between the machine and the operator is a man-machine interaction that is not unlike the relation between the spaceman and the space vehicle.

The second general function of the computer is to store information in known locations, so that this information can be recalled when needed. This function usually is described as the memory of the machine. In contrast to the human memory, the machine memory is perfect. It can locate and recall any information stored within it almost instantaneously. Its only limit is in its capacity—that is, the amount of information that it can contain.

The third general function of the machine is to perform the simple arithmetic operations of addition, subtraction, multiplication, and division. Since all these operations can be performed by a school child, it is obvious that a machine is not terribly intelligent in a human sense. On the contrary, the machine is basically an extremely simple device. If you speak to it in its own language it will absorb the information that you give it and perform simple operations upon it in the order required by the operator. It exceeds the human operator in only three things: its capacity, its accuracy of recall, and its speed of operation. The capacity of the machine is limited only by financial considerations. In theory there is virtually no limit to its storage capacity except size of the machine, availability of electric current, and so forth. Its accuracy of recall is perfect in the sense that a tape recording is perfect. If music is on tape, it will remain there as long as the tape itself remains intact and undeteriorated. If the tape is played back, the music will be perfectly "recalled" by the tape recorder. In this sense the memory of the machine is perfect and does not deteriorate over time to any significant degree. When physical deterioration does occur, the memory can be repaired or replaced by another memory unit, since it is mechanical rather than organic.

The speed of the machine is limited only by the ingenuity of the engineers who design it. The computer is basically an electrical apparatus. The speed of electricity approaches that of light. Therefore the electrical aspect of machine operation is almost incomprehensibly swift in human terms. It is not the electrical, but rather the mechanical, operation of the machine that sets the limits on its speed. The major mechanical problem in most machines is gaining access to memory. Since the memory unit occupies a certain space, some method of alignment is necessary so that the machine can reach the proper location in the memory required for a given operation. This may require the revolution of a drum as in the IBM 650, or it may involve the use of an electromagnetic process or the incredibly precise location on a small disk. In any case this operation is much slower than the actual electrical operations by which information is transmitted.

However, slower than this operation is the process of reading in and out of the computer. The first step in any machine operation is to transmit to the machine the program of operations it is to follow and the data on which it is to act. This feeding process is relatively slow, since the machine must translate symbols on IBM cards, holes on tape, or other coded data into electrical impulses. The rate at which either cards or tapes can be fed into the machine is limited by mechanical factors.

Similar mechanical problems exist in relation to the machine's presentation of its final results whether they are punched on IBM cards or are simply typed out on an electric typewriter. These operations require time greatly out of proportion to that required by the electronic calculations. For example, if one were to inter-correlate the scores of thirty tests taken by five hundred people on the Illiac, of the ten minutes required for the total operation, nine of these minutes would be taken by the input and output operations. The four hundred and thirty-five correlations themselves would be calculated in one minute's time.

We have previously said that the machine has its own language. It is now necessary to describe this language in order to complete the general description of the functioning of the computer.

The simplest distinction that an individual can make is between X and Y, or, even more basic, between *something* and *nothing*. Such a two way alternative is called a binary code. This is the language of the computer. With the exception of certain preset code operations, the machine language consists of nothing more than a complex series of something-nothing operations. At any given point in its sequence of operations, the machine distinguishes only between doing or not doing, something versus nothing, yes versus no. This is surely a very crude language. An infant uses such distinctions. It screams if it wants milk. It pushes it away if it does not want it. While the basis of the language is as simple as is conceivable, the results are far from simple. It should be added that this language is used only by machines known as digital computers. Other types of computers employ a different type of operation. For example, the analogue computer employs the principle of volume control. It is not all or nothing in its operation, but graduates its response to the strength of the incoming signal.

The digital computer is used primarily for numerical calculation. Most of the electronic computers that are used in the various sciences are of this type, since the central application of the computer at this time is numerical analysis.

In a rough sense human language operates on an analogue principle rather than a digital one. Language is designed to make a series of graded distinctions. However, the digital computer can make only one: something versus nothing. In order to communicate with such a machine it is necessary to translate or recode complex analogue human language into crude binary machine language. In practical terms this often means punching a given row or a given column of an IBM card. There are eighty columns on the standard IBM card, each of which has twelve rows. There are therefore nine hundred and sixty distinct locations on an IBM card. Each of these locations can represent an independent binary distinction. It is necessary to decide how these locations are to be used in each given instance when transforming numerical tests, or research data into code language. For this purpose it is necessary to make out a coding sheet that specifies the meaning associated with specific locations on the card. For example, the age of the subjects may be entered in column five. The twelve positions in the column will then be arranged to cover the range of ages in the sample. A zero punch may represent an age from 15 to 20, the one punch ages from 21 to 25, and so on. In order to translate raw data onto the IBM card it is necessary to record it in this manner. In some cases the data must be reduced, grouped, or condensed. In other cases this is not necessary if the scores range themselves from 1 through 10. Once the data has been recoded into digital form and punched appropriately onto IBM cards or tapes, the material can be fed into the computer as raw data.

A remaining question must then be raised: How does the machine know what to do with the data, where to send it, and in what order to process it? The answer to this question is that the machine does not know. It must be told. The instructions that the human operator gives to the machine must be formulated by a programmer and fed into the machine. In the earlier calculating machines these instructions were literally wired into the machines. Each machine contained the equivalent to a telephone switchboard that could be rewired by hand. For any given set of operations the machine could be appropriately wired by the operator. Such an arrangement was very time consuming and relatively inflexible. Later machines were built on the principle of programming the machine electrically rather than mechanically. In such a procedure it was necessary to break down any sequence of actions that the machine was to perform into a series of simple discrete steps. This series of steps was called the "machine program." The man who devised the steps was called the "programmer." Thus the man behind the machine is the programmer, since he tells the machine what to do.

The writing of a machine program is a highly skilled task involving logical analysis, artistic sense of design, and painstaking attention to detail. A new program of a fairly complex nature may require over six months to write and perfect. On the other hand, once it has been written it can be used indefinitely by any skilled machine operator, just as a textbook, once it is written, can be read by a great number of students.

It is not necessary to be able to write a program in order to be able to use it. It is only necessary to have some knowledge of the machine itself and some awareness of the kinds of mechanical and logical problems that arise in the use of computers.

Any program must be transmitted to the machine in the binary code. When this occurs it is necessary for the machine to be able to distinguish the fact that the material it is receiving is not a set of data but rather a set of instructions. This process is executed by using a special code card that precedes the program deck of IBM cards. This special card contains a code that automatically shifts the machine so that it will treat the information as a program and not as data. Another card code indicates to the machine when the program is over and data is being transmitted to the machine.

When the program is read into the machine each separate instruction is placed in a different location in memory as is each part of the data. Every instruction in the program is written in a special code. The instruction contains three pieces of information; first, the instruction tells the machine to obtain the data located in a given memory location; second, the instruction indicates what is to be done with the data at the given location; third, the instruction indicates where the machine should go for the next instruction in the program. In short each instruction says "go to x location and perform y operation on the data you will find there. After you are through go to z location for your next instruction."

These are the tools that the programmer uses to fashion the program. His skill lies in utilizing the available locations in the machine memory as efficiently as possible while reducing the number of different instructions to the minimum possible number in keeping with the given calculations that are to be performed.

The programmer is not usually a scientist, but he must be skilled in numerical analysis. His job is created indirectly by the computer itself, and the program that he produces usually can be adopted by scientific workers in many different fields, either directly or with suitable modifications.

As programs are written and distributed, various computer installations collect program libraries that are available to persons needing specific types of computations.

Unfortunately, the almost terrifying obsolescence of the technical and engineering features of computers has a parallel impact on the programs themselves. As new types of computers are devised, the old programs simply may not be suitable. Since programs are, in part, an artistic as well as a logical expression of the particular type of machine for which they were designed originally, they may be inefficient with a new machine, or simply inapplicable.

Until the design of computers approaches a stable state, there will inevitably remain a technical lag surrounding the availability of appropriate programs. And the programmers themselves continually will have to rewrite programs designed to perform standard numerical and statistical operations. Thus appropriate programs are not always available, and persons interested in computing are faced with a choice of using a less efficient machine that does have a given program, or writing a new program for a more advanced machine. These problems should hopefully be resolved as the basic design of the computer is stabilized in the course of the next few years.

The ingenuity of programmers defies any simple description, but it will be helpful to give a few illustrations of some of their more general technical short cuts.

For this purpose it is useful to utilize a specific example. Let us assume that we wish to write a program that is designed to obtain the square root of a series of numbers and then add them all together. The simplest procedure would be to write out a program in which each logical step constituted a separate instruction to the machine. Thus each number would be taken and the square root obtained and then the result stored in an appropriate location, and finally all the square roots would be added together. However, the simplest approach to programming is usually the most inefficient in terms of the use of machine space and time, so that a variety of short cuts are employed by the programmer. For example, instead of making each square-root operation a completely new instruction, it is possible to use only one instruction but systematically to change its address with each cycle of the operation. In order to do this it is necessary only to have the original data placed in a sequence of locations. For purposes of simplicity, assume that ten numbers are used, and that they are located in locations 1 through 10. In this case it is necessary only to add one to the address of the square-root instruction. Thus the first time the square root is obtained for the number in location 1, the second time the operation is performed on the number in location 2. Each time this cycle has been performed it is necessary to compare the address just used with some final address—in this case, 10—which will tell the machine to stop taking square roots. In this manner one instruction is applied systematically to all locations in which the data is located. A similar approach can be used to assign the results of the calculation to sequential locations without having to specify more than the first one in advance. When the tenth location is reached, the machine is programmed for a branching operation. Such an operation shifts out of the square-rooting operation to either printing out the final answer or entering into any new operations that might be required.

Another important method for simplifying the square-root operation is to utilize "subroutines." These are standard operations that are stored in the machine at a known location. Instead of having to write out program for obtaining a square root, a subroutine for such a purpose is already stored in the machine. The programmer need only say in the program, "Go to *x* address and perform the operation contained there." The address contains the first operation of the square-root subroutine, which operates and then returns to the next step of the program. In this way the programmer can build on relatively simple operations that are in common use and have already been programmed.

Programmers have devised a variety of aids including special codes that simplify the writing of programs by automatically translating certain English words into appropriate machine language. However the basic problem and the basic techniques remain as described.

Since the computing operation is a man-machine system, a variety of methods are used to enable the man and machine to interact at all times in the operation, from program writing to the final calculation of the data. To facilitate this interaction the machine is so designed that the human operator instantly can be made aware of what the machine is doing at all times and give it new instructions if such should be desirable. For this purpose calculators are provided with consoles of varying complexity. These consoles enable the operator to determine where the machine is, and enable him to shift the machine to a new portion of the program, back it up to an earlier step, or introduce a new instruction. Such man-machine interactions are vital in the trial of new programs, which never seem to work out quite as they are written.

It is also necessary for the machine to be able to stop itself. The machine does this when it receives an impossible instruction or when it makes an error that it can detect. An impossible instruction would be to go to a location on the machine that does not exist. A mistake in the machine might consist of the failure to recall or receive an instruction. A variety of internal checks exist in the machine that automatically alert the operator to an error and aid him in detecting its nature. Collectively these features of machine design have the important effect of reducing machine error to the vanishing point. The operation of the machine is almost perfect, and in this respect far exceeds the human operator. If the program is correct and is thoroughly tested on problems with already known answers, then the possibility of error is almost eliminated. In this way the computer is able to perform complex quantitative operations at an incredible speed and with a great degree of accuracy.

The form and function of the electronic computer have been described at some length in order to remove some of the mystery that surrounds these machines and their operations and to establish a concrete foundation for the discussion of their application to psychology.

STATISTICAL APPLICATIONS

It was stated earlier that computers are designed to manipulate quantitative data. In psychology most quantitative manipulation involves the use of statistics. There are two types of statistics that are usually distinguished; descriptive and inferential. Descriptive statistics are useful for reducing a large quantity of raw data to a few numbers that describe its important general properties. Inferential statistics are used to determine the likelihood that given data could be attributed to random variation. Put more positively, inferential statistics determine whether the manipulation of given variables produce any demonstrable effect.

Statistics are extremely important in the social and behavioral sciences because of the variability of the human subject that is studied. Modern statistical methods are designed to capitalize on this very difficulty faced by the behavioral scientists. The basic assumption made by these statistics is that all measures in psychology are contaminated by error, which produces uncontrolled variation in measurement. The purpose of the statistics is to specify the amount of error that is present and then determine whether there are other influences present in addition to this error. In psychological experimentation, where all variables except those involved in the experiment are controlled, any effect beyond chance variation is attributed to the variables under specific study. In order to determine whether differences obtained are to be attributed to these variables, it is necessary to apply appropriate statistical techniques. The choice of an appropriate technique depends on the nature of the data to be tested. However all statistics used for this purpose determine the probability associated with the actual event. If the probability exceeds a certain limit, the findings are attributed to the experimental manipulations rather than the random influences of uncontrolled factors.

Thus statistics play a central part in psychological experimentation. They constitute the test in terms of which the data is customarily evaluated.

Statistics play another important role in psychological studies that is not quite so obvious as their part in the evaluation of data. They influence the experimental design that is selected. Each statistic is based on a particular model that is appropriate for some data but not others. There are only a limited number of known statistical methods. Thus data cannot be gathered by indiscriminate methods in the hope that statistics will reveal something. They have to be gathered in a way that does not violate the model or models upon which the statistics are based. If they fail in this regard there may be no applicable statistical test for the data, and the experiment may be useless. In this way the methods of statistical analysis tend to dictate the forms of experimental design.

Statistics vary in a number of important characteristics. First, they vary in power—that is, in the number of cases or subjects required to detect a difference of a given size. The greater the power of the test, the fewer the number of subjects required. Second, they differ in the models that they use and the requirements associated with these models, such as normality of distribution, independence of samples, or homogeneity of variance. Third, and most important, they differ in practical utility.

The use of any statistical procedure requires a great deal of clerical labor. It is therefore important to insure that the proper technique is used so that the most information is obtained for the least effort. Many potentially important studies have not been undertaken in the past simply because the statistical work involved was overwhelming. The advent of the computer has changed the situation entirely. It has eliminated the need for any statistical calculation on the part of the investigator or his staff, and it has increased tremendously the speed with which calculations can be made. Both these effects are important and either would be sufficient as a noteworthy contribution to psychological research. To receive both advantages from one innovation was almost too much for psychological researchers to expect. Previously, for example, the industrial psychologists, interested in predicting success in a given occupation by the use of standard test scores, was faced with the dilemma of reducing the number of tests included in the statistical analysis to make it practical, or increasing the number of tests and using some less rigorous and satisfactory statistical approach. A choice was necessary since the statistical techniques required an enormous amount of labor. With the use of computers this dilemma vanished.

An even more outstanding example exists in reference to the statistical procedure known as factor analysis. A description of factor analysis is given in Appendix A. Computers have, to date, been used to factor analyze data more frequently than for any other statistical procedure. Using ordinary methods a factor analysis of more than forty test scores can be almost literally endless and the results uncertain. With the computer, the analysis is effortless and completed in a relatively short time.

However, a note of caution must be introduced at this point. All dramatic advances require payment, and the use of the computer is no exception. The economics of the computer are deceptive for several reasons. First, it is difficult to know what base line to use. The psychological researcher who does his own statistics does so as part of the over-all research operation. It is hard to determine just how much of his clerk's time is devoted to statistical calculations, rechecking, and so forth. Second, the availability of computers tends to increase the use of statistics in psychological research. The situation is similar to that presented by the consumption of electricity in the home. The cost of electricity remains the same or goes down, but the electric bill goes up as new appliances, gadgets, and fixtures are added.

The individual who is unfamiliar with computer costs is usually dismayed when he is told of them. A moderate-range machine such as the IBM 650 may cost approximately fifty dollars an hour, whereas more complex, high-speed computers may range as high as two hundred to six hundred dollars per hour. It is clear that some form of subsidy or support is necessary if one is to make extensive use of computers.

But it is not the cost per hour that is in itself important. It is the amount of work divided by the cost per hour. On the whole, the more expensive machines are actually cheapest when one considers their output per unit of time. However, there are many practical considerations that determine which machines are used and which are not. Among these problems are the availability of appropriate programs for the machine, an operator, money, and appropriateness of the machine for the problem. In practice most of the problems are resolved on a rather opportunistic basis. In any given location there are relatively few computers available. One takes what one can get and makes the most of it. Parenthetically, it should be noted that the availability of machine time may be a serious problem. Since the computer is being used for virtually all quantitative problems in the sciences, there is often a greater demand for computer time than there are hours in the day. Typically, computer time is scheduled by the hour, well in advance. If the required operation is not completed on time, it may be some days before another time period can be found to finish the job. A given project may require many days, though the computer time is a matter of hours.

Since the computer is a machine, and since its simple existence in any location is expensive, it is often scheduled for a twenty-four-hour day. This in itself is rather an innovation. The computer does not sleep, but unfortunately it does need an operator. It is not unusual, therefore, to hear the whirring, whining, and clicking of a computer throughout the night as the lonely operator fights sleep to keep the machine in operation.

Whatever difficulties are experienced in the present use of computers for statistical analysis, it is inevitable that such use will expand. Computers are too fast and too accurate to be denied. However, the specific factors noted above such as cost, availability of programs, and machine time, as well as a general technological programming lag, have tended to slow the widespread use of computers in psychological research.

Psychologists originally knew nothing about computers and slowly had to be educated as to their function and capabilities. This process is by no means complete. At present these machines are most frequently used where a trained computing staff programs and operates them. The researcher merely provides the data and indicates the statistical operations that he wishes to be performed.

Under such conditions the research psychologist need not know anything about how computers function. He uses them to do the statistical work and can turn his attention to other matters. This release of his energy is, in itself, a tremendous benefit, since his time can then be spent in data collection, analysis, and interpretation. However his blind dependence on computing centers limits his use of the machines and increases their cost, since he must pay not only for their use, but also for the operator's time, and perhaps rental of the program. In addition the psychological researcher is limited in his understanding of the machine's capabilities to the standard programs immediately accessible in the computer installation.

As the importance of computers in psychological research increases, it is probable that the study of computers will become part of the graduate curriculum in psychology. Such study will increase the range of problems that the researcher will be able to put to the computer, decrease the cost (since he may be able to run the machine himself), and increase the absolute amount of computing that he is able to do. The latter is particularly important since in many studies a variety of possible data analyses are eliminated because of manpower limitations. As computers are utilized more efficiently these additional analyses will become feasible, thus increasing the yield from any given batch of data. The situation is not unlike an improvement in farming methods. The amount of land remains the same, but the yield is increased.

There is one danger inherent in the extensive use of computers—namely, the abuse of calculation. In the past if a researcher was unsure of how to handle his data analysis he tended either not to undertake it or to do it in the simplest way possible. With the use of computers the researcher is tempted to try various techniques without giving much thought to any of them. This blind searching for results through overanalysis of data can occur if the researcher has the financial resources to support it. Usually he does not. In all probability the tendency to search blindly will recede as the computer becomes a familiar tool. At present it is somewhat like a new toy. The natural tendency is to play with it and see what it can do. Later this initial excess of interest and involvement will recede and a more realistic use of computers will probably result.

The computer can release the research scientist from doing his own computing. It can do it much faster than he could do it and far more accurately. All these benefits are bound to speed up the progress of research, since more findings can be accumulated in any given period of time.

In addition to this general advantage, the advent of the computer has had, and will have, an effect on the character of psychological research itself. In the past most psychological research has involved the systematic variation of one, two, or three variables. The degree of experimental complexity was suited to the experimental methodology and methods of statistical analysis that were available. More important, it did not place unreasonable demands on the investigator who had to calculate the statistics by hand, or with limited mechanical aid. The computer has removed the necessity for such limitation. It is now possible to design multivariate research involving simultaneous study of a number of different variables, limited only by the problems of logic, theory, and capacities for data collection.

The advantages of multivariate research are out of proportion to its complexity, since the amount of information that one can obtain increases rapidly as one adds variables to the analysis. Fortunately, the effort does not increase proportionately. In the simple two-variable experiment it is necessary to set up the experiment, obtain equipment, space, subjects, and so forth. This procedure must be executed regardless of the number of variables. However, once one has the space, time, and subjects, it is relatively easy to add a few more variables to the study. Most of the work is already done. Of far greater significance is the fact that multivariate studies enable an estimate of the relation between variables. If two variables affect one another when their influence on a third is measured, such an interaction cannot be discovered if they are tested separately in two experiments. When they are included in the same experiment it is possible and necessary to test for such interaction. Thus multivariate research is not only more efficient, but it also provides certain unique information about the interaction between variables that cannot be obtained in any other manner.

It is necessary to add the warning that the simple addition of variables may or may not add to the accumulation of useful knowledge, depending solely on their relevance to the situation investigated. If they are simply thrown into the research in the hope that they may amount to something, little can be expected. If they are included on the basis of previous research in the area, or theoretical considerations, their value should be great.

A number of statistical techniques have been known for some time, but received relatively little application because of the amount of labor involved. If these techniques are used, it is in a limited fashion and by the hardiest investigators. Such methods include factor analysis, multidimensional analysis of variance, multiple and partial correlations, and the exhaustive taking of cross products between all combinations of items. As these and other equally esoteric statistical techniques are used more frequently, because of the availability of computers, it is reasonable to assume that not only the absolute amount of findings will increase, but the nature of the research itself will be altered. Increasingly, the limitation on psychological research will be the ingenuity of the investigator, rather than the relative difficulty of his analytic techniques.

It is hard to anticipate the full impact of the use of complex statistical techniques in a routine manner. However certain trends are probable.

At first it is likely that, as with any new toy, computers will be overused where finances permit. This abuse will result in an overabundance of findings that are not clearly interpretable. This tendency will probably eliminate itself as the researcher realizes that he has bitten off more than he can chew, and certainly more than he can swallow.

Another more positive effect of the use of computers is that research itself will become multivariate, not as a matter of exception, but as a routine. Since the computer provides the means for such analysis, there will be little or no excuse for not increasing the efficiency of data collection by multivariate experimentation.

In addition, it is probable that the relative popularity of statistical tests will be realigned. Many excellent and exact tests such as canonical analysis that can relate multiple predicters of future behavior to various measures of that behavior in one simultaneous analysis will be used, whereas inferior approximate methods that had the advantage of ease of calculation will become historical relics.

A further impact of computer analysis will be an over-all reduction of computational error. While it is convenient to assume that the findings of all reported research are accurate, this is certainly not the case. When computations are carried out by hand, errors are inevitable. It is usually assumed that such errors tend to cancel each other out. This assumption may be incorrect, however, since the researcher might tend to make errors that would help to confirm his hypothesis. Thus computers will speed the execution and expand the scope of data analysis while reducing the errors that occur in such calculations.

THE SIMULATION OF BEHAVIOR

The second major contribution of computer technology to psychological research lies in the simulation of behavior. This behavior may vary from the action of a neural current to the interaction of a group member. In all cases the general procedure is similar.

When a computer is used for statistical analysis it is programmed to perform the calculations required by the statistical formula on the data that is submitted to it. When the computer is used to simulate behavior it is programmed to reproduce the behavior of the person or animal that is under study. In the latter case the computer is used as a dynamic model of the organism. If the model, as reflected in the machine program, is successful, the behavior of the individual will be reproduced in a realistic manner. The degree to which the computer falls short of this goal indicates to the psychologist the extent of his ignorance and the inadequacy of his model. More specifically the deficiency of the computer in the simulation situation suggests to the researcher specific areas where his thinking may have been incorrect, or specific areas where further research is required in order to make the program more accurate.

Simulation of behavior is possible because the computer has one characteristic that is not shared by any person, animal, or any living cell. It can be programmed for each step of its operation. Further, each of these steps can be altered at any time and its effect on the general program noted. It is therefore possible, using a computer, to study the anatomy of behavior in greater detail than by the direct study of any individual. The significance of this possibility is tremendous. It provides the psychologist with a tool of greater precision and power than he ever has had before. The gift is so great that he has been slow to accept it or to appreciate its importance.

One reason that the simulation of behavior has not been more widely applied or appreciated is that in its initial stages it is solely dependent on well-established knowledge for its formulation. In many areas of psychology this knowledge does not exist in sufficient detail to make even crude simulation possible. In other areas the problems of translating behavior into computer language have held back progress. But neither of these difficulties are permanent, and both inevitably will dissolve as knowledge accumulates and the functioning of the computer is more widely understood among psychological researchers. However, even at the present time, simulation has been undertaken in a variety of psychological areas, with varying degrees of success. In order to appreciate the problems and possibilities inherent in the programming of behavior on computers the progress in a number of areas will be briefly described.

For many years physiological psychologists have been studying the physiological correlates of behavior. The success of their efforts has generally been characterized by its lack of applicability to other areas of psychology, as much as by the amount of knowledge obtained.

Recently, however, the situation has dramatically changed. The results obtained from physiological exploration of the brain and nervous system have converged dramatically with the simulation efforts of engineering psychologists, learning theorists, and machine programmers interested in simulating human behavior on computers.

These separate lines of investigation were carried out in different areas by researchers with different backgrounds and using different experimental techniques. Their convergence is therefore of greater significance than might otherwise be the case.

In the present context our emphasis is on the contribution of simulation techniques to the problem of the neural organization and interpretation of behavior; but the physiologist and learning psychologist have made equal contributions to this problem.

As previously mentioned, there are two basic types of computer responses, digital and analogue. Most of the commonly used computers are of the digital variety; they either respond or they don't in a something or nothing manner. The analogue computer makes a graded response proportional to the incoming information that energizes it. In the simulation of neural and physiological behavior, as well as other types of human responses, both types of computer responses must be employed in various combinations.

In the limiting case all units can be interconnected so that an incoming signal affects them all in a constant series of reverberating waves. The exact effect depends on the previous state of the system, the way in which the signal is introduced, and its actual strength. When elements are interconnected they continue to react on one another until they re-establish the equilibrium that had existed before the signal was introduced from outside the system.

Into such a free and open system various constraints can be introduced in order to produce desired effects. Certain incoming signals can be delayed. Screening devices can be employed that limit the types of signals entering the system, and various forms of inhibition can be introduced into the system itself in order to reduce its reactivity. In addition the system can be limited by rearranging the circuits so that all elements are not interconnected. All these circuit arrangements are engineering matters, but as their complexity increases they tend to approximate certain types of neural circuits found in the body. In order for this to occur it is important to introduce into such circuits some type of feedback mechanism by means of which the circuit response is altered to fit some characteristic of the incoming perceptual signals. This adjustment between circuit and signal is a dynamic matching process. The circuit reacts to some aspect of the signal, this reaction is then fed back to the circuit, which reacts to this feedback until a match is obtained. The nature of this matching has to be built into the circuitry and represents the rules of perception of the circuit. Such rules describe the types of transformation from signal to circuit that are followed by the mechanism. Thus a light signal may be reduced to a simple measure of intensity. The measure describing intensity has nothing to do with the physical phenomena of light but can be used to control the reaction of the circuit to the light. It acts as a code for light whose success is proportional to its limitation. The circuit can respond to intensity and match its own response to the function of intensity.

In all cases it is the general abstract rule that determines the match and not any qualitative similarity between signal and circuit response. By such means various sensory information can be transformed in terms that are accessible to and transmissible by the circuit. These circuits can then respond to it by a series of feedbacks and interactions and until the circuit is tuned to the incoming signal as described by the rule or law governing the transformation. At this point the final response can be sent out of the circuit for further action.

The remarkable feature of this sequence of events is that physiological studies indicate that it describes the basic reception mechanism of the human organism. This mechanism has been given the name of TOTE, which stands for test-operate-test-exit. The first test represents the initial response of the circuit to the incoming signal. On the basis of this test the components of the system interact on each other in order to represent the incoming signal as governed by system transformation rules. This is the operate phase. A test is then made of the accuracy of this operation. If the test is successful, the representation as formed by the perceptual circuit is sent, or exited, to other circuits.

It is necessary to view the TOTE operations within the system as organized into a hierarchy of reactions as determined by systems laws. These hierarchies determine priority of response, its sequences and its limitations. Since the organization is hierarchical it can be modified continuously and selectively until a match is achieved. This match, which is in one sense an engineering event, is now believed to constitute a reward or reinforcement for the individual. As long as this match between signal and circuit eludes him he is dissatisfied and continues to search, order, and test in the sense that has been described.

Two types of reinforcing mechanisms have been described and isolated. In terms of computer programming they can be described as information gathering and information utilization. Both types of activity are necessary for problem solving to occur. These types of programs have their direct physiological correlate in the brain. The posterior system of the brain corresponds to the information-gathering system while the frontal intrinsic system involving areas of the cerebral cortex is concerned with the utilization of information gathered. Various neurological studies of brain injuries of an accidental or experimental character have confirmed these functions in the brain.

The sensory TOTE system is primarily of the first type; it is intended to gather information by matching signal to circuit state. In the brain all such incoming information is processed in the information-gathering center until the state of the brain is a realistic representation of all the separate pieces of information reaching it. This general mechanism is also a TOTE operation in the broad sense. When the match between signal and test is achieved, reinforcement of reward is achieved, and the brain is satisfied—that is, it has the correct knowledge.

In a similar manner the frontal intrinsic system organizes the knowledge in terms of past and present experiences of the organism as these relate to previously successful and unsuccessful problem-solving attempts in relation to the types of material currently presented to it. Thus when present information is related successfully to the various strategies stored in the brain on the basis of past learning, then the frontal system is reinforced.

This description must of necessity be oversimplified, but it is sufficient to demonstrate the way in which computer and neural descriptions can coincide.

In general, studies of the relation between neural mechanism and computer analogies suggest that the nervous system operates in the manner of an information-processing system that has a large storage capacity containing a great variety of programs that may be evoked if the stimuli reaching the system requires it. However, it is the stimuli that determines the nature of the strategy or programs that are tested. These programs are themselves the result of earlier efforts at problem solving that have been selectively reinforced. The neural system is active in the sense that it initiates impulses in the absence of stimuli and is engaged constantly in various matching procedures designed to fit incoming signals to the state of the circuitry that it reaches. Thus most of the neural activity that occurs is designed to search and compare earlier solutions with present situations in order to obtain the best fit possible, since the degree of fit is the determinant of reinforcement or reward.

What is most striking about this view of the nervous system is not so much that it resembles the working of many computers in actual operation as the fact that physiological investigation carried on in an independent manner and lodged in an entirely different tradition independently has come to the same conclusion. Thus in building computers man has helped indirectly to explain his own mechanism of neural operation.

Closely allied to the study of the neural mechanism of behavior is the study of thought processes. They are not, however, the same thing. Thought processes can be studied independently of their physiological correlates. In fact no one has succeeded in relating specific thoughts to any physiological measure. While the nervous system must exist for thought to take place, it cannot explain it.

There are two general approaches to the use of computers for the study of thought processes. The computer can be given a problem to solve and the processes in which it engages can be analyzed and the results evaluated. On the other hand it is possible continually to modify the machine program to approximate both the sequences and steps of human thought. While the latter approach is closest to the simulation of thought, the former is also instructive as an example of the use of machine methods to optimize problems-solving success.

An interesting example of the use of machines to solve problems is provided by the machine designed by IBM for solving geometry theorems in the Euclidean manner. The machine is provided with a certain number of theorems, postulates, and axioms and then required to prove a new theorem on the basis of the material with which it has been supplied. This problem is similar to that faced by all students studying the derivation of Euclidean geometry.

In order to reduce the complexity of the problem the machine is provided with a series of short-cut operations that are introduced into its program. These short cuts are in the nature of hints or clues suggesting, for example, that in a given instance one should begin with the nearest proved relationship, or look for other proved relationships containing one of the elements in the theorem to be proved; or to look at other theorems of the same general class, and so forth. These short-cut approaches are similar to the type of exploratory maneuvers engaged in by the human problem solver.

Another approach taken by the machine is to break down the larger problem into a series of smaller problems, each of which can be independently examined and later joined in sequence to solve the larger one. In this way the number of possible relations to be examined in any one problem is greatly reduced.

The geometry machine keeps a record of all the stages in its operation so that its action can be studied after the fact and reproduced in the future if desired.

As with all machines that study thinking or simulate any behavior, it is relatively easy to store successful solutions in the machine's memory, so that as it operates it steadily improves its performance by accumulating successful problem-solving maneuvers and learning to avoid those that do not work. Such a procedure is directly analogous to the human problem-solving operation in which successful solutions are related to the events with which they were associated for purposes of future recall.

It is this ability to improve with performance that initially differentiates the man from the machine. But as such an ability is built into the machine it becomes possible for the machine to learn with each problem that it solves to an almost unlimited degree.

One of the most interesting examples of learning by machines is the checker-playing machine. In this machine are stored all the possible checker positions that it meets, together with the outcomes that follow each move it makes. In addition to this large amount of information, the machine is programmed to generalize on the basis of its successes and failures and store these generalizations to be used as a basis for future action. Thus it learns to recognize classes of moves rather than treating each possible move as a unique event. This machine learns in a relatively short time to beat its programmer at checkers, and thus literally exceeds the capabilities of its own creator. While this demonstration is impressive, it must be remembered that checkers is a game with fixed rules and a limited set of possible moves. Thus it is a situation for which the machine ideally is suited.

The second general use of the machine in the study of thought processes concerns the attempt to duplicate the human by the machine action. In this instance the purpose is not to excell the human performer but to reproduce him. If the machine gets the same result as the person, then the processes by which the machine arrives at its answers can be studied as an avenue to the understanding of the human process. Such a program is not attained at one jump but can be arrived at only by a series of approximations. The problems involved are considerable. It is not enough for the machine to solve the problem; it must also make the same types of mistakes, and solve the problem in the same general manner as its human counterpart. Obviously, such a machine cannot be designed unless the nature of human problem solving is clearly understood.

The difficulties can be seen in a specific example. In a simple test of concept formation, the subject, or the machine, is shown a number of samples of some material or data and asked to determine whether each member or each instance belongs to a given class of events. The machine must first create a concept and then employ it, and it is much more difficult to create a concept than to use it— its use being no more than the application of a program that already has been worked out. Thus the concept "dog" is essentially a program that states if an event can be classified as being alive, having four legs, of a certain size, making certain sounds, and so forth, then it is classified as a dog. The problem involved in forming the concept of dog in the first place and arriving at a specific set of criteria by which the concept can be recognized is much greater.

An additional problem in concept formation is one of translation. In the previous section we described how perceptual information could be transmitted in a transformed manner by coding certain features of it according to the rules of the system. However, the perceptual problems involved in concept formation are extremely complex because the individual or machine does not know what he is looking for until the concept is formed. He must be able to take in as much information as possible to have an adequate basis for the formation. In the adult human being this process is automatic; he does not need to make an effort to see or hear. However, the process of transmitting pictorial data to a machine is a complex matter. Ultimately, the problem must be solved—by the engineer rather than the psychologist—by some procedure in which, as in television, the perception is reduced through a process of continuous scanning of a continuously varying signal that represents the point being perceived at any given instant. Each such point can be fed into the machine, which can then attempt to find patterns among these points that form the basis of the concept. However, the problem presented to the machine would be a very formidable one. Some guides or short cuts are essential both for the machine and the human learner exposed to new stimuli that they seek to relate by the means of a concept.

One approach is to study the types of concepts that can be formed; a number of these have been distinguished. There is the conjunctive concept, which describes the common characteristics shared by all its members. Dog is such a conjunctive concept. Second, there is the disjunctive concept, in which either of two different qualities may cause one to assign a given case to the concept. "Role" is a concept of this type; the role of mother, for example, describes someone who takes care of children and who also manages a home.

A third class includes relational concepts that apply to objects having no common characteristics but sharing certain fixed relationships. The relation between incoming perception and its recoding by the nervous system is of this type, as is the abstract concept of a circle.

A machine may be programmed to fit each of these three classes of concepts to the data it receives, applying one approach after the other. As the actual process of concept formation becomes more clearly understood in a logical and psychological sense, then the process of programming concept formation can be more highly differentiated. Such an approach can test new distinctions, and the results could lead to further refinement of our understanding of abstract thought.

One of the most natural areas in which to attempt simulation of human behavior is the small-group situation. The small group is usually described as a complex system in which the members interact in such a way as to satisfy their own needs through the action of the group. The successful accomplishment of whatever task the group sets itself generally provides a resolution of the complex forces at work and maximizes the satisfaction for all members.

The greatest similarity between the small group and the machine is that both utilize complex communications networks. The communications network of the machine already has been described. The communications network of the group is defined as the pattern of interactions that occur between group members. Hypothetically, by chance people would talk to each other in a random manner, all persons speaking to each other for approximately the same amount of time. In practice, however, a few individuals do most of the talking, and a large part of the conversation also is directed at them. When the possible number of communications-channels between members are related to those actually used, a communication network can be described. There is a clear analogy between such a network and the neural networks previously discussed. However, in many cases the small group is essentially independent of outside signals so that the attempts of the system to arrive at an equilibrium are complicated only by the nature of the individuals making up the group. In another sense each of these persons inject into the group a variety of relevant and irrelevant signals of a physiological, psychological, and social nature that require continual adjustment on the part of other members of the group, if the group equilibrium is to be maintained.

There are several ways in which a computer or a computer-like approach can be used in such a situation. First, the computer can be programmed to reproduce the known probabilities associated with various interaction sequences. Thus, if a person indicates agreement with someone else, the probability of various types of interaction following such a statement are known and can be programmed. Based on such probabilities the machine can generate sequences of interactions that can then be compared to those observed in actual groups. At the point in which the imaginary machine group deviates from the natural group, the programmer can introduce changes in the program and attempt to make the machine performance converge with the actual performance of individuals. These changes are the equivalent of experimental maneuvers with people, but they can be made rapidly and continuously on the machine with none of the practical difficulties associated with the manipulation of subjects.

The second major approach to the simulation of group experience involves the programming of the known facts relating to group behavior. Each of these facts determines, in some degree, the actual performance of individuals in groups. When all are considered simultaneously and given appropriate weight, the performance of the machine should tend to approximate the performance of an actual group. These relevant facts include such variables as task, personality of group members, setting of the group, norms of the group, leadership, communications network, developmental phase of the group, and the like. The limitation to this approach is the availability of well-established knowledge in the area. By bringing this knowledge together in one program, its practical importance can be tested by determining the extent to which it actually can simulate or predict group performance. Of equal importance is the fact that the weighting given to each relationship can be varied either systematically or in a random fashion in an attempt to maximize the predictive power of the simulation. This process will reveal the relative importance of the findings included in the program—an extremely significant fact that cannot be determined from an examination of the individual studies themselves. Thus the machine can be a testing ground, an area for new experimentation, and a hypothesis generator that may lead to new experiments on human groups.

There are a number of other areas in which simulation currently is being actively used. Large-scale organizations are under study from a simulation viewpoint. In the Leviathan project, currently being devised by the Systems Development Corporation, the simulation of large-scale organizations including businesses, schools, government agencies, and military organizations is being attempted. Interest also exists in the simulation of international events. Thus from the nerve current to the global event the challenge and opportunity of computer simulation extends its electrical hand.

Even in such a sacrosanct artistic realm as music, the attempt to simulate and perform compositions is currently under way, with at least moderate success. The thought of the composer of the future sitting at a card-punching console, rather than a piano, may be disturbing, but the elimination of the conductor and performers might result in the drawing together of composer and audience in a manner that has not been possible before.

Whatever the final results of the simulation of music or any of the various areas that we have described, it is certain that the impact of multivariate simulation on the experimentation and conceptualization of these areas is bound to be immense. The speed in which these areas will develop has to reflect in some small degree the speed of the computer itself.

Chapter Three

Teaching Machines

Teaching machines basically are simulated teachers. As such they are an application of computer methodology to the teaching situation. The ideal teaching machine is simply the ideal teacher who always says the right thing at the right time, adjusts the speed and difficulty of the material to the individual student, has an endless fund of patience, and is never bored, no matter how many times the same lesson may have been covered.

Interest in teaching machines recently has been stimulated by the increasing shortage of "live" teachers in the United States, and by the growing sophistication of our knowledge of the relation between man and machine.

The idea of a teaching machine is not new. It was first developed by the American psychologist Sidney Pressey in 1924,[1] though it had been described by the American psychologist Edward Thorndike as early as 1912.[2] The early teaching machines were designed automatically to present and correct test material as well as to provide new information and drill material. The actual machine was the size of a portable typewriter. The material was presented through a small window, and the subject indicated his response by pressing one of four keys. If he pressed the right key, the machine went on to the next item. If not, the machine recorded an error and did not advance. Teaching machines virtually were

ignored at this time, but Pressey was not discouraged and he continued throughout the years to devise simplifications and variants
of his original device. His efforts, however, fell on deaf ears and
were forgotten or ignored by psychologists and educators alike. The
historical climate was not conducive to the acceptance of such devices either as mechanical aids for the teacher or as harbingers of
a much broader revolution to come. As prototypes of teaching
machines, these devices were extremely simple and relatively crude.
It is understandable that the implications they contained were not
heeded.

It was only in the light of the development of computers during the Second World War that the power and flexibility of electronic calculators suggested to psychologists, technicians, and a few
educators that we might possess a sufficiently complex and flexible
technology to be able to fabricate the performance of a teacher.
Since the issues involved are practical as well as scientific, there has
been from the beginning an attempt to strike a balance between
economic possibility and theoretical complexity. This effort is understandable, but in some ways unfortunate, since it has resulted
in many "compromise" machines that are able to perform certain
teaching functions at a relatively cheap price. These machines have
tended to confuse the issue in the sense that they prematurely have
limited the possibilities inherent in teaching machines which, as a
result, sometimes seem more like extensive gadgets than educational
innovations. This kind of device tended to obscure the basic notion
that the purpose of the teaching machine is to simulate the teacher.

A number of issues are raised by the introduction of teaching
machines: What are their potential? Are they economically feasible? What are the repercussions on the process of education likely
to be? How should the development of these machines be handled?

Before any analysis of the moral, technical, economic, and educational implications is undertaken, it is necessary to describe in
greater detail the form and function of teaching machines as they
exist today, in order to provide a realistic framework for the discussion of present and future trends.

CURRENT TEACHING MACHINES

It is neither practical nor useful to attempt a description of all the kinds of machines currently on the market or in production, since several hundred already exist. All these machines, which usually are described as "hardware," can be classified into a few types, sufficient for the purposes of this discussion.

Perhaps the simplest teaching machine is not a machine at all but a book, or at least what looks like a book from the outside cover. On opening such a "programmed textbook," as it is called, the student is greeted with a rather unusual sight. In its simplest form the programmed textbook presents on one page a frame, or pieces of information and questions relating to them, and the answers are on the following page. The nearest equivalent to such a book is the ordinary student workbook, which presents a series of test items to the student for him to solve, with answers provided at the back of the book. However, the programmed textbook is a carefully thought out step-by-step progression of material that leads one through the subject matter, whereas no such thought has gone into the typical student workbook.

A variant of the programmed textbook is the scrambled textbook. On first appearance such a book looks like a confusing series of unrelated statements. In reality, these statements form a complex network of items and answers whose order is determined by the student's progress. If he is right on a given item, he is sent to one page; if he is wrong, he goes to a different page, and so on.

Somewhat more like a machine is the punchboard used for indicating answers to items. When the student punches the correct choice on the board, his pencil goes through the board. If the wrong answer is given, such penetration is not possible.

A more complex machine involves the use of a frame that presents the program item, a place for the student to write or otherwise indicate his answer, and a place for the answer to appear after he has made his response. In this case the student scores himself.

An even more complex and valuable machine allows the programming of prompts or hints for particular items and utilizes a drop-out feature eliminating items that have been answered correctly when the program is repeated by the student.

The most complex teaching machine currently available can present pages of material, or items, moving pictures, film strips, even sound. It thus involves multichannel presentation that incorporates maximum flexibility. It could also present taste, touch, and smell stimuli if there were any use for them.

Teaching machines are particularly intriguing to the American people who always are interested in new mechanical gadgets. However, they are only "hardware" and cannot produce any more than is put into them, regardless of their inherent flexibility. Thus the heart of the teaching machine's usefulness is not in the machines themselves but in the development of the material that they present. If the material is good, then the machines will be able to perform their task efficiently. If it is not, even the most complex machine will be useless.

THE PROGRAM AND THE PROGRAMMER

All teaching machines, in common with the computers discussed in the previous chapter, are dependent on a programmer for their operation. Neither the computer nor the teaching machine is intelligent. Neither knows what to do unless it is instructed. The programming of calculators depends either on the numerical analysis desired or the type of behavior one seeks to simulate. The programming of a teaching machine bears a similarity to both these approaches. Like the programming of numerical analysis, that of the teaching machine requires the presentation of a certain content predetermined by the nature of the subject matter itself. Like the simulator, the teaching-machine program is presented in a form that at worst mimics the teacher, and at best exceeds his or her virtues. The computer programmer tackles one or the other of these tasks at a time. He need not combine them. But the teaching-machine programmer attempts to do two things at once. The material that he covers in the program has a well-defined content.

However, the presentation of this material is guided by principles of learning psychology that are, to some extent, independent of the subject matter presented. The definition of the material to be covered in any teaching-machine program must be supplied by educators who are responsible for its formulation. The method of handling it is derived from research on learning, thinking, concept formation, and other related topics in basic psychology. From the viewpoint of the psychologist, the subject matter is more or less irrelevant. Only when the subject matter influences general laws is he interested in it. If shifts in content do not affect these laws, then content is of no further concern to him.

Programming a teaching machine is not unlike programming a computer. In both, the steps to be covered are broken down into small, distinct components. These steps are stored in known locations. The program can contain provisions for its own modification. For the computer program such modification is used to conserve computer storage space. In the teaching machine modification of the program is a vital element in the adaptation of the machine to the student by relating the program to the accuracy with which he responds. Both types of programs are logical in their development and designed to take into account and capitalize upon the particular features of the machines for which they are designed. Finally, both types of programs represent a compromise between technical limitations and artistic organization.

There are also differences between the two types of programming. The computer programmer who performs numerical analysis is concerned only with the final result. The end of any such program is the answer with which the researcher is provided. On the other hand, the teaching-machine programmer is not primarily concerned with the final product at the end of a long process. His concern is with the student's behavior. The student is slowly altered by his interaction with the machine until, at the end of the program, he has learned certain subject matter. Thus the machine alters the student, whereas the numerical analyst simply uses the machine as a means toward a final statistical result.

In addition, the basic problem faced by the teaching-machine programmer is different from that of the computer programmer. The latter knows the relative efficiency of various techniques at his disposal. They can be defined precisely in terms of time saved, storage space freed, and the like. The teaching-machine programmer is not in such an enviable position; he does not know in any exact sense the best way in which to handle the programming of a particular subject. His problem is more complex than that of the computer programmer since the programming of teaching machines must be based on a thorough understanding of (a) the process of learning in general; (b) the peculiar aspects of learning that result from man-machine interaction; and (c) the nature of the subject matter to be presented.

Psychologists and educators always have been interested in methods of teaching, as distinguished from content. But persons teaching educational methods have been relatively isolated from other related fields. Learning psychologists have had little impact on educational psychologists; and neither has had a measurable effect on the education of teachers themselves. The advent of the teaching machine has created a situation in which experimental psychologists are breaking into territory traditionally that of educational psychologists and educators. The result has been some resentment, confusion, and struggle for control.

A variety of basic issues in learning theory face the programmer as he attempts to transfer a certain kind of subject matter into a teaching-machine program. How much information should be contained in each stage of the program? What is the best method for obtaining the subject's response to the material presented by the machine? Should he push a button, write in his answer, or merely say it to himself? How difficult should the program steps be made? How, and in what form, should the machine feed back whether or not (and to what degree) the student's response is correct? To what extent does the subject matter dictate the form of the program? How flexible must the program be in adapting itself to the unique learning patterns of each student? Is self-pacing by the student more effective than controlled pacing by the machine or the programmer? Is one program equally effective with different types of students? What is the optimum order for the presentation of material? What is the optimum number of student errors that should occur in learning any given sequence of material?

Each of these questions is important, not only for the practical problem of programming materials, but for a thorough and deep understanding of the learning process as an interaction between student, teacher, and content.

It is evident that the answers to some of these questions would tend to determine not only the form of the program but also the very design of the machine itself. For example, if immediate knowledge of the degree of correctness of response is important, the machine must be able to provide this information. If it is important for the subject to create his own responses, the machine must allow him to do this, rather than forcing him to choose among fixed alternatives.

Since the central problem relating to teaching machines is that of programming, it is in this area that most of the active research is currently engaged. It will be interesting and helpful to review some of this research in order to gain a more intimate glimpse of the actual state of the science and art of the teaching machine. At the present time relatively little is clearly established. One firmly held principle is that information should be organized systematically in a logical or at least reasonable manner, employing both deductive and inductive reasoning as dictated by the material. However, a recent study has demonstrated that a series of machine frames randomly presented resulted in quicker learning than when they were presented in logical order. Such a finding is not general but applies to certain limited situations. It does, however, serve as a useful warning to the premature acceptance of a reasonable principle without experimental proof.

A further study on this issue has shown that a logical program organization may result in better acquisition of material, yet not have any great effect on its retention. Obviously, if the material is not retained, the speed and thoroughness with which it is learned initially is irrelevant.

Regardless of the form of any particular program, one of the vital links in the educational process is the way in which the student is required to respond to the information presented by the program. One such distinction involves the relative merits of using multiple-choice versus student-constructed responses to questions. Theoretically important distinctions can be made between the nature of these two types of response. In practice, however, some research suggests that multiple-choice responses take much less time and result in an equal amount of learning when compared to student-constructed responses.

A further refinement of this type of study involves the comparison of the nature of the response and the difficulty of the items. In one such study the findings suggested that simply reading the correct response was equally or more effective than writing a response. In regard to the difficulty of the items, the results raised some doubts in relation to the assumption that easy items are best because the subject can answer them correctly. Interestingly enough, the overt response by the student was most efficient with items of medium difficulty. With both easy and difficult items this approach was relatively ineffective.

A number of related problems exist in regard to the way in which the machine reacts to the student's response. One practical question concerns the importance of a drop-out feature. As mentioned earlier, when the student response is correct, the item is dropped out of the program. Preliminary research suggests the importance of this device in speeding learning and eliminating redundancy, but unfortunately the drop-out feature is expensive.

Another issue concerns the relative effectiveness of student-paced versus machine-paced timing of program presentation. At present, the research suggests that there is no difference, even though one would suppose that the student would do better if he paced himself.

Another consideration is the rate of student response. Studies have compared the relative effects of massed, intensive, long learning sessions versus short-spaced learning sessions. While there is a long and honorable history in psychological experimentation on learning favoring short, frequent sessions in relation to teaching machines, recent studies indicate that the distribution apparently makes very little difference. Of course, all these findings—or lack of findings—are extremely tentative. Further research may reverse them and certainly will qualify them. The results should, however, act as an antidote to the premature acceptance of teaching machines as "superscience" designed to solve teaching problems at a single blow. Perhaps the most important aspect of such machines at the present stage of their development is the questions they raise, rather than the success of the actual performance.

One of the key features in the design of teaching machines, and one of their unique capabilities, is the immediate feedback provided by the machine to the student. In general, the research supports the importance of feedback in the reduction of error and the improvement of learning. Such feedback is particularly valuable if an explanation is provided for incorrect answer. However, the form of this explanation seems to make little difference.

As with all forms of learning, the motivation of the learner is of prime importance. It usually has been found that motivation to work with teaching machines is relatively high. This is probably due to the machines' novelty as much as to their intrinsic nature, and such a favorable reaction may wear off after the initial fascination has ended.

Another important determinant of motivation is the quality of the student's performance. If he does well on the program, he tends to be motivated to continue. If he cannot follow the program, he becomes negatively motivated toward the machine. Thus comprehension and motivation seem to be, not unnaturally, related.

A final area of concern in the design and application of teaching machines concerns the study of various features incorporated in the machines themselves. Since there are great differences in the cost of the machines, their relative effectiveness is an important practical issue. The impact of various types of information presentation, the utilization of various sense channels, different types of display systems, and the ability to vary the program in accordance with student progress—all are fundamental issues that go well beyond the economic questions involved.

In part, the design of the machine is a problem for the engineering psychologist, who must determine the most effective way to transmit information and responses between student and machine. The studies of the different instrument displays carried out in aviation, space research, and by human factor psychologists are relevant to teaching-machine design. At present a large number of design alternatives exist. There is a great temptation to complicate the design of teaching machines simply because we are able to do so, but for the sake of the field as a whole and its future development, it is important not to overdesign such machines, both to avoid pricing the machines out of the market and also to keep their form within the bounds of known requirements.

The future importance of teaching machines depends mainly on the success and speed with which the above and similar questions are answered in the near future. Without clear answers, the programming of the machines will have little to recommend it other than novelty and the reliability it is possible to attain.

The programmer has at his disposal a variety of techniques that he can combine in various ways to aid in the presentation of material. The simplest approach is known as linear programming. The linear program is a fixed sequence of frames of information presented to the student in one and only one order, regardless of his response. Each frame leads into the next in a steady progression of small steps.

In contrast to this basic design is the branching program that bears at least a superficial resemblance to the machine programs used on electronic computers. A branching program is so named because the program sequence depends on the response of the student: if he answers correctly he is directed onward to a new frame of information; if he answers incorrectly he branches off the main program and is provided with special material designed to aid him in correcting his mistake. (An example of this is the "scrambled textbook" mentioned earlier.) When the material has been learned, the student may join the main line of the program at a different point. The branching program is more complex and generally longer than the linear program, though this depends in the last analysis, on the size of the program steps.

Regardless of its general form, the program must have some logical and systematic organization. While no one ideal system is known for the presentation of material, it is currently believed that the first step in efficient programming consists of the isolation of the rules or principles governing the organization of the particular subject matter that one wishes to teach. In some subjects, such as mathematics or spelling, these rules may be relatively obvious. In other areas, such as history or art appreciation, they may be relatively obscure. However, if the rules can be stated and arranged in a systematic table, each cell of the table will represent a unique example of the interaction of the rules in a given case. It is then the programmer's job to supply the examples that exemplify the rules in joint operation. Such an approach has the advantage of being systematic; but a good program is more than an exercise in logic.

A variety of supplementary programming devices are available, and more are bound to be discovered or created as the need arises. For example, the "prompt" and the "probe" have proved helpful in aiding the unsure student. The prompt is a hint about a given item; a probe is less clearly directed and is intended to initiate the student's re-evaluation of his response rather than direct him toward a new one. Prompts may be specific verbal statements, or they may employ only the use of indirect verbal context that suggests an answer by the process of verbal association. Thus in the item "We are going to the ———" the answer must be a noun. The thematic prompt is provided, in this case, by the rest of the sentence.

A similar approach that is helpful in certain types of visual material is the "fading technique." In this approach various aspects of the material are dropped with each repetition of the cycle. Thus in the first cycle a whole map may be shown in detail. Then a few lines are left out, then the names are dropped altogether, and so forth. This approach can also be used with strictly verbal material, using the full description first and then dropping facts a few at a time with each repetition of the program.

A final example of programming technique is usually referred to as "item" or "program" density. The denser the program, the more the student is required to learn in a given sequence. In part, density is a function of difficulty. In a different sense, the density is inversely related to the redundancy of the program. The less the redundancy, the greater the density. By varying density in a systematic manner the program can be adapted to students with different degrees of ability.

The programming of teaching machines, like the programming of computers, takes a great deal of time and effort. This is true even for a bad program. A good program is a work of art. In the haste to get programs on the market, most manufacturers are unprepared for the special problems inherent in the process of

programming itself. This job has almost no precedent. No textbook writer ever undertook such a task, and certainly no teacher
has attempted it. In some areas, such as elementary reading or
arithmetic, the specific steps have been spelled out with some precision. But in general the programmer has little to go on except
the facts themselves as they are presented to him by an educator
or through the medium of the textbook. Thus the selection of
suitable programming units is a problem for experimental research. But whatever the units, the subject matter must be broken
down in a logical and systematic manner.

The importance of such a task certainly exceeds the immediate
implications of writing a program. It requires that someone sit
down and think through all the systematic implications of a given
subject matter, organize it in logical terms, and divide it up into
digestible steps. Such a task is essentially the analysis of teaching
content, which most teachers avoid, but which lies at the heart
of the teaching process. In answer to the question, "What are you
trying to teach?" most educators are rather vague, or fall back
on achievement scores. The programmer must, however, be specific. His task is most important since the program that he writes,
if it is widely accepted, will establish empirically the content in a
given area. His position is rather like that of a successful textbook
writer: the subject is defined by the book he writes.

But, unlike a textbook, a program cannot merely be written,
though that task is extremely complex and arduous in itself. A program must be thoroughly tested, retested, revised, and finally validated. Its testing resembles the standardization of a psychological
test rather than the publication of a text. After the programmer has
finished with his work, and made some preliminary checks to
insure reasonable clarity of meaning and logic of sequence, it is
necessary to carry out fairly large-scale applications of the program
in order to test its effectiveness and isolate its trouble spots. Such
a testing process requires the use of the program in various educational settings under reasonably controlled conditions, and it will
inevitably suggest revisions that must be incorporated in the original program, or at least in a second edition. Of even greater significance is the opportunity that is presented for determining just
how effective the given program is in teaching its defined content.

A record of the number and kinds of mistakes, the total time required to learn the material, and a standard test of achievement in the area can establish the general effectiveness of the program for given types of students using it for specified lengths of time. Such information would be of great value to educators in planning any program of study. Present teaching materials do not lend themselves to such exact evaluation because of the variation in the way in which they are used by different teachers. Any evaluation of teacher effectiveness is always complicated by the difficulty of separating the effectiveness of the teacher from the effectiveness of the method he or she uses. The teaching machine overcomes this technical problem since the machine is the method. No personal element except the student's own rate of progress can alter the teaching procedure.

The evaluation of the program is necessary in order to establish its effectiveness. This kind of testing also has the added value of adding to our knowledge of the effectiveness of different types of teaching procedures. In this sense each new program is both a research project and a test standardization. This is why the work involved in producing adequate and useful teaching-machine programs is much greater than most people—including publishers—suspect. It may be helpful to the reader to look at a section of a specific program in order to gain a clearer conception of what is involved. Such an example is given in Appendix B.

THE ECONOMICS OF THE TEACHING MACHINE

Publishers who produce educational materials are currently investing heavily in teaching machines. It is this economic intervention of publishers that has done more than anything else to focus widespread attention upon teaching machines and what their implications may be.

The publishers who have become interested in this area have a natural desire to make money. They have invested in these machines in the expectation of a rich harvest. By doing this they have almost singlehandedly contributed to a self-fulfilling prophecy, which is, of course, what they intended.

The shift in publishers' attitudes on the future of teaching machines has been very abrupt. As recently as 1960 the major publishers looked on the machines as a temporary fad. However, the following year this opinion was sharply revised and major financial resources were committed to the machines. It is now estimated that teaching machines may be a billion-dollar business by 1970.

It is difficult to state why this shift should have come so suddenly. Presumably the forces responsible for it were building up for some time until they suddenly passed the critical point and produced the sharp change in climate. In part, the enthusiasm for and interest in teaching machines reflect the nature of our economy, which thrives on novelty, new models, and new techniques. Moreover a bandwagon effect forces publishers to compete after a few have made the initial investment. Whatever the motivations, the results are forthcoming in a tremendous variety of programs covering virtually every subject for which there might be a demand.

The disinterested spectator watches all this activity with some misgivings. It may represent a premature spring that ends in frost. On the other hand it may simply represent the immature manifestation of an important future trend.

Competition among programs is never likely to be great, because of the effort, time, and skill required for their design. Therefore, they must achieve a level of excellence from the start or the effectiveness of teaching machines will be seriously crippled.

Unfortunately, economic pressures force publishers to put programs on the market prematurely. The result can be only disappointment and discredit to the machines themselves.

A teaching machine of reasonable flexibility is expensive. As with a computer a great initial investment must be made for the machine itself, unless it is rented from a manufacturer, and the present rate of obsolescence is almost terrifying. The machine that is bought today may be superseded by a breakthrough in design the following year. This in itself, is not necessarily crucial, but unfortunately, also as with computers, change in design may imply change in programs, which is a crucial problem.

In general the expense of a teaching machine presently exceeds the cost of hiring a teacher to do the same job. Where budgetary limitations are paramount, such machines will not be adopted. However, mass production of these machines and the weeding out of those not fit to survive should bring costs down and quality up.

These costs will probably have two opposing effects. On the one hand manufacturers will attempt to produce simplified machines on a mass basis, with cheaper and poorer programs. On the other hand, the cost of all machines, plus the rapid changes in programming technique and design, will cause the prudent administrator to pause. He will tend to wait until the accumulated weight of evidence, or parental demand for the latest in educational method, forces him to commit his hand and his budget.

The first of these trends should lead to some disenchantment with teaching machines among early enthusiasts. If this period is weathered, it is probable that mature, flexible, well-programmed, but relatively expensive, machines will become available.

As to the question of cost, public expenditure is relative. We will spend any amount on destructive weapons or on systems to counter destructive weapons, but proportionately little for direct progressive efforts, including housing, the arts, or education. However, as has been noted, the American people have an ingrained affection for and interest in technical devices, from the automobile to the Automat and teaching machines appeal to this pragmatic interest. While machines may cost far more than the teachers they might partially replace, this cost is small as compared to other expenditures. Under certain conditions the whole structure of educational finance might rapidly shift. For example, if it were demonstrated that the basic sciences could be taught faster and better on machines than by lectures, our long-range competition with the Communist nations might force a rapid employment of teaching machines by popular demand. It is conceivable that Congress would insist upon it.

A less immediate but no less inevitable situation is the increasing teacher shortage that helped to focus public attention on the teaching machine in the first place. The teacher shortage is a fact. It could be solved by a general increase in teachers' salaries and a change in their social status. However, neither of these steps seems likely under private auspices. Educational costs already are relatively high, and it is difficult to change the social status of a given role such as a "teacher" without changing the whole society in the process. Of course, massive government aid could increase the number of teachers in training, but a variety of political and historical factors have impeded attempts to provide such aid in the past and seem likely to do so in the future. In the light of current conditions, however, it is not unlikely that government subsidy will be forthcoming for the purchase of machines. Such aid would, of course, sharply reduce the cost of programmed instruction to the school system and would not be noticeably resisted, because the government would not tell the school systems what machine programs to use, but only provide them with the possibility of using those that they choose. Under such an arrangement, teaching machines easily might provide an answer to the teacher shortage, if they could be sufficiently perfected.

Government funds already are supporting most of the fundamental research that forms the basis of programming teaching machines. If the need for such machines continues—and it seems that it must increase—this money may also increase. Thus the federal government may, and probably will, finance the development and the distribution of such machines on a large scale and at a cost that would appear negligible in terms of the over-all budget, though it might be prohibitive to each local or state school system.

In the early stages, at least, only well-subsidized research organizations or large publishers will be able to afford the investment required. Unfortunately, most of the public is unaware of what to expect in terms of teaching-machine programs. Their only protection will be an education in the nature of teaching machines and the way in which the machines' programs are designed. In this manner the public may learn how to spot inadequately tested programs, or those of intrinsically poor design. However, in the long run, the future of teaching machines lies in the hands of psychologists, though the adoption of machines is an administrative educational decision. The effectiveness of the teaching machine depends on its program. An adequate program must be based on knowledge of the principles of human learning. If the psychologist can advance rapidly enough in this area to supply the needed principles, teaching machines should flourish. If not, they will founder.

From a different point of view the advent of teaching machines has given a great impetus to learning psychology, stimulated new research, and made available new sources of funds for such research. Whatever the future of the teaching machine itself, its effect on the development of learning-theory research in psychology can only be good.

THE TEACHING MACHINE
AND THE EDUCATIONAL PROCESS

The general public is usually either attracted or repelled by the notion of a machine that teaches. It appeals to their mechanical bent as a complex toy, but it is repellent to their notion of personal liberty and freedom of interpersonal exchange.

Both these reactions are misguided and arise from a misunderstanding of the nature of teaching machines. These machines are intended to act as personalized tutors for the individual student. An ideal machine would not seem mechanical to the student working with it; it would be interesting, flexible, and intriguing.

The effect of teaching machines on the educational process in general, and on the employment of teachers in particular may be very far-reaching.

At present, school personnel engage in a variety of administrative, educative, and caretaking functions. Teaching machines can affect all these functions in varying degrees.

In educational administration various low-power calculators and other specialized accounting machines are presently used to file student scores and maintain efficient, easily accessible records of various kinds. Financial payments are made using various kinds of automated equipment. Thus the use of machinery is common and increasing all the time in the administration of education organizations.

The caretaking aspects of school maintenance require human performance, often aided by various automatic or semiautomatic machines designed for cleaning, polishing, heating, lighting, and so forth.

Neither the administrative nor the maintenance function is directly affected by teaching machines, except as they influence the use of the school by students, or the assignment of space to facilities, personnel, and records.

The most direct impact of the teaching machine is on the teacher, particularly the traditionally trained teacher covering well-defined subject matter. Presumably, the physical-education teacher would not be directly supplanted by a teaching machine, though a large variety of electrical equipment already is available for such purposes, as one can see in many health clubs.

The teaching machine is designed to act as a substitute for the teacher's central function: the transmission of information to the student. If the machines are able to perform this function, they may replace the teacher in this respect. However, the teaching machine cannot conduct a seminar; it cannot have a personal conference with the student; it cannot initiate field trips; it cannot plan school projects; it cannot sponsor various social activities and clubs; it cannot act as a substitute for an athletic coach, nor can it conduct a laboratory session.

In addition, it is probable that teaching machines will not be kept up to date, because of the time required for programming. Thus, in the more advanced topics, where progress is rapid and continuous, a teacher may be needed to supplement standard material presented by the machine.

So, the teaching machine is not a substitute for the educational process, as some have feared. On the other hand, it increasingly can take over the traditional teacher's role of transmitting information, and it is probable that this substitution can, under proper safeguards, be accomplished with an increase in effectiveness and efficiency. As pointed out earlier, the teaching machine never forgets, never makes a mistake, and can be adapted to the speed and intelligence of the individual student. Beyond these advantages, the machine can cover any subject for which it is programmed with approximately equal ability. The same hardware can be used for a great variety of subjects, and persons in the same room can study different subjects using similar machines, which should greatly increase the efficiency with which school space is used.

There will always be teachers who are able to present a given subject more effectively than a teaching machine, but they are the exception. A program that has been developed with sufficient care ought to be more effective than are the vast majority of teachers in any given area.

Those who are actively engaged in the production and design of teaching machines usually make a point of avoiding any statements that machines might take the place of teachers. While this is true in a broad sense, it is also true that if the machines are designed correctly they *will* take the place of teachers as they have functioned traditionally.

When teachers come to realize this, a strong reaction is bound to set in. The teaching machine does to the teacher what industrial automation does to the factory worker. It threatens his particular niche in the vocational framework. However, the teacher is in a much more fortunate position than the industrial worker. While the former's area of competence may be specialized, his methods are not. A teacher is not limited to the presentation of factual materials. He has at his disposal a variety of other, more modern and generally more interesting procedures that he can use. In this sense, the teaching machine can free the teacher for more interesting and creative tasks. If the introduction of teaching machines is handled in a gradual and democratic manner, teachers will probably realize the benefit they can bring and welcome them. However, it is more likely that machines will be imposed from above, in which case teachers may actively or passively fight them. Then, the quality of education probably would be temporarily impaired and the effectiveness of the machines themselves reduced.

It is unfortunate that in most locations teaching resembles the civil service: it doesn't pay very well, but there is compensatory job security. These conditions foster long-term dedication, but they do not create a suitable climate for the introduction of new techniques and ideas.

There is virtue in a gradual application of teaching machines from the viewpoint of perfecting the machines, developing and testing adequate programs, and reducing the teachers' resistance to them. Whether history will allow the luxury of such an approach remains to be seen.

Psychologists can do little to guide the application of teaching machines once they have been put on the market. Their main point of influence is in the basic research that stands behind the programmer's technique, and in setting of standards for the proper pretesting of programs, so as to minimize the appearance of inadequate programs. The latter problem has concerned the American Psychological Association, which recently formulated certain preliminary notions regarding the standards to be set for programming. It was stated that in general: (a) a teaching machine needs to be evaluated not only in terms of its mechanical reliability but also in terms of the quality of the programs available for use in conjunction with the machine; (b) any program should be subject to preliminary testing in order to determine its teaching effectiveness, just as any test must be standardized in order to measure its reliability and validity; (c) pilot experimentation with teaching machines in school settings should be encouraged prior to their widespread adoption.

However, it will require more than a statement by psychologists to put standards into effect. Educators, publishers, and government agencies must all agree on formal or informal standards. Such agreement on a nationwide basis will not be easy to obtain, and it is not likely to occur until a pressing need is felt by all parties. At the present time no such need is felt. Psychologists do their research and report their findings; publishers seek to capitalize on a new boom by quick production; educators watch developments with feelings of elation tinged with despair; and the government watches benignly from a distance, providing moderate encouragement to basic research.

It is in the midst of these conflicting and disconnected reactions that teaching machines have emerged from the laboratory, through the programmer, into the classroom.

In terms of the present educational models, the teaching machine would appear to fit most easily into a progressive-school type of curriculum. This kind of education already has emphasized a variety of approaches to learning, of which the transmission of information is only one. Teachers accustomed to this flexibility gladly would relinquish a particular function to be able to devote time to others that are potentially more rewarding and stimulating.

The nature and significance of teaching machines ultimately will have to be taught in the teachers' colleges themselves, if the machines are to be used in a sympathetic and effective manner. But the diffusion of ideas as well as techniques will take time.

If extensively adopted, the machines would have a strong impact on teacher training. The teacher of a number of subjects would be a more appropriate goal for such training than the specialized teacher who is produced today. Except at very advanced levels, the teacher's knowledge of a particular subject matter would have little importance, and great importance would be attached to his familiarity with educational techniques. From this viewpoint the teacher would become more of a technical specialist in educational methods than a transmitter of knowledge. This shift in emphasis would simplify the training of teachers, and probably attract a different group of people to the teaching profession over a period of time. Such a change would emphasize the importance of learning and educational psychology and require even greater research in educational methods than exists today. Thus the indirect effect of the teaching machine would be to require not only the study of learning principles but also a general study of other educational methods not specifically used by the machine, but employed by teachers who supplement its activity.

It is also important to realize that teaching machines need not be limited to a school setting. Since programs are standardized for the machines a nationwide standard for subject matter at any grade level could be achieved with relative ease. With such standardization, students could easily study at home, if they had a machine and programs available. Home study is of limited value for the normal student but of significant value for sick or handicapped students. Of greater importance may be the traveling student who takes his machine with him or rents one wherever he goes. If educational standards are ultimately measured in terms of academic achievement, there is no reason why the student has to stay in one place to study. In colleges and universities, for example, it might well be possible to re-establish the medieval system of traveling scholars. In this way one might be able to study at several centers of learning connected with one's field of interest and still cover the required subject matter. On the college level, teaching machines might make a number of interesting scholastic programs practical realities. Various patterns of work and study could be devised easily. Students could combine travel in foreign countries with teaching-machine study. Moreover, they could progress through college at their own pace in keeping with their abilities and rates of learning.

Perhaps the greatest significance of teaching machines on the college level is that the machines would make the goal of equal educational opportunities for all a realistic one. If machines and programs were financed largely by the government, it would be appropriate and logical that they be available to all who could use them. As long as education is privately endowed, a college education will not be available to the individual solely on the basis of his ability, because of the economic factors inherent in the operation of private colleges. But with government support such machines should belong to the people and be available to all, as is public education through high school. Such a development would be logical and of great importance to the future position of our nation.

IMPLICATIONS OF TEACHING MACHINES

In this discussion of teaching machines, American society has been used as the point of reference. However, a machine works equally well in any country. It is probable that these machines would have greater importance in underdeveloped countries suffering from a chronic lack of trained personnel than they would in more advanced societies. Through the use of proper translations, a form of international education could be developed as an aspect of machine-age technology.

None of these developments is unlikely, given the widespread acceptance of teaching machines. Whether such acceptance will, in fact, come about, depends on the many factors already discussed.

There are two types of dangers inherent in the development of teaching machines. The first is that they might be discredited due to premature publication and marketing. Disenchantment due to poorly designed machines and programs would be extremely unfortunate, in view of their possibilities.

The other danger is that teaching machines might be too successful. In such a case, they might produce a new era of regimentation in education. All students would be required to learn a specified set of facts in a particular order. Such a system would lend itself to a totalitarian approach with great ease. But this is no reason to avoid teaching machines. It is just a danger latent in their misuse. In any case, it is certain that totalitarian governments will use such machines for their own purposes regardless of the course that democracies follow. Safety lies not in ignoring the machines but in using them in keeping with our tradition of freedom under the law.

The spectrum of educational techniques should be expanded by teaching machines rather than reduced. If other methods such as field trips, seminars, and laboratory experimentation do not prosper under the use of the machines, then something is wrong with our approach; machines should fertilize other educational methods, not lead to their atrophy.

The teaching machine is distinguished from audio-visual aids in its ability to supply continuous feedback of student progress, and its flexibility in adapting itself to the progress of individual students. It does, however, lend itself to use in conjunction with such aids. Thus a lesson in physics on a teaching machine could be followed by a televised program presenting a demonstration-lecture covering the same area. What audio-visual aids lack in flexibility, they add in the physical impact of the experimental demonstration coupled with human explanation.

The proper combination of teaching machines, audio-visual aids, and various teacher-led methods opens a new horizon for education research. However, such combinations are as yet untouched territory for future investigation.

The study of man-machine relations, as conducted by military and engineering psychologists, should provide some initial guidance in this area in terms of analyzing the problem and providing research methods for testing the effectiveness of various combinations of men and machines in the classroom.

The adoption of teaching machines is destined to institute a reformulation of our educational principles. The machines themselves will cause a re-evaluation of subject matter in each area that they cover. Collectively, they will require educational psychologists, educators, and the general public to re-evaluate the nature of public education. It will be necessary for all these groups to reconsider how much of our educational time should be spent in learning new subject material, how much in supplementing factual learning with group discussions, laboratory experiments, field trips, audio-visual aids, and the like. More generally, what place shall sports, socializing, clubs of various kinds, school projects, and other non-intellectual aspects of the school program have in the school of the future? These questions cannot be solved by the teaching machine, but they must be solved for its proper utilization in the school program.

The psychologist cannot decide these issues, since they are problems of social policy that lie beyond his professional competence. He can however, test the relative effects of different decisions and offer a guide to others who are responsible for decision-making.

In recent psychological literature, increasing attention has been given to the factors involved in such decision-making. In drawing together the various strands that are related in one way or another to the advent of the teaching machine, it is helpful to use a decision-making model as a basic descriptive device.

The basic principle of decision-making theory is that any decision involves costs, risk, and rewards. A proper balance of these variables determines whether a given decision should be expedited or avoided. In technical decision-making theory an attempt is made to make quantitative each of these variables so that a fairly exact decision can be made. In the present instance this is not possible.

The decision to be faced by psychologists, educators, and the public is whether to encourage the widespread use of teaching machines. This decision need not be made today, but it will probably arise in some form tomorrow.

Such a decision involves a number of complex issues, many of which we have discussed. For the sake of simplicity, let us assume, however, that nothing more than the one basic question is involved—that is, whether or not to adopt teaching machines. Let us review the preceding discussion by briefly considering the costs, risks, and rewards involved in this decision.

The cost of adopting teaching machines can be broken into a number of dimensions. First is the financial cost of the machines and the programs. Under present conditions the cost exceeds, and is likely to continue to exceed, the cost of equivalent teacher time. In another sense cost refers to the impact of teaching machines on teacher performance. Any technical innovation is accompanied by various social difficulties and resistances. These are inevitable and can at best be minimized but not eliminated.

The risks involved in the adoption of teaching machines come from at least three directions, as we have already observed. First, the machines may be adopted before they are perfected and thus lead to disappointing results; second, widespread use of such machines may lead to a standardization and mechanization of education; and third, government sponsorship of teaching-machine purchase and distribution might lead to government control of education itself.

The rewards that are latent in the application of teaching machines are many, as we have previously suggested. The teacher is released from the simple transmission and testing of information for more interesting and creative methods and activities. The student can proceed at his own speed. The level of education can be generally raised. Equal access to educational materials can be provided for all. Improved education can be provided for backward countries. And flexibility of all educational planning can be greatly increased.

These are some of the costs, risks, and rewards. A simple listing of them is not, however, sufficient for decision-making. Each risk, cost, and reward must be weighed by some appropriate means in order to arrive at a final resolution. This weighing can be made directly and indirectly, by the psychologists who provide basic research information, by the manufacturers, the programmers, the educators, the government, and ultimately the general public, in the coming years.

In describing the application of teaching machines to the school, it is easy to venture into possibility and leave established fact far behind. Therefore, in concluding this discussion of teaching machines, it may be appropriate to describe some futuristic work in the incorporation of machines in schools that actually exists at the present time.

The most interesting application of teaching-machine methodology to the total school setting currently is being conducted by the Systems Development Corporation, an organization devoted to the study of man-machine interactions. The major feature of this investigation is "CLASS," an appropriate abbreviation that stands for the Computer-based Laboratory for Automated School Systems. This laboratory consists of three separate areas: a principal's office, a guidance office, and a classroom large enough to accommodate twenty students. Each of these rooms is connected to a central electronic computer. Information from the computer can be displayed in each room and information and instructions can be fed into the computer from each room. Otherwise, these three locations are intended to serve their normal school function.

At any moment the principal can communicate with the computer and obtain various information pertaining to daily school administration such as registration, bus scheduling, attendance records, individual grades, financial accounts, or any of the numerous teachers' records. This information routinely will be stored in the computer as it is obtained, and the computer thus will serve as the filing system.

Similarly, in the guidance office the past record of all students will be available instantly, including grades, performance on standardized tests, reports of interviews, and observations by teachers and other professionals. It should be noted in passing that having this information already stored in the computer would facilitate greatly any statistical analysis that the counselor might wish to undertake of individual students or of the total group. Various types of profile comparisons easily could be made, as well as exhaustive comparisons of the relations among all test results. Factor analyses of the individual easily could be carried out and probably would provide uniquely interesting and valuable information. Further, multiple correlation with known test criteria could be conducted in order for the counselor to utilize all known actuarial methods in making predictions of student performance in various academic and social occupations.

In the classroom itself provision exists for various forms of audio-visual display that can be controlled directly by the computer. These include closed-circuit television, film-strip display, films, and language laboratory equipment. However, the most important feature of the classroom consists of electric typewriters by means of which the student communicates with the computer. Because of the complexity and large storage capacity of the computer each student can study a different subject at the same time. All programs are stored in the computer and can be initiated by an appropriate request from the student. In this sense the computer is a program library that transforms one classroom into a whole school in which each student can study a different subject at a different rate.

Two things must be emphasized about the CLASS installation. First, it exists. It is not a projection into the future or a dream. Second, it is extremely expensive. Therefore, while many of its features sound very appealing, its cost would prohibit any widespread adoption in the near future. CLASS is experimental. However, from it will come the practical modifications that may determine tomorrow's more advanced educational techniques, particularly if it can be demonstrated that students in such an installation learn at an appreciably greater rate and over a broader range than in more traditional settings.

The teaching machine casts a long shadow over the educational horizon. Its advent may cause the field to take quite a different direction from any envisioned by the wildest proponent of progressive education only a few years ago. If properly handled this development may benefit many individuals and strengthen our whole society. But if misused, teaching machines either will disappear and be remembered as a fad, or will add to the increasing weight of automation already overpowering the individual.

Chapter Four

Psychological Implications of Communications Theory

Communications theory, or "information" theory, as it is often called, is relatively new. It was originated by a scientist working in the Bell Telephone Laboratories and reported on in an obscure engineering journal in the year 1948.[1]

Its significance was appreciated by only a small group of communications engineers who saw in it a solution to many of their conceptual and quantitative problems.

The later reception that communications theory received was probably as much of a surprise to its creator, the American communications engineer Claude Shannon, as to anyone else. His interests were limited at the time to describing in mathematical terms the properties of communications sent over noise-laden channels such as the radio, telephone, or any of the standard means of communication. The expansion of his initial concepts into virtually every area of science constituted a scientific breakthrough the extent of which was only comprehended in retrospect.

When such a breakthrough occurs in science it follows a more or less typical but dramatic sequence of events as it influences high-, middle-, or low-brow types of scientists.

With the upper echelon of high-brow scientists, it is the quality of the idea that counts, and the degree to which it suggests quite new directions for theory and speculation. Their interests are scientific rather than practical and they would prefer a new, unusual generalization to a plodding conclusion.

For the middle-brow scientist new concepts have validity only if they can be used as practical tools for solving otherwise unsolved problems. The new language and symbolism associated with the breakthrough is not appealing to them. They are essentially oriented to problem solving rather than theorizing or generalizing.

Finally, there are the scientific low brows. These men are unlikely to hear of the breakthrough in the first place, since they do not tend to read the journals in which such ideas generally appear. The low brow is a limited technical specialist who may be threatened by the re-evaluation of his field that might be caused by the breakthrough, since it might undermine the importance of his specialty.

It was through this mixture of scientific types that the original description of communications theory filtered in 1948. During the next three years this material became the focus of excited academic gossip and speculation in such institutions as MIT and Harvard. From these centers the ideas traveled along normal academic communications channels, themselves an interesting phenomenon. These channels are not geographically limited, since prominent scientists are likely to have extensive national and international connections. Thus in a relatively short time a wide network of leading figures and creative minds become aware that a new and possibly important reformulation of an old problem has appeared. The breakthrough is then a reality.

The basic concepts of communications theory are relatively simple. The theory itself is a mathematical expression of the relation between these concepts. Fortunately, the mathematical aspects of the theory can be largely ignored in the present context.

The fundamental idea of communications theory is that any communication is characterized by a sender who transmits information to a receiver through the medium of a communications channel. The information transmitted has two components: the intended meaning of the sender, and error, or noise. This noise may be produced by mechanical interference in the channel, just as static interferes with radio transmission, or by a variety of individual and technical factors.

It was by using the telephone conversation as a model that this description of communication was devised. However, the definition applies to any communication, whether carried on in person or not. It can describe communication between machines, between men, and between men and machines.

This model has been used profitably in such diverse fields as physics and physiology. In physics, communications theory has been related to quantum mechanics. Physiologists were able to re-analyze the action of nerve networks in terms of these new conceptions. Further applications were made in almost every conceivable area, with varying degrees of success. Sociologists used the concepts to explain organizational communications patterns, and papers have appeared relating communications theory to anthropology, political science, philosophy, biology, genetics, and a variety of other fields. Even library science has been started off in a new direction!

During the initial stages of this development only economics appeared immune from the general contagion, because of the peculiar isolation of its content from that of other disciplines. But it appears to be only a question of time before it too becomes involved in the general re-evaluation of subject matter brought about by the widespread adoption of communications theory.

THE LANGUAGE OF COMMUNICATIONS THEORY

The power of this theory is thus far in excess of the expectations of its originator. Among its various contributions, it provides an integrative framework for the preceding sections of this book, since computers, teaching machines, and to some extent space travel are essentially problems involving the relation between men and machines. In each case the crucial problem is the communication between man and machine. This problem has proved particularly thorny because men and machines do not speak the same language. Communications theory provides a common element or unit to which both languages could, in certain instances, be reduced. This marvelous unit is called, prosaically enough, a "bit," short for binary digit. Technically a "bit" of information is defined as the amount of information that we need to make a decision between two equally likely alternatives.

The bit is the basic element in the language of many machines, including digital computers. The operation of such computers involves nothing more than a distinguishing between a series of yes-no alternatives, each of which constitutes one bit of information.

While the language of many machines may be expressible easily in terms of the number of bits involved in any given sequence of operations, it is certainly not obvious how language or other aspects of human behavior can be translated easily and systematically into the same terms. The main value of communications theory is that just such a translation is often possible, even though its form may not be obvious initially. When this translation is performed, men and machines literally speak the same language, and the same general communications theory can be applied to both. Such a theory can then become the basis for the analysis of any man-machine system, such as we have discussed in connection with space travel.

The teaching-machine program, a prime example of man-machine interaction, easily can be reduced to bits of information, particularly if it is presented in the form of multiple-choice responses in which the number of comparisons or alternatives is fixed. However, the number of bits of information associated with any frame in the program can be determined only by examining the item. If the question is whether Columbus did or did not discover America in 1492, only one bit is required. Two bits would be required if the student had to choose between four equally likely alternatives. The first bit would distinguish between the first two alternatives and the second two. Having identified the right pair, the second bit would be used to distinguish between the two alternatives in that pair. The relation of bits to equally possible choices is simple. The number of alternatives is equal to some power of two. The exponent of power is the number of bits. Thus four alternatives equal two to the second power, or two bits. In a more complex situation involving thirty-two alternatives, two has to be raised to the fifth power in order to equal thirty-two; thus five bits of information are required to distinguish between thirty-two equally likely alternatives.

HUMAN PERCEPTION OF INFORMATION

The concept of bits of information can be applied even more easily to human perception of information coming from the environment than it can to teaching-machine programs. The advent of communications theory literally has created a new kind of research in psychology that determines the number of bits of information that can be sensed by the human observer using various sense modalities. This research resembles traditional studies in psychophysics designed to relate changes in physical stimuli to changes in perception. However, if such studies are redefined in terms of the number of bits of information supplied to the observer, both the physical stimuli and the observer's perception of them can be defined in terms of the same units, and all sense modalities can be reduced to a single framework.

One of the simplest examples of such a study involved the absolute judgment of tones. The experimenter sounded tones of different frequency and assigned numbers to them to be used simply as identification tags. The tones were then played again, and the subject was asked to give their assigned number. Under these conditions the subjects had no difficulty whatever in distinguishing three tones. Four tones usually were distinguished. However, when from five to fourteen tones were chosen from a range of one hundred to eight thousand cycles per second, the subjects became confused in varying degrees. If the success of the subject in identifying tones is plotted against the bits of incoming information, it is found that he can distinguish about two and a half bits of information. This limitation is called the "channel capacity." It apparently represents an inherent limitation in the human ability to distinguish different absolute sounds from one another. If we retranslate the two and one-half bits into alternatives, we find that the subjects can identify about six different tones.

This does not seem like many, considering the range from which they are drawn. However, the results, except in the case of someone who has perfect pitch, are relatively unaffected by the spacing of the tones or variation in their range. If, for example, a person can identify correctly five high tones in one series and five low tones in a different series, it might be supposed that if all ten tones were combined in one series, he could identify most, or all, of them. If the tones are combined, however, he still can identify only about five of them.

When similar experiments have been performed using loudness of tone rather than pitch as the basis of discrimination, similar results have been obtained. While the problem of equating frequency range with decibel, or loudness, range cannot be solved easily, studies have shown that about five different loudness levels, or 2.3 bits can be discriminated.

The intensity of taste sensation also has been studied. The results suggested that about four such taste discriminations, or 1.9 bits, could be made—slightly less than the range that the ear can discriminate; but the sense of taste is generally less sensitive than the sense of hearing. The remarkable fact is that of the degree of similarity, rather than the slight difference.

If the sensitivity of the sense modality is related to the amount of information the sense can discriminate, then we would expect sight to have the highest channel capacity, since the eye is the most sensitive receiving instrument. Studies of the discrimination of visual position have indicated that about 3.25 bits of information may be received. Other studies of such visual characteristics as object size, hue, and brightness all have reported channel capacities of from 2 to 3 bits. Similar results have been obtained for measures of skin sensitivity to vibration, involving the variation of intensity, duration, and location of such vibrations.

Further studies of certain variables associated with visual displays such as area, curvature, length, and direction have also produced results falling in the 2-to-3-bit range.

It seems therefore that the study of a variety of unidimensional measures of human perception provide a remarkably uniform result. While small differences exist between different senses, the differences are less striking than the limited range of channel capacity common to them all.

If this is the case, then how are we able to make discriminations between hundreds of faces and thousands of words? The answer, of course, is that we use various sense dimensions simultaneously, and not one at a time, as in the previous experiments. When two or more sense dimensions, or channels, are used simultaneously, what does this do to the over-all channel capacity?

Numerous studies have been made of this problem. When two dimensions are used simultaneously—for example, when the position of a dot in a square is systematically varied—about four and a half bits of information can be transmitted. The square in which the dot is located is literally a two-dimensional figure, so that the example is appropriate. If a point is located on only a line, three and a quarter bits of information can be transmitted. Thus the addition of another dimension increases the information transmission, but it does not double it to a value of six and a half bits, as might be supposed. This, in general, is the finding in relation to the effect of combining any two dimensions.

In most realistic situations we make use not of two but of a great number of such dimensions in order to discriminate between objects. Therefore it is necessary to study the way in which such highly complex situations affect the transmission of information. In one study of sound, frequency, intensity, rate of interruption, total duration, and spatial location all were presented in various simultaneous arrangements. Under these conditions 7.2 bits of information were transmitted, corresponding to 150 different alternatives. These findings are typical of other multidimensional experiments. They continue to suggest that the addition of sensory dimensions facilitates the transmission of information but follows the law of diminishing returns.

Similar patterns and limitations have been obtained from the study of memory and recall. We can recall only about seven numbers in order, if they are randomly presented to us. However, if we can group them in various ways, then the recall of numbers can be expanded by this process of recoding. Language is, in this sense, an elaborate device for recoding perceptual data of a com-

plex character in symbolic form. A similar recoding process is
used extensively in computer programming. A single symbol may
come to stand for a whole subroutine that awaits recall in a convenient storage location.

The study of channel capacity is more complex than can be
indicated here. But its nature and general significance have been
documented sufficiently to provide a practical illustration of the
application of communications theory to a psychophysical problem.

LANGUAGE AS COMMUNICATION OF INFORMATION

One of the earliest applications of communications theory in
psychology was devoted to the analysis of language as a vehicle
for the communication of information. This analysis was possible
because of previous work by specialists in psycholinguistics, who
had exhaustively analyzed the written and spoken elements in
many extant languages. As a result of this analysis, fundamental
units of language and meaning were isolated. These were called
the *phoneme* and the *morpheme*. The phoneme is the smallest
unit of spoken language; the morpheme is the fundamental unit
of meaning. In English the phonemes are represented, in their
written form, by the twenty-six vowels and consonants of the
alphabet. However, an analysis of the unique vocal elements that
are used as the building blocks of the spoken language generally
can be reduced to about twelve, regardless of the language.

In English and in many other languages morphemes can be
identified with individual words, but in other languages a word
may constitute a whole sentence, or there may be no written words
in the usual sense. However, in all languages there are rules for
the combination of morphemes that take into account the structural meaning of the sentence as well as the components that
constitute it. Language has an organization that determines how
morphemes are to be combined in order to transmit meaning; for
example, in English the fundamental unit of a completed thought
is the sentence.

All the preceding findings are the product of linguistic analysis. They are introduced to set the stage for the application of information theory to language. In order to apply information theory it was necessary first to reduce language to its fundamental units, so that binary two-way decisions could be expressed in terms of these units. Thus the morpheme or phoneme is the equivalent of the punch on the IBM card. It is either there or not there.

The major application of communications theory to the study of language was an analysis of the redundancies in language. In an ideal sense, the less redundant any system of communication, the more information can be transmitted by a given number of signals. An analysis of the words constituting a language indicates, even to the untrained, that all combinations of letters are not used equally. Such redundancy is actually very large. It has been estimated that printed English is at least 75 per cent redundant. All combinations of letters are not employed systematically in the construction of words. "Th," for example, occurs more frequently than "tz." The justification for this inefficiency of coding information into symbols is that the greater the redundancy of the code, the less likely it becomes for error in code interpretation to occur. As we learn to take probable combinations for granted, it becomes easier to guess what a code ought to signify without actually studying all of it.

Because of the redundancy of information coding in language units, is is possible to predict and build language on a statistical basis simply by programming the probabilities of any given word or symbol being followed by all other possible ones. Such probabilities can be obtained from studying samples of language. Once such probabilities are combined with known rules of grammar and syntax, a computer actually can synthesize sentences that make sense for the most part.

This process can be approximated by a group of individuals without the use of a programmed computer. All that is necessary is to obey the following procedure. Give to the first person a common word such as "it" or "he" and ask him to note down a sentence using that word. The word that he uses following the given word is then noted down and given to the second person with the same instructions. The second word is also retained as part of the simulated sentence. In this way each person contributes one word to make a simulated sentence that may end whenever one runs out of people, or at some predetermined time, based on the desired length of the sentence. When this method is used, the likelihood of a given word's following the word before it is approximately equal to the actual statistical probability associated with the words in English usage, since each individual is actually programmed, as it were, to associate words in terms of their probable sequence. The results of the process will bear little resemblance to an ordinary sentence but might read as the following: "The bear me and I am the quick." However, if the rules are changed progressively, so that each person is presented with two words rather than one, or three or four or five, the result becomes nearer and nearer to an actual sentence. The more information an individual has about the context of the word he is to contribute, the less latitude is left him, so that it is more likely that his contribution will make semantic as well as statistical sense. When five words are given to each individual, sentences such as, "Greater notice has been given to eating but usually in regard to disease and to the changes in young children" will result. Here we are on the verge of a sensible sentence, but something is still amiss. As more and more contextual words are added, the approximation becomes ever closer. In this way each new word helps to determine and overdetermine the meaning to follow, because of the inherent redundancy of language. Communications theory is able to describe the relation between coding redundancy and error in transmission and thus provide a precise measurement of the efficiency of language as a means of communicating information.

SOCIAL INTERACTION AND COMMUNICATIONS THEORY

In a less rigorous sense, communications theory has influenced the study of individuals in groups and not only the language that they use. The most essential feature of such groups is the interaction between their members. These interactions can be conceptualized in terms of communications theory with little or no difficulty. Under ordinary conditions the channels of communication among group members are uncontrolled except by structural group factors, such as the nature of the task or the group power structure. The personality of individual members also does much to determine the nature and extent of interaction among persons.

From the viewpoint of communications theory, it is not the interaction itself that is important, but the way the message is understood by the recipient as compared to the meaning intended by the sender.

Studies of the relation between sender and receiver in social situations have been conducted by controlling the channels of communication. Group members have been arranged in patterns such as a circle, a wheel or a chain to determine the effect of placement within the communications network on member satisfaction and general task performance.

Generally, the more centrally placed the individual is in the network, the greater his satisfaction. These studies have not been undertaken specifically within the communications-theory framework, but they can easily be placed within it, as a generalization of the two-person conversation originally visualized in communications theory. In any network, regardless of its complexity, information is transmitted and noise or error interferes with the transmission. The experiments that artificially limit the direction of flow of communication introduce structural group elements into the simple two-person analysis, thus measuring how control of communication influences other group characteristics.

In a related area, studies of rumor transmission lend themselves to a reinterpretation in terms of information theory. In these studies the first person in a chain is given certain information and asked to transmit it to the next member, who passes it along the chain until the message reaches the last person. The original message is then compared with that reported by the last member. The distortions that have occurred reflect the various sources of noise in the communications channel. Generally, these sources of noise are uncontrolled; they are produced by the personality of the members, by the setting, or by the nature of the message. However, all these variables can be controlled. When such control is introduced, the communications chain can be subsumed within the general model of communications theory and subjected to the same laws.

As was discussed previously in relation to the simulation of a group, group interaction tends to take place through selected channels. These are not imposed from without but rather grow from the group experience itself. They reflect the differentiation of status and role that characterizes the group. The relation between the nature of the network and the amount of information transmitted has been studied in a general way in terms of interaction categories. When this is done, each statement made by each individual in a group is placed in an appropriate interaction category, such as "providing an opinion" or "expressing satisfaction." Such studies have suggested various regular relationships involving the use of channels. For example, the use of a communications channel in one direction generally is proportional to its use in the other. Further, channels are arranged generally so that high-status people such as business executives communicate frequently with each other, using friendly types of communication. When high-status persons do utilize communications channels connected to low-status persons, such as assembly line workmen the character of the interaction is quite different. Generally, the high-status person transmits orders whereas the low-status person attempts to be agreeable and accept suggestions. From these studies the necessity of characterizing the information transmitted in terms of its content as well as its quantity is clearly brought out. However, studies of small-group interaction have not emphasized the amount of information actually transmitted in any given interaction, so that the results cannot be directly compared to other aspects of research on communications theory.

An indirect but interesting effect of communications theory has been the emergence within social psychology of a strong interest in interpersonal perception. Interpersonal, or social, perception concerns the way in which people perceive and understand each other. Most work in this area has been devoted to the study of distorting factors in interpersonal understanding. These distorting factors logically can be considered to be noise disturbing the understanding between persons. The message in this instance is not a particular communication but rather the total impact of one individual on another. On this level of analysis, the message loses its specificity, but it gains in importance. Interpersonal perception is concerned with the understanding of the structure from which the specific communication emerges and the context within which it is interpreted. Thus interpersonal perception reflects the adequacy and accuracy of social communication, whether this communication occurs through the medium of language or is the direct sensory impression of various nonverbal cues and signals.

Originally, interest in this area was stimulated by a theoretical concern with the behavioral and personality correlates of being able to take the viewpoint of another person. However, as the field has become more sophisticated, the basic problem in the area has become one of differentiating noise from information. The initial assumption was that a person's ability to respond as another person responded was a measure of his accuracy of social perception—or, to use a more familiar term, of his "empathy." However, an analysis of the methodology involved in such research revealed that this response was contaminated with an unknown amount of noise.

This noise obscured the interpretation of the results because there was no way to tell which part of the message was to be attributed to real information and which to various sources of contamination and error. In order to explain this observation it is necessary to describe the model for a study in social perception. This model is extremely simple. Individual X participates in a standard situation that may consist of nothing more than filling in the answers to a test. Individual Y then fills out the same test, attempting, as he does this, to answer the various items as he thinks they were answered by X. The two forms are then compared to determine how accurately Y is able to guess X's responses.

This approach to the problem appears simple, but it is also ambiguous. Just because Y attempts to put himself in X's place does not necessarily mean that this is what happens. Maybe he only answers the test questions as he himself would do so, whether there was an X or not. Or perhaps he answers the test questions according to some stereotype that he has in his mind, rather than in the way he imagines some unique individual X answered them. In fact, no one knows what the predictor, Y, actually is doing when he fills out the test forms, and therefore the interpretation of the result is confused.

The problems involved in the analysis of interpersonal perception have been analyzed carefully by the American psychologist Lee Cronbach in terms of traditional tests and measurement concepts.[2] This analysis has to do with tests and items, their variations, and averages. However, in another sense it concerns the separation of equally likely alternatives, in order to distinguish how many and what kind of bits of information are being transmitted when Y attempts to predict the responses of X.

Specifically, Cronbach points out that one can break down the predictions made by Y into a number of dimensions or classes. These classes are concerned with the individual items of the test considered separately, and the total test considered as the summation of all its items. Each test and each item has, for a given population, an average answer and a certain amount of variation, describing the differences in response associated with the test as a whole or with a particular item in it. In analyzing this situation Cronbach points out that the total test score of social perception, which equals the test results of X subtracted from the predictions made by Y, consists of a number of different factors or dimensions that must be considered separately. When they are all lumped together the total accuracy of prediction is a conglomerate of the mutual influences of these factors. Since the proportion of the factors in any particular case is unknown, it is impossible to interpret total scores describing the accuracy of the prediction.

Cronbach breaks down the separate elements along the following lines. For each individual item in the test there is an average score for a given sample of subjects and an average amount of variation from person to person. The ability to predict either the mean value of the item or the variation associated with it has nothing to do with unique interpersonal perception but reflects the predictor's understanding of general group trends. On the other hand, if the predictor can predict on which side of the item mean X's response on a given item falls—that is, if he can predict the direction of his variation—this would reflect genuine empathy.

If we turn from the individual items and look at the test as a whole, again we note that the total test has an average score for a sample of subjects, as well as an average amount of variation about this mean for the same group of subjects. The ability of the predictor to predict either the mean—or the degree of variation around the mean—of the total test score has nothing to do with social perception but reflects his general understanding of the norms of the test. But if he can predict the way in which the particular subject deviates from the norm, this does reflect genuine interpersonal perception.

In summary, the apparently simple measure of interpersonal perception that was, until recently, widely adopted, is literally saturated with contamination and ambiguity. Until the various components of this measure are separately analyzed, its meaning really cannot be determined.

In terms of information theory, such studies have failed because of the confusion between the information that was being measured and the error involved. What Cronbach has done is to clarify what information actually is provided and how it can be separated from the error.

MAN-MACHINE INTERACTION

As mentioned earlier, one of the most significant applications of communications theory lies in the teaching machine, though the connection is not always overt.

The teaching machine involves man-machine interaction. Most machine programs are arranged to present a few new bits of information in each step. Whatever the precise arrangement, the programmer controls the number of bits in each part of the program. He may make provisions for varying these bits in terms of the student's response, or they may be fixed.

The student communicates with the machine in terms of the channels that the machine provides. Usually, his response is in terms of one bit (yes or no) or several bits (multiple choice). In any case the numbers are controlled by the nature of the machine. In one sense any error on the student's part can be interpreted as noise in the transmitting circuit. The machine is then programmed to adapt to the amount of noise or degree of error by the various stratagems described earlier, such as repeating a cycle, dropping material, or analyzing the nature of the mistakes and rearranging the material accordingly. The noise that arises lies within the student and may be due to fatigue, stupidity, anxiety, boredom, and the like. The more the machine can interpret the source of noise and adapt to it, the more successful will be the student-machine interaction. Further, the machine programmer makes use of modified redundancy in order to minimize error and provide the student with reinforcements.

What is true of the teaching machine is true of any man-machine interaction. Because of the nature of the machine the input (transmission to the machine) and output (the machine's response) are precisely defined, and man's communication channels with the machine similarly are determined. Thus a radar station and a spaceship both can be described in terms of the same general model.

The proper relation between communications variables in any given situation can be studied through experimentation, and the effectiveness of various noise-reducing maneuvers can be determined. In a radar station, for example, the importance of simultaneous feedback as an error-reducing device has been clearly demonstrated. This principle is also incorporated in the teaching machine.

COMMUNICATIONS THEORY IN PSYCHOLOGY

Communications theory has been of the greatest help and significance in situations in which bits of information actually could be measured, since the theory is basically a set of mathematical relationships. There are, however, a number of areas in psychology in which communications theory has been applied loosely as a convenient means of organizing and reorganizing diverse material with varying degrees of success.

For example, psychotherapy increasingly has been visualized as a conscious and unconscious exchange of information utilizing verbal and nonverbal cues. The success of psychotherapy depends, at least in part, on the accuracy and quality of this information exchange. As long as the patient maintains his customary methods of transmitting and processing information, he also will maintain his defenses and his illness. In a sense the psychotherapeutic process is designed to first create a situation in which new types of information can be transmitted. This information is generally of a personal and anxiety-provoking nature. At the same time new methods are learned by the patient for processing or interpreting this information so that he gains a new perception of himself and his experiences.

Psychotherapists usually talk in terms of repressions and defenses rather than information and error. Nevertheless, perhaps the most obvious and significant psychological difference between the "normal" and the "abnormal" person is in the kinds of information he transmits to others and the peculiar way in which he interprets the information he receives. Defense mechanisms actually are descriptions of maneuvers engaged in by people to distort information or limit its reception (create noise), because such information threatens some aspect of their personality structure. Unless the therapist can find a way to modify the intake and processing functions, any change that he induces is bound to be temporary, since the patient still maintains his customary patterns of interpreting communication, which reinforces his old behavior.

If this description is correct, then therapy can be viewed simply as a specialized communications process whose function is to alter the rate, type, and process of the patient's communication. Presumably the therapist's function is primarily catalytic, though some therapists will admit that they too are changed, but to a lesser degree than the patient.

The preceding analysis indirectly suggests that psychotherapy might benefit from a more explicit reformulation of its goals in terms of communications theory. Such a translation would have the value of lending precision to a process that has tended to be complex, difficult to describe, and heavily weighted with an artistic element. Thus patients would be described in terms of the way in which they received and processed information. These processes are relatively overt and could be measured from time to time to obtain an objective estimate of change. It seems probable that specific communications deficiencies would suggest specific therapeutic techniques. For example, the patient's tendency to process information in such a manner as to place himself in a guilty light might suggest the therapeutic tack of consciously transmitting varying opinions about the patient, showing him that whatever he, the therapist, says, the patient interprets it in the same way. Little has been done along these lines, but the possibilities appear extensive.

Before the treatment of patients must come their diagnosis. The description of individuals is a problem that goes far beyond the realm of psychotherapy. Personality description is a fundamental problem for all psychologists. While communications theory does not by itself constitute an explanation of personality development, it does suggest an interesting and possibly significant method of describing individuals. A description based on communication and information processing has two general advantages: first, the measures are relatively objective and could be reliably quantified; second, these measures also can be applied to machines, so that men and machines could be described in the same general terms.

If such an approach is taken, it holds out the promise of matching men to machines in terms of their own unique information-processing capabilities. Far more important, however, is the possibility of formulating some general theory of organization that describes men and machines within one general theoretical framework. The need for such a formulation becomes increasingly apparent. The description of machines as communications facilities is at a relatively advanced level; it is the description of man in the same terms that remains to be accomplished. The reason that it has not been attempted to any appreciable degree is that personality description has had a different historical development, tied to depth psychology, behaviorism, or phenomenological gestalt emphasis. (Gestalt psychology emphasizes the principles of wholeness and behavior organization.) But it is clear that any individual can in fact be described in terms of the way he transmits information, the way in which he processes it, and the characteristic types of error that he introduces into this process. These errors are due to his physiological limitations, his previous experience, and his general personality. However, it is his actual communicative behavior that forms the logical focus of investigation in order to interpret the other less clear and less measurable characteristics.

This fact has been recognized by researchers who attempt to measure interaction in terms of an appropriate set of categories. However, no one has used a category system built directly on communications theory. Perhaps the nearest general approach to the significance of communication and data processing is provided by general semantics, but the connection is not explicit. In the study of general semantics great emphasis is placed upon the processes by which information is interpreted and the nature and causes of its misinterpretation, but a different descriptive language and a somewhat different theory is used for this analysis.

In quite a different area, communications theory has been applied roughly to certain higher learning processes such as symbolization, generalization, and creative thinking. These can be described as specialized forms of information processing. The use of symbols involves the grouping together of a number of bits of information into one large configuration, which then represents them. Without such a process we would be severely limited by the low channel capacities of our sensory apparatus. Generalization is closely allied to symbolization but it involves the relations among symbols as much as among the raw elements of information. The clearest example of such generalization is a mathematical axiom or postulate that ties together mathematical symbols already abstract in their content.

Creative thinking as a problem of data processing represents an intriguing frontier for exploration, and will be further examined in the next chapter. In the present context it can be noted only that creativity seems to imply an ability to repackage known components of information into unusual or unique forms.

The study of communications channels in social situations already has been described. A more challenging application of communications theory to such interaction has not been widely undertaken. This approach would involve the measurement of natural communication as it occurs in uncontrolled groups of various types. A wide range of systems is available for classifying such interaction. Each of these classifies units, variously defined, into one of a limited set of categories. Each classification represents a bit of information, and the system of classification that is used determines the qualitative range of these bits. While it is not usually spoken of in these terms, the study of interaction in normal and laboratory groups consists of measuring and classifying the bits of information transmitted by group members.

Similarly, studies of the process of psychotherapy involving the systematic analysis of the therapeutic interview also reduce the data to bits of information for purposes of analysis.

The difficulty in both instances is that the basis of classification is arbitrary to some degree. Further, in any natural human inter-action the actual amount of information transmitted is difficult to determine or control. What the observation systems do is to char-acterize a statement, thought, phrase, or gesture. These are seg-ments of action and can be coded reliably. But they each may con-tain *many* bits of information, in the strictly technical sense. Thus these observations could most properly be said to deal in chunks rather than bits of information. With this limitation in mind, it should still be possible to transmit some of the more rigorous ideas of communications analysis into these areas of human complexity.

For such an undertaking, however, it is not enough to measure what is transmitted. It is also necessary to determine what was in-tended by the sender, and what was received by the receiver. These three aspects of any communication are not necessarily equivalent. Presumably there is a closer relation between what a person intends to say and what he says than there is between what he says and what is received. Intention and reception are more difficult to quantify than transmission, which is objective. Reception can be inferred by response, and intention usually is assumed to be re-flected in transmission. It is assumed that a person means what he says unless he gives evidence that this is not the case.

The most natural approach to the problem is to analyze any message into units of information and relate the nature of the mes-sage to the nature of the response. From such a viewpoint the efficiency of various types of communication in social situations can be determined.

The perception and transmission of information has been studied widely in psychology but not in the context of communications theory. Emphasis has been placed on psychological, physiological, and social sources of distortion in information reception.

For example, studies have examined whether poor children estimate the size of a standard coin to be larger than do rich children. In such a study the effect of social and personality factors on the processing of information is examined. In a more traditional sense, however, this is merely a study of the effect of personality on perception.

The classic instrument for the investigation of the influence of personality on the perception and processing of information is probably the Rorschach inkblot test. In this test the information transmitted to the subject is literally meaningless, so that any meaning attributed to it by the subject must reflect his own predisposition when processing data rather than any clear attribute of the stimulus itself, since the Rorschach card is nothing more than an inkblot.

The Rorschach is but one example of a multitude of instruments all of which share the common characteristic of presenting to the subject an ambiguous set of standard stimuli consisting of pictures, sounds, shapes, and so forth. While the material in these tests varies widely, the principle remains the same. In essence these tests are designed to measure the types of processing errors that are characteristic of the individual, though they usually are not described in just this way.

Another approach to the study of human data-processing tendencies is employed by gestalt psychologists interested in studying the way that people organize the information they perceive. These psychologists investigate the types of perceptual interpretations that individuals characteristically impose upon the stimuli reaching them. These interpretive tendencies exist because of the basic nature of human data-receiving and processing equipment, which organizes perceptual data without the conscious awareness or consent of the perceiver. An example of such a tendency is the law of *Prägnanz*. This somewhat exotic-sounding law refers to nothing more than the fact that we tend to see things in terms of "good" forms—that is, as symmetrical, balanced, and complete. An almost complete circle is seen as complete, a crudely drawn right angle is seen as perfect. In order to make such revisions of reality it is necessary for human beings to fill in gaps that exist in the figure, straighten lines, and smooth out deviations from the ideal pattern.

A similar tendency in the realm of motion perception accounts for our seeing the motion picture as a continuous action, even though intellectually we know that it is a series of discontinuous photographs flashed on the screen in a predetermined order.

Another fundamental organizational tendency imposed upon incoming information is known as the figure-ground relation. In any perceptual field, visual, aural, or tactile, a certain group of sensations is seen as prominent, whereas the rest form a background. This tendency is most clearly noted in the sense of sight. When we look at a word or a person, all other facets of the visual field temporarily recede from our attention, and the word or person stands out.

Even more general is the tendency to perceive stimuli as a whole rather than as discrete entities. Every sensation that an individual has is unified. The nature of the organization may shift, but one basic field of activity is always seen, just as a photograph always represents one scene. To put the matter differently, it is impossible to perceive two different visual images simultaneously. When this is attempted artificially by feeding different images to the right and left eyes, the person sees first one scene and then the other, alternately. But he cannot combine them. This alternation is not inherent in the information that is being received but imposed upon it. The perception of one field at a time is a basic precondition for perceiving anything at all.

Psychologists have isolated other predispositions, tendencies, influences, and determinants of perception, all of which can be classified as principles of organization and distortion. They do not belong to the incoming bits of information that we receive but are imposed upon them.

These studies are of interest and significance in themselves. They also may aid the student of man-machine relations as he attempts to maximize information transmission and minimize error.

However, it is not only the man but also the machine that can introduce error into communication. In some ways the machine is analogous to man. It has circuitry (nerves), memory (brain), a source of power (metabolism), and various other components bearing some resemblence to the human body. The care of these components is the job of the engineer and the maintenance specialist. However, the effectiveness of the machine is in part a psychological problem. This problem is constantly faced by the programmer who formulates his program, not only in terms of the required operation, but also with the limits of the machine's capabilities in mind.

Further, the machine may malfunction while in operation, due to mechanical or electrical failure. When this happens it must communicate its breakdown to the operator, who then needs to identify the source of the trouble and correct it immediately. In contrast to a human, most machines are made so that they automatically stop when an error is detected. Such a step is necessary because the computer's speed of operation is so great in comparison to that of its operator that the man could not otherwise correct or repair it.

The psychological and social determinants of accurate perception and transmission of information uniquely are associated with human behavior. Machines are not defensive or influenced by social norms. However, a few suggestive observations of the human behavior of machines have been made. Under certain conditions computers have been observed to behave in a neurotic manner— that is, they persist in solving a given problem in an incorrect or inefficient manner. Of course, there is at the bottom of this behavior some technical, mechanical, or electrical difficulty. Occasionally, it seems to machine operators that computers have a temperament all their own; sometimes they want to work and sometimes they don't: they blow a fuse, eat up the IBM cards, fail to count all the digits, or do one of a hundred other things that stop their operation. Whether these examples represent projection on the part of the operators or intended behavior on the part of the machine cannot be determined. On a less complex level, however, most people have felt, at one time or another that a machine such as an automobile, washing machine, or even a screw driver was against them. But whether we deal with human reactions to machines or accidental simulation of human behavior by machines, it is the human element that must be taken into account.

All these man-machine problems are involved in communications, but they are not suitable for communications-theory analysis. It is only when they can be specified exactly that they may be reduced to the appropriate form for such treatment.

For such a purpose it is necessary to be able to state just how much of a given perceptual personality or social factor affects just how many bits of information in what way. If this can be done, it may be possible to translate many previous findings of psychology dealing with the reception and processing of impressions and information into a single, general framework. These various influences are significant only in as much as they affect communication. They can be compared from this general viewpoint and ordered. Usually they are considered one at a time, which prevents general comparisons and decreases the likelihood of cumulative findings.

COMMUNICATIONS RESEARCH AND SOCIETY

Beyond such a slow process of reinterpretation of known facts into a new context, it is necessary to say something about the impact of communications research on society in general.

The development of communications theory runs parallel with the rapid and almost incredible development of the mass-communications media, including radio, telephone, television, and tape recorders. These instruments have, by their very presence, changed the character of modern life by increasing the absolute amount of communication that takes place and reducing the importance of the factor of distance as a determinant of communication.

These technical achievements have made great impacts on most organizational structures, from businesses and schools to the military and the government. The greater complexity of organization that characterizes most modern institutions is made possible by the increased flow of communication due in part to these technical advances. Beyond such technical improvements, with which we are all familiar, the increased ability to communicate, and be communicated with, has had a number of effects on the fabric of society and on psychology as it concerns the interpretation of man to himself.

The process of communication has changed in a variety of ways. It has transcended the boundaries of space, time, and culture. Its cost has become continually cheaper as its amount has increased. Correspondingly, the likelihood of error because of lack of information or misinformation due to technical failure has decreased. Mistaken decisions are not due primarily to lack of communication but to deficiency in the human understanding and application of this communication.

While communication has rapidly increased, only a small portion of this information actually is crucial for the orderly functioning of social institutions. The remainder is used for leisure-time activity, socializing, and the development of hobbies. These activities reflect the indirect impact of automation on society.

For the purpose of clarifying the current situation, it is helpful to distinguish among the major types of communication that can be observed. First, there is interaction between persons who are in face-to-face contact. This type of communication has been going on since the dawn of history and does not seem likely to be eliminated by newer methods. Second, there are one-way interactions between men and written or printed matter. The transmission of material in this manner again has a long and noble history, dating from the first written manuscripts to the paperback volume of today. Third are the one-way interactions between men and machines that include the reading of dials, gauges, looking through optical instruments, and man's communication with the machine by levers, dials, and switches. Fourth, there are person-to-person interactions with interposed machines such as telephones, closed-circuit television, and the like. Finally, we have simple machine-to-machine communications that occur, for example, in the inner workings of a computer as it solves a problem. These modes of communication are changing at different rates.

The person-to-person interaction remains fairly high and slowly increases, due to the increased efficiency of social organizations, and greater transportation mobility.

Reading has increased constantly in the face of stiff competition from radio and television. Its growth has been possible because of the continuous reduction of printing costs and the fact that most important information is reduced to printed form at the present time. In the future, records may be stored in machines and the over-all amount of books consequently may decrease.

Man's interaction with machines is slowly increasing as he uses them to explore his environment. In addition these communications are used to determine what the machine itself is doing or what it has done.

The most startling increase in communication is in the category of man-to-man interaction with machines interposed. More and more of our communication is performed through a machine rather than directly with the person concerned. This increase is efficient in the sense that we do not have to be present physically to talk with a given individual. It also enormously increases the amount of absolute communication that can reach us and broadens its range to an almost inconceivable degree.

The only form of communication that seems likely to exceed that of man to man with machines interposed is that among machines themselves. There seems to be no fixed limit to such communication except the costs of the machines. Since these costs continue to decrease, the amount of machine-to-machine communication is bound to rise. This type of communication may, in fact, take on the characteristics of an explosion.

It is fairly clear that the absolute amount of communication is rising and will continue to rise, though some forms will rise more rapidly than others, and machine-interposed communication partially may replace direct man-to-man communications. If this is so, and there is no reason to doubt it, we are faced with a serious problem in communications saturation. In the studies of communications channels previously discussed, the limited nature of sensory channels was described. There is a corresponding but less definite limit to the total amount of information that can be processed when all available means of recoding are used and the maximum number of cues and dimensions are employed. Little is known about the effect of such saturation on men, though its actuality is already upon us. But when machines receive more information than they can handle, a variety of interesting behavior patterns is observed: messages become jammed; more errors are transmitted; and messages don't go to their intended destination. Sometimes the machine alters its pace, going slowly and then going extremely fast. This condition gradually becomes worse until the machine breaks down altogether.

These mechanical reactions certainly are suggestive of behavior observed in human beings in complex social structures. Anyone familiar with the workings of a large organization is familiar with the communications problems of message jammings, messages going to the wrong place, and even the strange condition of lethargy followed by hectic periods of activity.

On a more scientific level, studies have been conducted to determine the nature of human limits for absorbing and processing information. Expert pianists, for example, can read musical notes at the rate of about 22 bits per second. Rapid calculators can perform mathematical problems at the slightly higher rate of 25 bits per second. A similar rate can be achieved by the silent reader.

Several observations have been made of the effect of pushing an individual beyond his processing capacity. Under such conditions individuals either tend to emphasize speed at the expense of accuracy or hold back speed in the hope that they may strike an easily processed section of information that will allow them to speed up again. Others attempt to balance speed and accuracy with varying degrees of success.

A different approach to the problem involves the study of the behavior of successful persons in the communications field or those who are exposed, because they are in executive positions, to great amounts of information. A variety of techniques is employed by such persons. Some use elaborate filing systems so that they can identify any new case with one just like it and reduce its complexity in this manner. Another alternative is the delegation of information processing to others, who evaluate the facts and then report their findings and conclusions. In other cases specialists are used to handle the communications from the individual to the world. Public-relations experts, for example, are responsible for communicating their client's intentions, or his image, to others, while he remains free to accomplish other tasks.

The typical communications-saturated individual does not seek solitude in his leisure hours, but rather participates in a number of social and community functions that fill whatever time he has that is not taken by his family responsibilities. It is perhaps more common to find such individuals in America, but the communication level is probably higher in this country than elsewhere, so that these two facts may be a reflection of the same condition.

Eventually, the communications-saturated individual must vary his routine or suffer a minor or major breakdown in his efficiency. Even computers periodically must be overhauled. In the case of the communications-saturated individual, a vacation will often be used as an excuse utterly to cut off all contact from the social world. In other cases he may rise an hour early to think things over, or he may purposely break his round of activity with some relatively noncommunicative hobby.

Beyond such limited observations, the problems that have been created by the communications saturation in which we and our metal brothers, the machines, are involved hardly have been identified.

The challenge to psychology that these events present is largely unrealized at this time. Psychologists are generally too busy helping mentally ill individuals or studying abstract variables to realize the impending nature of the situation, which has tended to develop so quietly, but with such rapidity, that it is taken for granted as a great benefit or a necessary evil, depending on the nature of the communications and one's point of view.

It is clear that the effects of communication and overcommunication need urgent study. Any mechanism, man or machine, can absorb and process only so much information at a given time. Methods for extending this limit must be the focus of intensive investigation. At the same time the effects of oversaturation on the individual untrained to meet it need to be determined more exactly.

It is hard to say at this point how many of these problems can be traced directly to the conceptions formulated in communications theory, and to what extent they relate simply to communication as a generalized activity independent of precise measurement and theory. However, communications theory has made us aware of the capabilities and limitations inherent in data-processing equipment, including ourselves. Further, it has indicated some of the ways in which bottlenecks in communication analysis can be resolved through recoding, strategic delays, and the use of additional dimensions of sensory discrimination. All these findings are bound to be important in the reformulation of various psychological areas into a common machine-man language, and the study of the impact of communications processes on human behavior.

Chapter Five

Intelligence and Creativity

THE MEASUREMENT OF INTELLIGENCE

The description and measurement of intelligence has a relatively long history in relation to the lifetime of modern psychology itself. Starting with the pioneer work of the French psychologist Alfred Binet in 1905, the measurement and description of human intelligence has occupied the careful attention of testing, vocational, and clinical psychologists.[1] It is assumed generally by the public that the issues related to intelligence testing are settled and that the subject matter itself is at a relatively mature level. Some time ago this description might have been accurate, but in recent years it has become increasingly obvious that the measurement of human abilities in general, and intellect in particular, was a complex matter that raised more questions than could be answered easily.

Parallel with the study of intellectual ability there has been a slow but steady interest in the nature of creativity. For many years it was believed that creativity was largely a function of intelligence, and the topic consequently received little specialized attention. However, with an increasing need to utilize talent in the most efficient manner for the national good, this assumption has come to be questioned.

The nature of creativity took on new proportions as our idea of the nature of intelligence itself was reformulated and redefined from a single characteristic to a complex entity. Thus intelligence and creativity at the present time are being redefined both in respect to their earlier formulations and with regard to their mutual relationship. These developments have important practical implications for the detection and cultivation of human resources. It is therefore timely to reassess these topics as they are defined at the present time.

In the early days of intelligence testing, psychologists assumed that, in the absense of precise knowledge of the nature of intelligence, it was the better part of wisdom to use a variety of tests that would sample collectively the various aspects of intelligence and arrive at some average performance score. Thus these early tests, which were designed for children, used many items of a diverse character, ranging from those suited to low-grade idiots through those for intelligent upper-elementary-school children. They included, for example, coordination of hand and eye movements, execution of simple orders, counting, and distinguishing among abstract terms. This general strategy of heterogeneous items was a useful one in its time. It is still used in preparing tests designed to measure intelligence as a generalized entity, where more specific discriminations are not required.

The turning point in the measurement of intelligence came in 1932 when the American psychologists Louis Thurstone and his wife, Thelma Thurstone, began to apply factor analysis to the study of intelligence.[2] The application of factor analysis to psychological data has had sweeping consequences, though even today the extent and importance of such investigations are not realized fully. However, for many years factor analysis was applied only to intelligence-test scores.

A brief description of factor analysis is given in Appendix B. For our present purposes it is sufficient to describe factor analysis as a mathematical method for determining whether a set of relationships can be reduced to some simple form. More technically, it determines whether a group of correlations can be simplified without losing any of the information that they contain; this reduction is made in terms of factors.

In the physical sciences the problem of factors does not arise. The factors are "given" electrons, elements, compounds, and so forth. Upon such basic components the laws and relationships of these sciences can be built. In psychology no one knows what the components of man's personality, ability, or intelligence may be. They are not obvious, and must be determined inductively. The purpose of factor analysis is to test whether such factors do exist in any given set of relationships—or, on the other hand, to describe the best set of components that can be fitted to a given group of data. Factor analysis takes two general forms, or rather uses two kinds of models. The *orthogonal model* attempts to isolate factors that are independent of each other. Scores made on the testing of one factor do not in any way predict scores on another. The *oblique model* formulates factors in terms of density of tests rather than uniqueness of relationship. In oblique factor analysis, factors may be related to each other. They are drawn in such a way as to describe the common variation of test scores in the most economical manner. Thus oblique and orthogonal analysis have the same purpose. However, the oblique analysis does not incorporate the condition of factor independence.

All this may seem somewhat confusing to someone who hears about it for the first time. An illustrative example may clarify the situation. Suppose that we have three tests of mathematical ability and wish to determine whether they measure the same thing. If all three tests are given to the same group of subjects and the resulting scores are factor analyzed we can find out. In such a case, we might find that two factors were being measured: the ability to do arithmetic and the ability to reason mathematically. Such knowledge would aid us in interpreting the test results and in designing future tests.

In their early work with factor analysis the Thurstones were interested in how many types of intelligence could be found. To be able to explore this question they gave people a number of different tests and factor analyzed the resulting correlations among test scores. A correlation is a statistic describing the relation between two scores. The larger the absolute magnitude of the correlation, the larger the relationship.

The success of any factor analysis is determined partially by what is put into it. The Thurstones therefore attempted to include as many kinds of intelligence tests as they could find. As they repeated the test administrations, they included new tests and, after factor analyzing the resulting scores, they began to find certain kinds of factors recurring from study to study. At one point the Thurstones described the basic factors of intelligence, using the following names: verbal reasoning, spatial reasoning, number, word fluency, memory, perceptual speed, and motor ability.

There is nothing sacred about these or any other factor names. They are merely labels for a particular configuration of test scores, giving greater weight to those scores that contribute more heavily to the mathematical definition of the factor, and less weight to those that contribute less. One individual may use a slightly different name for a given factor than another. However, there is no ambiguity about the factor itself, merely about the name given to it. A factor is defined in terms of the tests that are related to it. This definition is precise, even if its English equivalent is not.

Since the time of the Thurstones' pioneering work in this area countless similar studies have been executed in order to determine the structure of intellect and devise appropriate measures for this structure. The more research that has accumulated, the more imposing and confusing the results have become.

THE MODEL FOR THE STRUCTURE OF
THE INTELLECT

Perhaps the most ambitious and systematic series of studies on this problem has been carried out at the University of Southern California under the general direction of the American psychologist Joy P. Guilford.[3] The results of this research have been conceptualized in terms of a three-dimensional model that has been called "the structure of intellect." This model is visualized as a cube. The first dimension of the cube is called "operations," the second "contents," and the third "products." The nature and further subdivisions of these dimensions will be described shortly.

Before this is done, however, it is necessary to explain why such a model is either necessary or desirable. From what was said about factor analysis, it would appear that the study of intelligence ought to involve nothing more than the isolation of the number of factors involved in intelligence and the standardization of tests designed to measure these factors. While this is true in a general sense, the search for these factors has suggested a certain order among them, just as the search for elements in chemistry was facilitated greatly by the realization of their periodic nature. It is this recurrent order that Guilford and his associates have attempted to visualize and formalize in their model. The nature of this model will be described in some detail, since it represents the most complete current account of intellectual functioning. It should not be thought, however, that this model is invariable. Future work will certainly modify it and may even fundamentally change its nature. But at this time it is the best that is available.

The first dimension involves operations, which are divided into the five major subgroupings of cognition, memory, convergent thinking, divergent thinking, and evaluation.

Cognition involves the recognition or discovery of relationships. Memory involves the retention of cognition. Both divergent and convergent thinking are involved in various types of productive problem solving. Divergent thinking involves the search for solutions in new directions; convergent thinking involves the search for the best fit or conventional answer to a given problem. Finally, evaluation concerns the assessment of the correctness or quality of what has been produced, what is remembered, or what is known through cognition. Thus the five classes of operations are intertwined with each other and taken together involve the active processes of intellect.

The second general dimension of intellect, or the second way of classifying intellectual factors, is the content in which they operate. These contents are divided into four groups: figural, symbolic, semantic, and behavioral. Figural content consists of perceptual material, such as a picture that represents nothing but itself. Symbolic material is composed of letters or numbers organized into various general systems, such as language. Semantic content concerns the meaning of the material organized in symbolic form. Finally, behavioral content involves the observation of social behavior. While behavioral content is noted, it is excluded from the general model because most factor studies have not measured this kind of variable.

The third general method of classifying intellectual factors concerns the products that result from a certain operation's being applied to a specific content. Products are described as units, classes, relations, systems, transformations, and implications.

The definition of different products varies somewhat with the material being analyzed, but general distinctions between them can still be drawn for purposes of analysis. The unit, such as a specific word or object, is the most simple type of product. The class is the organization of units, which may be classed according to common conceptual meaning or the possession of similar formal characteristics. Relationships among products concern not so much the classification of units as relations between different types and classes of units. Systems involve the description of the over-all pattern of a number of relationships. Transformations can deal with changes or modifications in the meaning, organization, or the arrangement of units. Finally, implications concern an extrapolation, or the ability to foresee certain conclusions or problems not explicitly given in the information presented.

In order to apply this model of intellect employing operations, contents, and products, it is necessary to realize that each of these types do not constitute factors. Rather, any given factor is represented by one operation working on one content and resulting in one product. It is for this reason that the three basic dimensions of this model are arranged in the form of a cube. Any point in the volume of the cube is defined in terms of all three dimensions; thus, any given factor is characterized in terms of its operation, product, and content.

To the extent that this model is correct, it should aid in summarizing and relating known factors into a single structure and help to indicate where undiscovered factors may soon be found, just as the chemical periodic table of the elements has predicted the discovery of elements that were unknown when the table was first formulated by the Russian chemist Dmitri Mendelyeev.

As with any model, a perfect fit is not to be expected. In some cases there may be more factors than had been predicted, and in others, there may be no known factor, even if one had been predicted.

The model states, in effect, that for each operation there are three types of content and six types of products that occur in all possible two-way combinations, a total of eighteen unique configurations. Since there are five operations each associated with these eighteen variations a total of five times eighteen or ninety different factor types exists.

In order to indicate how this model is applied, some of the factors falling in specific categories will be described. This should help to specify a rather abstract approach to intelligence, as well as indicate the complexity that is masked under the concept of intelligence as a unified entity.

Perhaps the most widely studied operation is cognition. It is therefore convenient to focus on cognition in order to demonstrate how one operation relates to various contents and products. At present factors falling in fifteen of the eighteen cells made up by these dimensions are known. These will be described systematically, by keeping each of the products constant while varying the contents.

The first factor configuration involves the cognition of figural content arranged in unit products. This factor is illustrated by such material as incompleted pictures, auditory figures, or kinesthetic forms, in which persons perceive specific imperfect objects that they translate into completed forms. The second factor involves the cognition of symbolic units, illustrated by incompleted words to which letters must be added or scrambled words whose letters have been arranged in the wrong order. In order to be able to see the word correctly the individual must realize what it is. Finally, the cognitive semantic unit is nothing more than verbal comprehension. It is not recognizing the word as a written symbol, but rather understanding its meaning. Since short-answer intelligence tests have been based on nothing more than this factor, under the heading of "vocabulary," it is presumably one of central importance in measuring the general meaning of intellectual performance, though it occupies only one of the ninety cells in the Guilford scheme.

Next in order are factors involving cognition of classes. The figural context of class products is tested, for example, by the presentation of several drawings sharing a common property that the individual is asked to name. For the semantic test, the individual is provided with groups of letters organized on some unspecified basis and asked to select which groups belong to a general class and which do not. On the symbolic level, the individual is presented with real words and asked to organize them in a class on the basis of their meaning rather than their formal properties.

On the next level are cognitive factors involving relations among units. To measure either the figural, symbolic, or semantic contents a test as "*a* is to *b* as *q* is to ?" can be employed. If the items refer to figural relations, geometric shapes may be employed; for symbolic relations, nonsense words are used; and if semantic relations are measured, then real words are substituted in the general test formula.

There are several different ways to test the cognition of systems. Any test involving the visualization of a series of objects arranged spatially constitutes a measure of cognitive figural systems. A symbolic system test might involve an arrangement of letters in a square or a pyramid on the basis of some periodic relation; the individual is then asked to fill in one or two blanks in the arrangement on the basis of the information presented. Testing at the semantic level involves what has been called the factor of general reasoning. It can be described as the ability to describe a process of arriving at an answer without actually carrying out the process, such as describing the method of solving a mathematical problem without carrying out the actual computation.

Transformation of cognition on the figural level involves what is known as the power of visualization. Symbolic transformations are measured by tests of similarity; the subject is requested to name the similarity between two items such as a fish and an apple that do not initially appear similar. Only by a shift in their mutual relationship can he arrive at a meaningful answer.

On the final level of implications, the figural level is well illustrated by a paper-and-pencil maze test. On the semantic level implications are measured by a pertinent-question examination. The subject is asked to describe the types of problems that might occur in a new situation, such as starting a new business or visiting a foreign country.

This concludes the description of the content and product dimensions associated with cognitive operations. Parallel combinations exist for memory, divergent thinking, convergent thinking, and evaluative operations. In some cases known tests exist for each combination, while in other cases no tests have yet been developed. In general, the operations of memory closely parallel those of cognition except that the material is recalled rather than presented. However, other operations present interesting contrasts.

Divergent-thinking abilities are of importance because of their close connection with creativity. The central feature of divergent response is variety. Thus on the level of divergent thinking involving classes of ideas one would ask a subject to list all the uses he can think of for "fieldstone." This measure is called spontaneous flexibility. Another example of divergent thinking involves the use of figural contents on the transformation level. The old puzzle of taking a given arrangement of matches, removing three of them, and arriving at another specified arrangement tests this ability. A further interesting factor involves the transformation of semantic rather than figural material. For example, a subject is asked to think of as many titles as he can for a given short story. The number of different types of meaning that the subject provides measures his adaptive flexibility for semantic material.

An interesting example of convergent-thinking ability is the Picture Arrangement Test, in which scrambled pictures must be arranged to tell a coherent story. This is a measure of semantic systems involving convergent thinking.

Finally, an example of the evaluative operation, involving in this case semantic transformation, is the Judgment Test. In it the subject simply is asked to give his opinion as to which of five solutions is the most practical for a given problem. This task requires the evaluation of solutions, each of which represents an attempt at problem solving through the rearrangement of the nature and meaning of the given problem.

In this way each cell in the Guilford model describes an intellectual factor as well as suggesting the means by which it can be measured. Collectively, these cells form the structure of intellect.

This three-dimensional model of intellect has recently been criticized by the American psychologist Lloyd Humphreys in a rather interesting manner.[4] Most of his argument is fairly technical, but the central points can be indicated.

Humphreys questions whether ninety factors are required to define intelligence. He points out that the factors obtained in any analysis are dependent on the materials put into the analysis. Therefore, the results of different factor analyses may be on quite different levels, even though the same statistical process has been applied to them. Humphreys feels that Guilford has tended to look at ever more specific, narrow, and unimportant factors in his attempt to match factors to specific types of tests or items.

There is no question that the results of factor analysis represent factors in the mathematical sense. However, the meaning of the factors in terms of a general system is not thereby determined. It is possible to refine, splinter, and purify factors by associating them with more limited test materials so that they measure ever smaller and less significant domains.

The main point that Humphreys makes in regard to these variations in factor levels is that factors may be organized in terms of a hierarchical arrangement. In this case the factors described by Guilford may belong at the lowest end of the hierarchy where greatest specificity is reached. However, this lower level may not be the one that should be studied, since it may be too specific for many problems.

For example, in describing the domain of mechanical information it is possible to differentiate four levels of complexity: (a) information about specific tools—for example, the hammer; (b) information about specific types of tools having a similar function —for example, kinds of saws; (c) information about certain content areas, such as carpentry; (d) information of a general mechanical nature drawn from several areas, such as plumbing and electrical work.

In this model there are fewer factors as one goes up the hierarchy. The more general the level, the simpler the terms used to describe it. The process of determining whether, in a given case, such a hierarchy of relationships exists is a fairly complex matter. It involves oblique and orthogonal factor analysis with a hierarchical transformation. However, the basic notion is quite simple. In many sets of test data dealing with intellectual performance, the resulting factors can be arranged in a hierarchy resembling the structure of a tree. At the most general level is the tree trunk. Next come the main branches. From these come small branches and, finally, twigs. Humphreys believes that Guilford may be studying the twigs, which may be unduly limiting since different scientific and practical situations might require different types of factor measurement. Certain fairly limited practical problems might best be met by focusing on "twig factors." However, it is probable that many problems involving prediction to classes of events rather than specific situations would use the midrange, or "branch" factors, for simplicity and ease of calculation. Some very general purposes might employ the "tree-trunk factor" of general intelligence, or whatever it might be called.

If this analysis is correct, it would indeed simplify the testing problem. In many cases the hierarchical model appears adequate. However, in the multitrait, multimatrix approach to test validation, which will be described in Chapter Seven, this approach breaks down. This approach involves the study of different traits, each of which is measured by a variety of instruments. In this arrangement a given twig factor may be related to more than one branch, and thus the hierarchical arrangement would break down —that is, a given measure would be related to other instruments measuring the same thing and would also be related to other instruments having the same form but measuring a different content.

Humphreys' ideas form an interesting and critical foil to those of Guilford and his associates. They both cannot be fully correct. But at this point in the description of intellectual function there is insufficient evidence to enable us to choose between them. Guilford has the advantage of a systematic and carefully conceptualized position resulting from a series of systematic investigations that he has carried out during the last ten years. Humphreys utilizes a more eclectic approach and suggests a number of alternatives rather than any direct systematic approach to compare with Guilford's structure of the intellect.

These differences of opinion are not in themselves bad. They will stimulate new research in the area that may either reinforce a special position or, as is more probable, aid in the combination of diverse elements that now appear either hopelessly separate or contradictory.

THE USES OF INTELLIGENCE PREDICTION

The study of intelligence has come a long way in less than sixty years, when Binet, naïvely and intuitively groping, put together some tests that he thought might aid in the measurement of intelligence. The rate of progress has paralleled the development of psychology itself. The present sophistication of the methodological and theoretical disputes stands in remarkable contrast to the simple beginnings of intelligence testing that lie within the life span of the average individual.

At this point the reader should be convinced that the measurement of intelligence is not a simple matter. But the rewards of clarification should be an improvement in the prediction of intelligence and performance. At present, tests of mental abilities are used widely as both school-admissions criteria and as predictors of successful performance in jobs partly or totally dependent on measures of ability. Aptitude tests to predict future performance are generally useful only when one has an excess number of candidates that one wishes to whittle down on a sane and simple basis. For the individual candidate an aptitude score is a very approximate guide to future success, since the correlation between the test score and the measure of actual success is usually fairly low.

The isolation and organization of the components, or factors of intelligence, should enable far greater precision in prediction.

Of equal importance to any increase that occurs in the predictive value of intellectual measurement are the implications that such intellectual components will have for education. From Guilford's viewpoint the three-dimensional structure of intellect describes the types of learning of which the individual is capable, and these form the frame of reference for any educational program or method. However, the hierarchical model puts the problem in a new light, by suggesting that it is not only the component but also its level that needs to be considered in the selection of educational methods. There is no need to be concerned with lower-level components if one can train the more complex higher-order factors that subsume them. For example, rather than train an individual to use different tools as a separate segment of mechanical information, it might be possible to deal directly with the use of tools as a more general factor that would, in large part, obviate the need for more specialized instruction.

Before education can be related fully to intelligence, the trainability of various intellectual components must be determined. This information, along with the accumulated evidence of predictive studies using intellectual criteria, will help to indicate which components are both socially important and amenable to development. Thus, those factors that, in fact, predict success in various social and occupational situations and in which people have been shown to be trainable will form the logical focus for educational development.

In this manner the study of intelligence will help to guide our educational objectives, and aid in bridging the gap between academic psychology, as studied in the laboratory, and education, as applied in the schoolroom. This bridging has already occurred with regard to teaching machines, but not with regard to the training of intellectual abilities, as distinct from the accumulation of factual knowledge. In principle, there is no reason why teaching machines cannot be programmed to develop certain of these intellectual abilities through appropriate exercises.

For example, the test items concerned with general reasoning as described by Guilford involve the outlining of solutions without actually executing the steps that are necessary to obtain them. The items that measure this ability are suitable for programming in a sequence of increasing difficulty, designed slowly to train the individual in the use of such procedures.

Certain other abilities, such as those involved in social intelligence, will not lend themselves so naturally to machine training. Whatever the procedures used, the important point is that this training can be planned and carried out on a rational and systematic basis, with regular provision for evaluation and reassessment of goals. Since the factors can be measured, a method is automatically at hand for the evaluation of success in the training of people in any one of them. Such rationality is scarcely characteristic of present-day education and could represent a major contribution of psychology to education, in terms of aims, means, and measures.

While the most general approach for the educator is to develop all factors of intelligence in the student, it seems probable that in particular programs some factors would be emphasized more than others. The selection would be determined on the basis of the goals of the program. When the educator has at his disposal a full array of intellectual factors, he can plan his strategy in over-all terms and decide which facets of his program should either be neglected or given greater emphasis in terms of social needs. In this way abstract psychological investigation can help to guide social and educational development and provide the basis for rational training procedures.

THE MEASUREMENT AND CULTIVATION OF CREATIVITY

The study of creativity usually has been associated with the study of intelligence, since it was assumed that a direct relation existed between the two. However, in recent years creativity has come into its own as an independent topic of investigation.

With the acceleration of the rate of technical and scientific development, an increasing premium has been placed on scientific creativity. International political conditions also have stimulated our need to identify, measure, and cultivate creative scientific abilities.

Naturally enough, much of the research on creativity has been conducted in the schools. Progressive education has placed a premium on the development of initiative and the execution of original projects. Stimulated by these aims, educational psychologists, teachers, and educators have conducted a considerable number of studies of creative and noncreative students, seeking to distinguish between them and to learn whether creativity can be developed or whether it is a fixed ability. Unfortunately, a good deal of this work has been too trivial and too uncontrolled to be of much value, except in confusing the issue. For example, a teacher will rate class members on creativity and then administer a personality test to determine the relation between personality and creativity. However, no one will ever know if her definition of creativity resembles anyone else's, or whether her class members are typical or not. The results of such research generally lead to confusion because they are contaminated by various sources of error.

A further problem in this area is that there is little agreement as to the nature of creativity either as a conceptual entity or as a psychological measure; there is, however, little doubt as to its importance, whatever it is and however it can be measured.

At present there are two general approaches to the measurement of creativity. The first involves the identification of persons who, it is commonly agreed, are creative and then studying their personalities, life histories, intelligence, and aptitudes. The problem with this approach is that the judges must agree on whom they consider to be creative, even if they do not know precisely what creativity is.

The second approach involves an analysis of the nature of creativity itself. The components of creativity are specified, and the relation of various combinations of components to other aspects of personal performance are then studied. This procedure involves a great deal of initial effort. The nature of creativity must be analyzed carefully; separate tests must be devised for measuring each component; and, finally, the relations among these components must be determined. However, even in this approach, social agreement remains as the final test of any measurement of creativity, regardless of how the measurement of creativity is obtained.

Generally, the first way has been adopted in studies of creativity in order to avoid the methodological problems inherent in the second. The quality of the studies produced by this approach depends mostly on the correlates of creativity that are measured rather than on the measure of creativity itself, since this is merely a matter of social consensus. As in all experimental research, it is important to draw an adequate sample. If the individuals studied are not really creative, nothing can be found. Further, the study of a creative group of people is of no use unless a control group of average noncreative people also is studied in the same way. Otherwise, one can never tell whether a given relation between measures is due to a high rate of creativity or just simply to normal personality development. In many of the more ambitious studies normal control groups are studied in parallel with the creative groups. Fortunately, in other cases, this is not necessary. If standard tests are used, norms often are available for the general population. These norms act as the control group since deviations from these norms suggest the influence of creativity, if the creative subjects are otherwise similar to average persons.

In one example of this approach a sample of creative artists and writers selected on the basis of national eminence by librarians, editors, and other experts was given the Personality Factor Test, and the results were compared to the test norms.[5] The test itself is an assessment of sixteen factors at the level of self-description. In this study, writers and artists were found to be more intelligent, emotionally mature, adventurous, sensitive, dominant, bohemian, self-sufficient, generally radical, somewhat more tense and enthusiastic, and less influenced by group standards than the average individual. The difficulty with such a study is that being a successful writer or painter involves more than creativity. It involves certain definite skills without which creativity cannot manifest itself successfully. These skills are not the equivalent of creativity. A good technician in the arts can produce flawless work, but it has no spark. It is not creative. In studying the whole person the technical requirements of successful performance tend to become confounded with the effects of creativity. However, the findings presented by this study are generally in the expected direction. They are congruent with the popular stereotype of artists as radical, self-sufficient, and adventurous. However, in other aspects the findings are surprising. Artists as a group are not usually seen as emotionally mature or necessarily dominant. These characteristics may, however, be either the effects or causes of successful artistic performance rather than the correlates of creativity.

Countless studies of this general character have been undertaken, with varying results. In one similar study of artists and nonartists projective tests were used to compare creative and noncreative groups.[6] While it is not clear if the persons interpreting the tests knew to whom the records belonged, the results are generally reasonable. Artists, in comparison with nonartists, were found to be original, sensitive to themselves, able to establish a multiplicity of identifications with other persons, and better able to tolerate ambiguity.

The accumulation of correlates of creative versus noncreative people does not lead too far, except in the few cases where the results are not as expected; this approach only tends to confirm the obvious.

A variety of theoretical explanations have been given for creative ability, varying from depth interpretations of unconscious germination and ego flexibility to an extension of normal problem-solving abilities. These explanations may contain partial truth but they do not lend themselves readily to measurement or test.

A more precise and systematic approach to the problem of creativity has been undertaken by Guilford and his associates. This represents a logical extension of the three-dimensional structure-of-intellect model.

Guilford takes the position that if the general description of the structure of intellect is approximately correct, then those elements that collectively go to make up creativity must be found within the model itself.[7] He has, therefore, searched through the cells of his model in order to isolate those intellectual abilities that particularly seem to be associated with creativity. It is his hope and intention in this way to arrive at both a precise method of measurement and a more detailed and clearer concept of the nature of creativity itself.

His basic position is that creativity is not a unitary ability but rather the product of different factors working together. Some of the components are relatively obvious. Among these he includes fluency, flexibility, and originality. Other components are less obvious and may vary with the type of creativity involved. In general, however, creativity is placed under the heading of productive thinking and under the more limited subheading of divergent rather than convergent thinking. A further important distinction is made between creativity and successful creative performance requiring abilities other than simple creativity for its consummation. Further, while creativity may be a function of a relatively consistent constellation of abilities, it also may be associated with other intellectual abilities that are not constant—that is, there may be a hard core of creative abilities surrounded by others of less importance or generality.

Guilford has described those factors of intellect that he considers to be central in the definition of creativity. He views these factors in the general context of the creative act, involving both cognitive understanding and the production and evaluation of a product. In this sense creativity is an intellectual performance like any other.

As has been stated already, the general abilities of fluency, flexibility, and originality are those most closely identified by Guilford with creativity. Three types of fluency are itemized. The first is verbal fluency, the ability to name words that meet certain formal characteristics. For example, this ability might be measured by seeing how many words beginning with "s" an individual could name in a minute. The parallel ability involves conceptual rather than verbal fluency, and can be measured by such tasks as "providing a given word with as many synonyms as possible in a given time period." Finally there is ideational fluency, which involves the ability to express oneself by putting ideas into words. The technique of "brainstorming" involves such an ability—giving as many ideas on a given problem as one can, regardless of their implications or practicality.

Under the heading of flexibility two major forms are distinguished: spontaneous and adaptive flexibility. Spontaneous flexibility refers to the tendency to seek—without special instructions—for new modes of expression, the avoidance of verbal repetition, and so forth. Adaptive flexibility, on the other hand, involves the use of different types of strategies in the solving of given problems. It does not occur spontaneously but only in the context of specific problem-solving situations.

Only one measure of the final major factor associated with creativity, originality, currently is available. This measure concerns the ability to give uncommon or remote responses on such tests as word associations.

In addition to this central core of abilities, Guilford also suggests that a number of other factors are related to creativity, at least in artists and writers. Among these he includes visual and auditory memory, verbal comprehension, spatial orientation, logical evaluation, perceptual evaluation, experimental evaluation, and visualization.

Thus the picture of creative ability presented in this analysis is fairly complex, even in its preliminary formulation. Since nothing is stated about the way in which these factors are related in given instances, we really are dealing with raw elements in unknown quantities.

Some research has been done to determine the validity of this conceptual scheme. The results have tended to lend it partial, but by no means complete, support. It is best to view Guilford's analysis as an interesting example of the approach it typifies, rather than as any final statement of the nature of creativity itself. Since Guilford has, as we know, provided the means of measuring each of the factors he describes, other investigators can incorporate these measures in their work.

One example of the use of these measures is provided by the studies conducted by the American psychologist Frank Barron, on the correlates of creativity in normal persons.[8] In this study Barron adopted a compromise position between identifying creativity as the behavior of creative people and the identification of creativity in terms of its elements. Barron gave his subjects a number of tests, including Guilford's "creativity battery." These tests could be used to measure various aspects of creativity and also other aspects of personality. Thus a number of creativity measures could be obtained independently and later pooled, or kept separate in the analysis, as fitted the needs of the investigation. By comparing personality characteristics with these measures of creativity, Barron was able to suggest some characteristics of creative people. In this work the influence of intelligence was eliminated by appropriate statistical manipulation, so that the relation between personality and creativity was not obscured by the influence of intelligence. Under these conditions it was found that creativity was associated with the ability to integrate various stimuli, general energy, self-assertion, and domination, responsiveness to impulse and emotion, feminine interests, and general effectiveness of performance. These findings are in keeping with those already described and suggest that creativity is a generally desirable characteristic when viewed in the context of its correlates.

A more ambitious investigation of creativity is currently in its final phases under the general guidance of Donald MacKinnon at the University of California.[9] These series of studies are of particular interest because of their high quality and their utilization of an excellent validating criterion of creativity—namely, studying only those persons who have been recognized by others as successfully creative in their own field.

A broad range of creative persons has been studied. Each such group was investigated separately so that generalizations could be made from study to study, each investigation replicating, in part, the previous ones. For this purpose persons of recognized stature in the fields of creative writing, architecture, mathematics, industrial research, physical science, and engineering were successively studied. These groups represented artistic, scientific, and technical creativity, including all of the major types currently thought to be significant.

At present the architects' group has received the most intensive study. The results obtained from these data serve as a model for other investigations in the series and as an excellent summary of their general trend.

Architects occupy a peculiar and interesting position between the engineer-technician on the one hand, and the creative artist on the other. Because the architect must combine both artistic and engineering ability along with a generous dash of human-relations skills, it is felt that creativity in architecture may have wide implications for the many other fields on which it borders.

In order to obtain a sample of creative architects, the researchers followed the simple expedient of asking five professors of architecture independently to draw up a list of the forty most creative architects. A total of eighty-six different names were obtained by this procedure. Those on which there was least agreement were eliminated and the remaining sixty-four names were submitted to eleven editors of architecture journals, who again rated them on their creativity. These sixty-four architects were invited to California to participate in the study. Forty of them accepted. These forty were asked to rate all sixty-four names of the original list including themselves. Their ratings were correlated with the ratings of the architectural editors. A correlation of .88 was obtained, indicating a remarkable amount of agreement among these experts about the relative creativity of different architects, in spite of the fact that no common definition of creativity had been adopted by them.

One problem that arises in any investigation in which a group is invited to participate is that of deciding whether those who refuse are different from those who accept. In the present case there was no difference on mean rating of creativity between the accepters and the refusers. In order to be sure that creativity was used as the basis of selection rather than some other general characteristic, such as age or geographic location, two additional groups were obtained that matched the chosen creative group on age and location. Ratings of these two groups on creativity clearly differentiated these two groups from the creative sample, indicating that an appropriate sample of creative architects had indeed been obtained. These two noncreative groups subsequently were assessed by the same procedures used for the creative group, to provide control groups in testing for the unique effects of creativity.

The forty creative architects who accepted the invitation to participate in the study flew out to the Institute of Personality Assessment and Research at Berkeley, California, for a weekend of testing. There they were subjected to a barrage of paper-and-pencil tests, interviews, problem-solving experiments, and situational tests. When the weekend was over, they had been tested thoroughly. The analysis of the data obtained from this intensive two-day session provided the following experimental findings.

In contrast to other less creative members of their professions the creative architects were characterized in the following terms.

They had, in general, a high opinion of themselves and their ability, but also greater self-acceptance, indicated by their willingness to speak of themselves critically and frankly. They stressed their individuality, enthusiasm, and determination.

Remarkably, no relation was found between creativity and intelligence, except that general intelligence had to exceed the feeble-minded level for creativity to manifest itself. This finding was replicated for writers, industrial researchers, physical scientists, and engineers. Only in the case of mathematicians was a small positive relation between intelligence and creativity obtained. This finding has remarkable implications for the concept of creativity as an independent entity to be distinguished from general intelligence. Further support recently has been provided for such a concept by the American Psychologists Jacob Getzels and Philip Jackson, who studied the relation between creativity and intelligence in several hundred school children.[10]

The personality of creative persons has been the subject of many informal comments, ranging from an assertion that geniuses were near to insanity, to the less extreme statements that the more creative a person was, the better adjusted he tended to be.

In the present studies of MacKinnon, a variety of personality and vocational inventories were used to study the personality of the architects in order to relate personality to creativity. The findings were relatively clear. The more creative an individual is in his work, the greater is the tendency for him to possess an openness of emotions, a sensitive intellect, self-understanding, and a broad spectrum of interests including some thought of as characteristically feminine.

In addition, various instruments designed to study artistic preference and perceptual organization clearly indicated that creative persons prefer complex, asymmetrical designs rather than symmetrical ones. Such complexity seems to challenge their creative capacity to supply bonds among diverse elements.

Another interesting finding involves the comparison between a perceptual and judgmental attitude toward experience. The perceptual attitude primarily is concerned with extending awareness, whereas the judgmental attitude places emphasis on coming to a conclusion. Persons can be characterized as tending toward one or the other of these poles. The majority of creative writers, mathematicians, and architects tended toward perceptual awareness. Only in the case of creative scientists was there a clear preference for the judgmental mode, and even among this group those who were most creative preferred the perceptual approach. Further, an associated measure of the use of intuition in the perception of situations and objects showed that, whereas the average person employs such an approach approximately 25 per cent of the time, the various creative persons studied used it in from 90 to 100 per cent of the time.

Studies of the interests of creative persons included in the sample revealed that, in general, they were uninterested in small facts or in details for details' sake. Rather they were involved in meanings, implications, and the cognitive and verbal skill necessary in communicating with others, combined with a relative disinterest in controlling either their own impulses and images or those of others.

Further data suggested that creative persons have the ability to combine the esthetic with the cognitive. Problem solving for them must be not only rational but also beautiful.

One interesting finding that relates to some of Guilford's work on the structure of intellect is that unusual mental associations on a word-association test were found to be one of the best indicators of creativity. The word-association measures correlated as high as .50 with the ratings of creativity made by the architects and editors. This test is a measure of divergent-semantic thinking on the symbolic level in the Guilford model.

One problem that remains unanswered by the research of MacKinnon is whether the characteristics of successful and mature creative persons are the same as when such persons were younger and not yet successful. One partially acceptable approach to this problem, which was used in this study, is to ask such persons about their earlier life, in an effort to pinpoint important events and influences. Unfortunately, such self-reports are open to numerous sources of bias. They can be accepted as suggestive, but certainly not definitive.

A review of such self-descriptions obtained from the architects' group suggested that creativity in adulthood was related to the amount of confidence and respect granted to the individual by his parents when he was a child. The architect's parents tended to assume that their child was independent, and could be expected to act in a reasonable manner. Associated with these expectations was a certain lack of emotional closeness between the child and one or both parents. As part of this pattern there was a certain lack of clear identification of the child with his father that might account for the relative predominance of feminine interests in creative persons.

At the same time the families from which these creative people came were characterized by clear codes of conduct that were enforced uniformly. Discipline was consistent. Emphasis was placed on the development of a personal code of ethics, rather than the adoption of a particular religious system.

Families of creative persons tended to move more often than the average and consequently suffered from some cultural estrangement from their neighbors. This condition added to the breadth of the child's experience, but insulated him from the full impact of the social norms of society, since he was not closely associated with the neighborhood in which he lived.

Virtually without exception, all the architects showed skills in painting and drawing at a very early age. Moreover, one or both of their parents had similar abilities and encouraged the child. However, strong pressures to develop these abilities were not applied. The child was left to pace his own development to a large degree.

The studies of creative individuals under the direction of MacKinnon are still under way at the present time. The results for all groups may not be parallel in every respect, since the basic skills of such professionals as the research scientist and the creative writer are different.

It is evident, however, that even at the present time, studies of creativity have forced us to revise our understanding of the creative process and its cultivation. In practical terms a variety of new principles in nurturing and educating the young person appear to be suggested by the studies of creativity.

One of the most striking and important findings about creativity is its lack of relation to intelligence. This finding is very interesting from the viewpoint of personality and learning theory. In addition, however, there are certain practical problems that this finding suggests. In many situations intelligence is used as the criterion of selection. Most educational experiences are directly dependent on performance either on an intelligence test, or with respect to tasks that are heavily weighted on the side of intelligence. If a person is highly creative, but only of average intelligence, it is clearly imperative to identify him as such, so that he may have proper training. Many potentially creative people undoubtedly are deprived of proper training by the use of an intellectual selection criterion.

Another conclusion that is suggested by the research described in this chapter is that in the training of individuals to become more creative it is clearly important to allow them the opportunity to experience both the world and themselves without too much premature limitation. While discipline is necessary in creative expression it must not cripple the continuous exploration of new possibilities and attitudes. All that is closed, finished, and known tends to cripple or discourage the establishment of a creative relation to a given subject matter. A difficult balance between the presentation of known information and the encouraging of a questioning and open attitude toward new possibilities is essential.

In this regard, there are two general approaches to learning that can be differentiated. The first emphasizes learning of new facts by rote and assigning them to memory. The second involves the generalization across fields of knowledge. The first receives the lion's share of attention because it is easier to apply and clearer to understand. It is also more susceptible to testing after the fact. However, it is the second that appears more essential for the training of creative expression. For this approach it is necessary to stress transfer of training, generalization, the use of analogies, and application of all possible sensory and intellectual modalities, in order to broaden the perspective and deepen the understanding of underlying relationships in a certain manner.

The latter approach is not possible without the former. Unfortunately it is usual to stop with the acquisition of facts, which is only the first stage of training in creative expression. Facts are the building blocks of knowledge, but for the understanding of relationships between facts, the creative faculty is required in order to reconstruct the perceptual and cognitive field. Experience suggests that it is extremely difficult to teach both facts and transformations. It takes, in fact, a creative person to do it. Teachers as a group are not known for their high degree of creativity, although fortunately exceptions do exist.

On the other hand it must be admitted that a creative student is not always easy to handle. A person who can see beyond the present fact to new possibilities is often, by chance or design, placed in conflict with the standards and authorities of his time. If such persons have the characteristics of self-confidence and dominance that seem to go with creativity, they may challenge accepted standards and prove difficult to teach and disruptive to classwork.

All the studies of creativity and the implications they suggest do not tell us specifically how to train creative individuals. At best they suggest general objectives. Clearly, an altogether different type of effort is necessary to formulate and test appropriate techniques for the development of creative ability. Logically and strategically it is important to study the nature of creativity before attempting to foster it. But the next logical step, as these descriptive studies proceed, is a parallel effort devoted to the formulation of methods designed to increase creative ability in all persons, regardless of their inherent gifts. It is hard to overemphasize the importance of such an effort.

Because of the turmoil and uncertainty that must be generated by any training in creativity, it is reasonable to suppose that real improvement of creativity is possible only in a tolerant democratic society—if we take creativity to mean not only scientific investigation but artistic expression. It is therefore in this area that the superiority of democratic government may be manifest, if such training actually is evolved and applied. If it is not, we may be overwhelmed by external political events or by the impact of automation from within our own society.

Chapter Six

ESP, Prognostication,
and PK

Psychic phenomena probably represent the oldest frontier in psychology. These phenomena have been with the human race in various forms throughout recorded history. Tales of thought transference, precognition, contact with the dead, and the movement of objects without physical agencies recur in all cultures of the past and present.

In a more modern sense the investigation of psychic phenomena dates from the time of the origination of modern psychology. But unlike the general field of psychology, psychic phenomena have remained in the shade of controversy, suspicion, doubt, and ignorance.

Thus in the early 1900s William James, the first great American psychologist, was able to predict that in the coming decades the investigation of psychic phenomena would constitute the area of greatest importance for the development of psychology. This prognostication has not proved correct. While interest in the scientific evaluation of psychic experiences of one kind or another has continued, it has not grown and has not found acceptance in the scientific community.

In our day we do not use the term "psychic phenomena," which has about it certain archaic overtones, but prefer to break down these phenomena into more scientific-sounding titles such as extrasensory perception (ESP) and psychokinesis (PK), and refer to the whole area as parapsychology rather than psychic investigation.

Parallel with the development of a new vocabulary, the methods of research in this area have been extraordinarily refined, in comparison with early efforts. But these changes have not altered the fact that ESP, PK, and related phenomena are, at best, tolerated and generally are ridiculed among psychologists.

There are many psychologists who may feel that a chapter on parapsychology does not belong in any account of the frontiers of psychology. From their point of view parapsychology should not be accepted as a part of modern psychology at all. Other psychologists are indifferent to parapsychology. They do not believe in its validity, but are at least willing to consider reported results with a skeptical eye. Another group of psychologists is interested in parapsychology as a general topic but would not seriously consider performing any studies in the area. A very, very small group of psychologists, something in the nature of $\frac{1}{10}$ of 1 per cent, are actively interested in the subject, and either perform work themselves, or, more likely, encourage others to do so.

The reader should bear in mind, therefore, that in discussing parapsychology we are going against the tide of current psychological thought and belief. It seems to us, however, that the topic should be discussed in this context for several reasons. First, the subject matter itself has important general implications for psychology. Second, the subject matter is intrinsically interesting to the general public. Third, the development of ESP and related researches in the last thirty years is an interesting illustration of the application of strict scientific methodology to an area that would seem to be peculiarly resistant to any methodology.

With all of the foregoing in mind, a brief description of the development of a systematic interest in psychic matters will first be presented as an historical frame of reference for the more detailed examination of the status of psychic research at the present time.

In one sense modern studies of psychic phenomena must be associated with the founding of the British Society of Psychical Research in 1882. Significantly enough, while a number of professional persons, including physical scientists, were involved in the formation of the society, psychologists were not represented. In America a parallel society was formed shortly thereafter, and both groups have remained active to the present day. The studies, cases, and records kept by these organizations are voluminous and in many cases fascinating. Unfortunately they either describe unique natural incidents or crude experiments, which, from a modern viewpoint, might be explained as due to error, deception, or bias. Thus, while these groups have kept interest in their subject matter alive, they were not responsible during the first three decades of the 1900s for introducing scientific methods into the study of psychic phenomena to any great extent. Whatever the literary and philosophical interest of the documents they produced during this time, their contribution to the scientific study of psychic research was germinal rather than substantive.

In the last thirty years this picture has changed materially. As in anthropology, the simple collection of new case records has lost much of its vigor and importance. It is now necessary to establish under conditions of scientific control, whether the phenomena that form the bedrock of psychic investigation can be demonstrated to exist in an objective sense. There is, of course, no question that they exist in a mythological sense, just as no one doubts the reality of dreams. The question is whether psychic research represents more than a projection of man's hopes and wishes, or is simply another example of a kind of primitive, partially unconscious mechanism of the mind.

STUDIES OF ESP

The beginning of modern research in ESP is usually associated with the early work of the Rhines at Duke University. Both the Americans Joseph Rhine and his wife Louisa were originally biologists who felt dissatisfied with biology because it was too limited for their interests and needs. For a while they considered careers in religion, but then they decided that psychic research would combine both scientific method and a broad range of focus, in a topic that had both religious and philosophic implications. In a mood of dedication and daring they quit their posts and threw themselves on the mercy of Professor William McDougall, who was then Chairman of the Department of Psychology at Duke University. Their choice of a benefactor was fortunate. Professor McDougall was then very much in the minority of American psychologists, since he was the last of the vitalists, believing that life is in part self-determining, in an age of behaviorism. He was sympathetic to psychic research not only for its own sake but as a way of identifying himself with an interest that his colleagues refused to consider seriously. With his aid the Parapsychological Laboratory was, after a time, founded at Duke University. In this laboratory the study of psychic phenomena was undertaken for the first time in a relatively systematic, scientific manner.

In the early years the Rhines devoted their attention more or less exclusively to the phenomena they came to call extrasensory perception (ESP). This term was meant to be a scientific synonym for "telepathy," but in time it extended beyond it.

The general form of the Rhines' early experiments was extremely simple. A subject was seated across a table from an agent who administered the experiment. The agent had in front of him a pack of cards. Each card contained one of five possible symbols: a cross, a square, a circle, a star, or a wave. The agent would, after looking at the cards, present them to the subject one at a time, face down. The subject was asked to name each card in turn. In this way an objective and simple measure of the ability of the subject to read the mind of the agent was obtained, or so it seemed at the time. By chance, the subject would guess correctly one out of five times. If he did better than this, the probabilities could be calculated exactly.

On the basis of such work Rhine published, in 1934, his preliminary findings.[1] His data indicated that a small ESP effect generally was found for all subjects, and in a few rare persons accuracy of guessing was so high as to be unexplainable on a chance basis.

On the publication of these findings a battle ensued, due, in part, to the resistance of psychologists to parapsychology as a topic of research investigation. Unfortunately, this resistance was partially justified by the many possible forms of error that had not been controlled in many of these early experiments.

It is necessary to examine some of these sources of error, because they had an unfortunate effect on the progress of parapsychology and also because they serve to indicate the methodological problems that still plague researchers in parapsychology.

Perhaps the most severe criticism of this work deals with the issue of sensory cues. The subjects could see the back of the cards. Each back is a little different from the next, differences so small as to be almost imperceptible, but all the more significant for this reason. Such cues could, of course, help subjects identify the cards. Even more damaging is the fact that the symbols were heavily printed on the cards, so that it was possible for the subject to have seen through the back. These obvious sources of error were, of course, corrected in later work by simply not letting the subject see the cards at all.

Other types of error were present. The agent could provide the subject with various visual and aural cues without even knowing he was doing so. He might engage in unconscious whispering—that is, as he was thinking and looking at the card he might say its name softly to himself. Further, he might use vocal inflections when asking the subject to name the card that were helpful to the subject. These sources of error may seem farfetched to the reader, but they have been demonstrated as possible and not unlikely in certain cases. Magicians, for example, have worked out elaborate codes with their assistants to enable them to identify objects when they are blindfolded, simply by the phrasing of the responses made to them by their assistant. Of course, no such code exists between subject and agent, but one may be built up unconsciously in time, since ESP tests may be repeated thousands of times with a given subject. The obvious solution to this problem is to eliminate any direct communication between agent and subject. Thus the deck of cards may be prearranged, so that the agent can merely turn them over one at a time, indicating by a mechanical signal when a new card has been turned, without otherwise communicating with the subject.

A further problem concerns the arrangement of the deck. If the agent chooses which of the five symbols he is to select next, the order is not determined solely by chance factors. In this case the use of probability statistics in evaluating the data is not fully justified. In Rhine's early work, the agent *could* choose from one of the five symbols that were laid out before him, so his order of choice was not random. In particular he would not tend to repeat a choice of the same card as often as this would occur on the basis of random selection. This error also can be easily corrected. It is necessary only to use a table of random numbers in arranging the deck. In this way the human element can be removed.

A more serious and general form of error that can creep into such an investigation is the bias of the agent. It may reasonably be said that most, if not all, serious parapsychologists believe in the reality of the phenomena that they are studying. The pressures against such work are so great at this time as to make it unlikely that any but an extremely dedicated person would pursue such research for any length of time, since all he will get for his trouble is suspicion and abuse, or blind acceptance from the faithful.

Because of this positive bias on the part of the investigator, any errors of scoring and recoding that occur are likely to be in favor of ESP rather than against it, and such errors do occur in scientific work. The greater the belief of the scientist, the more likely their occurrence. The basic problem can perhaps be eliminated by using two experimenters. The first records the answers given by the subject while the second arranges the deck. In this way the experimenter who records does not know whether a given response is correct or not. However, this does not correct possible errors in the final comparison of the scores with the actual arrangement of the deck. One solution is to have such scoring done mechanically. This actually has been done in one large-scale study done by the American scientist S. David Kahn as his Ph.D. dissertation at Harvard University.[2] Kahn had his subjects attempt to predict which of five spaces on an IBM card column was the correct one. An IBM machine was then used to compare the subjects' responses with the key card that had the correct answers on it. In such a procedure no possibility for scoring bias was present. This study, it should be mentioned parenthetically, demonstrated a slight but statistically significant tendency toward ESP. A total of forty-three thousand responses indicated that the correct identification reached a level that would occur by chance only one in two thousand times.

However, this is really not terribly impressive, since the greater the number of cases, the easier it is to demonstrate significant deviation from chance.

A further problem in Rhine's early work, which continues to the present, is the atmosphere in which he conducted his experiments. Rather than demonstrating the cold impersonality that is usual in such experiments, Rhine went out of his way to be friendly, casual, and to some extent careless in his procedures. He built up to the final experiments by slow degrees. In the intervening period various sources of error could enter. The problem was that it was not always clear as to precisely what conditions prevailed during the collection of a given set of data.

In all fairness this procedure was not the product of carelessness on Rhine's part, but rather the result of his conviction that subjects had to be relaxed if they were to perform effectively. For this reason he introduced them to the procedures gradually and in a friendly and warm manner. This in itself is certainly not objectionable if the data collection does not begin prematurely under less-than-ideal conditions. Unfortunately, there is no way of telling whether or not such premature data collection might have occurred.

Perhaps the most striking discovery made by Rhine in his early experiments was that a few individuals possessed an extraordinarily high degree of ESP. These "stars" could be studied extensively under various conditions to determine the effect of changes on their ESP ability. The main subject with high ESP found at Duke was a student named Hubert Pearce. Under proper conditions Pearce could identify the cards correctly at two to three times the level expected on a chance basis. Of equal interest was the fact that it appeared to make no difference whether the agent looked at the card or not. When the agent did not look at the cards Rhine believed that he was testing clairvoyance—the ability of the subject to know the arrangement of the pack directly. Whether or not this was the case is not so easily established, but clearly the ability is different from that which would be required if the agent knew the identity of the card.

Rhine also provided a limited demonstration of the fact that it made no difference whether Pearce was in the room or some distance away when testing for ESP. In one experiment the subject was placed at one hundred yards' distance and given a signal when to begin, with the understanding that a new card was to be presented every minute. These conditions did not reduce the quality of his performance.

The findings reported by Rhine generated a great deal of methodological criticism but they generally were ignored in this country by psychologists. In Great Britain, however, they stimulated other researchers to attempt to replicate his results.

The results of these replications were dismal indeed. No matter how hard they tried or how long the British psychic researchers worked, they found nothing. One of these workers, Donald West, experimented for twelve years without results. Regardless of his initial enthusiasm, his disappointment and skepticism about Rhine's results naturally grew under such trying and heroic conditions. And then, when all hope of success seemed out of the question, he discovered a "star," an individual who uniformly exceeded chance levels to a great degree.

Another British investigator, the Mathematician Samuel Soal, worked for an almost equal length of time, testing one hundred and sixty different persons without apparent results. Then a colleague suggested to him that he reanalyze his data to see if he was getting dispersion effects in which persons tended to guess the card that already had been shown or the one that came next. When Soal did this he discovered to his great surprise that two of the individuals he had been studying were "stars," but their predictions were not for the card being tested but the one behind or ahead of it.

The ESP accuracy of these subjects approached fantastic probabilities. One of these subjects, a Mr. Shackleton, predicted with an accuracy that could occur by chance only once in ten million, million, million, million, million, million times. This type of finding is, perhaps, the most convincing evidence for ESP at the present time. Unfortunately, the results obtained from three or four of those highly responsive subjects uncovered after endless investigation and data collection scarcely are acceptable in a scientific sense. Any general law in science must be applicable to all things and persons, and capable of replication. ESP cannot easily be replicated, nor can a subject with high ESP be selected beforehand. Thus we have before us a few remarkable cases whose accuracy cannot be explained on the basis of chance; but a few utterly unique cases possessing a quality that no one can predict or interpret do not make a scientific discovery in the usual sense. We do not appear to be dealing with a general human property.

The studies of ESP, as mentioned earlier, tend to confound telepathy with clairvoyance. Mr. Pearce, could do as well when the agent did not know the identity of the cards as when he did. This facility suggested that there might not be too much difference between the two abilities. However Dr. Soal, working with his two stars, was able to demonstrate that when clairvoyant conditions were introduced into the experiment without their knowledge, the accuracy of both stars fell to a chance level. This provided a fairly clear demonstration that the two abilities are not equivalent.

A number of other interesting demonstrations were made with the high-ESP subjects discovered by Dr. Soal. Mr. Shackleton already has been referred to. The other equally remarkable subject was a Mrs. Stewart. Mrs. Stewart uniformly was able to guess correctly about 28 per cent of the time over a series of seventeen thousand trials when by chance she would only have got 20 per cent correct.

Once the basic ESP ability has been established in this subject, Dr. Soal then began to vary the procedure. He allowed the agent to look at the order of the cards for thirty seconds before the experiment, which was long enough to see them but not long enough to memorize them if he had wanted to. During the test itself he did not know which card he was handling. Mrs. Stewart did equally well under these conditions, suggesting that the conscious concentration of the agent was not necessary for success.

In another variation, the necessary information was placed in the possession of two different agents. The first knew the arrangement of the random numbers previously selected as the basis of arranging the deck. The second knew the code that told which number went with which card symbol. In order to be able to guess accurately both sets of information were necessary. Under these conditions Mrs. Stewart did as well as usual, indicating that it was as easy for her to get the information from two persons as one. Interestingly enough, however, when she was told that only one agent was involved, while actually two were being used, her results fell to below chance level. When she was told the truth, her accuracy rose sharply.

In an interesting confirmation of a result achieved by Rhine on the effect of distance on ESP, Soal took advantage of a holiday trip to Belgium taken by Mrs. Stewart. A time signal given by the BBC was used in order to coordinate Mrs. Stewart with the experimenter. The cards themselves were arranged by a system of random numbers that was not worked out until the ESP session itself. The results under these conditions approximated Mrs. Stewart's usual level of accuracy.

The results obtained from the analysis of the data produced by these high-scoring persons are interesting and suggestive, but they cannot by themselves be taken as proof in a scientific sense, because they are based on a very limited number of highly specialized cases. On the other hand, as for the value of the ESP accuracy obtained by these individuals, there is no question that these results cannot be explained on the basis of chance alone. It is possible, however, that they possess some ability in extreme form that is responsible for their accuracy, but which is not ESP but something quite different. In the past results of apparent ESP have been reduced to various instances of bias and error. It is conceivable that these responsive subjects represent an unusual instance of such misinterpretation of effect.

How error and ability may be confounded is illustrated by the effects of refinements that another British investigator, George Tyrrell, introduced in working with Miss G. J., a "star" whom he found. Tyrrell used five small boxes with open backs to test psychic ability. He placed a pointer through the hidden back of one box. The subject could not see the stick but was asked to guess which box it was in. Miss G. J. was able to do this 30 per cent of the time. When it became evident that Tyrrell might not be placing the stick in various boxes in a random fashion, six different agents were used. In this series Miss G. J.'s accuracy fell to 25 per cent. Finally, the equipment was arranged so that lights were used inside the boxes. These lights were so wired that the agent could not tell, when he pushed a button, in which box the light would go on. Under these conditions, more clairvoyant than telepathic, the accuracy fell to 23.5 per cent. This was only a little above the chance level of one in five, or 20 per cent. Even at this point other sources of error were possible. Thus as experimental technique was improved, the accuracy fell, indicating that the results were at least in part due to error.

A number of interesting studies of the correlates of ESP ability have been made both with normal subjects and with the higher-scoring ones. For example, one study conducted in the United States has shown that believers in ESP tend to be higher in ESP than nonbelievers. When the subjects were reclassified according to adjustment, only those who were well adjusted scored either very high or very low on ESP tests. However, an attempt to replicate these results failed. A similar study conducted at Duke showed that expansive personality types tend to be lower in ESP. Here again the results could not be replicated when the study was repeated in England.

Certain data suggest that some agents are much more successful than others in finding high ESP in given subjects. There is no explanation for this fact, but it has been demonstrated in cases in which various agents have worked with a given subject.

Another interesting and significant observation about ESP is that the subject has no better explanation of what is happening than anyone else. While he may correctly suspect that he has ESP ability, usually his beliefs concerning its emergence and accuracy are wrong. Conditions that he believes will help him usually have no effect.

Sometimes when working with the high-scoring subjects surprising or unanticipated results were obtained that set the investigators off in quite a new direction. In one notable instance Pearce was asked to predict the order that the cards would have after he had shuffled them. He was able to exceed chance level in this surprising feat, apparently involving the ability to predict the future.

Unfortunately, as so often seems to happen in psychic research, it was later demonstrated that if persons are allowed to shuffle a pack of cards until they feel that the order of the pack matches some prearranged order, they can do this in excess of chance. Such

a phenomenon is interesting in itself, but it eliminates the necessity of resorting to prognostication or prophecy as an explanation
of Pearce's ability to predict the order of the cards before he had
shuffled them. It is regrettable that a mechanical shuffler was never
used with Pearce to enable a foolproof test of his prognostic ability.
Further tests that have been run at Duke have been inconclusive
regarding prognostication.

However, European researchers using "stars" have produced
interesting, though never conclusive, proof of such an ability.

In the previously mentioned work of Tyrrell with Miss G. J.,
using the boxes with lights inside, the experiments passed from
tests of ESP to precognition when the circuit was rewired so that
the light would not flash on until the box actually had been opened.
Under these conditions she was able to perform successfully. Unfortunately, the selection of the buttons controlling the lights was
not fully random, but was determined by the agent. Even though
he didn't know which light would go on, he still controlled the
pattern of lights by the way in which he altered the buttons that
he pushed. If a mechanical random selector of buttons had been
used, the objection would have been overcome, but unfortunately
it was not.

The most famous research instances of prognostication were
uncovered by accident after the fact and have already been mentioned. Dr. Soal had tested one hundred and sixty subjects without
any results. At the suggestion of the British psychic researcher
Whately Carrington, who had been doing related research, he reanalyzed his data to see if anyone had been predicting one ahead
or one behind the target card. It was discovered that two subjects
had, in fact, been doing just this. In one case, that of Mrs. Stewart,
the ability had disappeared by the time it was discovered. In 1935
she had displaced one before or one behind. By 1945, however,
she was accurately predicting the target card. Fortunately, Mr.
Shackleton, the other case, maintained his ability between the time
that he first manifested it and the time that it was discovered. Dr.
Soal found that Shackleton regularly could predict ahead by two
cards. Actually, Shackleton was predicting two to three seconds
ahead in time; by an adjustment of the rate of card presentation

he could be made to predict either one or two cards ahead. However, when he did this, the list of random numbers that determined the order in which the cards would be drawn had already been picked. If by telepathy he could gain access to this list apparently he could predict the future. In order to eliminate this possibility the order of selection was determined by reaching in a bowl and pulling out a number for each card selection. While this procedure eliminated the problem, the resulting selections were not truly random, since all numbers were not equally accessible at any given moment. Unfortunately, a simple randomization machine was not yet available so that Dr. Soal could not apply an entirely foolproof test of Shackleton's ability to predict the future event.

In summary, the evidence in relation to prognostication is interesting but not conclusive, even for a given case. One feature of the testing procedure should be noted, however, in assessing the results obtained. The subjects were not asked to predict a normal social event, but were required to guess at a future event whose very nature could depend only on chance factors. This is an extremely stringent test and far exceeds the normal meaning of prognostication. To predict an individual's future is done all the time by psychologists in the sense of correlating known forces that are presumed to be operating with known future events, such as job performance. While these predictions are never perfect, they can be helpful, since social events occur due to known and controllable causes. However, the arrangement of cards using a randomization machine is not due to any cause at all, and in this sense it should be the least predictable thing imaginable. If, in fact, it were possible to predict an event whose outcome is due solely to chance, the foundation of modern statistics would be destroyed. However, the evidence for prognostication is not striking at this time. Only the isolated instances of star performers help to suggest the possibility, whatever its eventual explanation.

A number of theories have been suggested to explain ESP and prognostic effects. However, these theories all seem to be putting the cart before the horse, since the existence of ESP as a general phenomenon has yet to be demonstrated conclusively and prognosis has not been demonstrated conclusively even in an individual case.

In general, there are two types of ESP theory: physical and mental. Physical theories rely on some material apparatus such as a neural radio to transmit and receive the thoughts of others. These theories generally have been discredited by certain obvious facts. First, no such mechanisms are known in the brain or elsewhere in the organism. Brain waves could not be associated with ESP since their magnitude is so small that extensive electrical amplification is required for their detection. Further, ESP appears to be unaffected by distance, whereas all known physical radiation varies in intensity as the square of the distance from its source.

The alternative is some mental model of telepathy. Such theories usually involve two steps: (a) the reception of common thought patterns by the group mind; (b) the emergence of these thoughts from the individual's unconscious, with which this group mind is presumably connected. This emergence follows the pattern associated with the emergence of all unconscious material. The various forms of distortion familiar to psychoanalysts analyzing the dreams and fantasies of their patients occur here also. Thus the ESP impression is filtered through the personality of the individual receiving it and is distorted by his own needs and motivations. The group mind is inherently unknown just as the unconscious mind is unknown and by definition unknowable. However, the contamination of content that occurs in the emergence process is characteristic of various ESP productions. Many ESP researchers have been struck by the strange and often capricious conditions associated with ESP emergence. The motivation of the subject often has been observed to affect the outcome. If the subject grows bored, self-conscious, or fatigued, his accuracy may decrease. Many subjects have peculiar personal habits of prediction that interfere with their accuracy.

What is perhaps more interesting is that even the best ESP subject never comes close to being 100 per cent correct. Usually they average about 30 per cent, when the chance level is 20 per cent, though higher short-term runs have been noted. If ESP exists, why cannot an individual be 90 to 100 per cent correct? This very interesting question carries some searching implications about the nature of ESP. It is as if there was some force holding back ESP ability from manifestation. This notion is not too far-fetched. If ESP ability emerges from the unconscious, it must overcome the repressive forces that the individual uses to maintain his own conscious identity. In this sense the manifestation of ESP is but another example of the complex dynamic relation of the personality to the various hidden and unconscious memories and motivations that it rejects as threatening to itself and its image. ESP, if it exists, would certainly threaten the personality structure of virtually any person. Who could stand to know what others were really thinking? It would undoubtedly be a very shocking and disturbing experience. Thus, it is suggested that the individual generally does not manifest ESP ability because it would threaten his personality structure to do so.

If we shift our thinking from ESP to prognostication, the theories that have been proposed are both premature and unsatisfactory. If prognostication really could be demonstrated to exist, we would have to revise our basic understanding of the nature of time and the freedom of future events. Such a fundamental revolution in human thought is not likely to be brought about by a few cases that can be interpreted away to some extent as various forms of error. On the other hand the enormity of the problem should not discourage experimentation, particularly since, in the few exceptional cases, there has been at least a suggestion of some results.

While studies of ESP remain in many respects unsatisfactory their results do indicate that ESP is an aggregate of interpersonal psychological phenomena affected by the state of the subject, the nature of the agent, the degree of faith in the process, and the surrounding environmental and social conditions. In this sense parapsychology has come to belong to psychology whether psychologists like it or not. ESP then must be related to other interpersonal processes involving many of the same sources of distortion and error. Fundamentally extrasensory perception may be viewed as a form of communication. Perhaps in the next few years a daring soul will attempt to apply communications theory to ESP results, determining how many bits of information were transmitted and how various forms of noise affected the transmission of information.

PSYCHOKINETIC RESEARCH

Since the inception of Rhine's work in the 1930s a number of new types of experiments have been attempted, such as influencing the growth of living things, from plants to microbes, by psychic processes. But, with one exception, these efforts either have been fruitless or ignored by others, so that little data has accumulated. The one major exception to this state of affairs has been psychokinesis (PK), the ability to determine physical events by mental effort. Such phenomena have long been produced by mediums in seances in which objects move without any apparent physical cause. However, it was not until 1942, almost twelve years after the first studies of ESP, that, once again at the Duke Parapsychological Laboratory, the subject was approached in a controlled, scientific manner. Since that time over two hundred studies of this phenomenon have been reported, so that PK has, by the sheer magnitude of the effort, competed with ESP as a subject for investigation in parapsychology.[3]

The general hypothesis guiding PK research is that psychic forces can influence physical events. Specifically, the investigation usually concerns the ability of the subject to make the fall of dice follow a prearranged pattern. Since the probability associated with the fall of dice is directly determined by the nature of the dice themselves, it is relatively easy to calculate whether a given series of throws deviates from the pattern that would be produced by the operation of chance factors. For this reason dice were used extensively in many studies of this kind, though many similar objects could be and were used at a later time.

Two general measures were employed to determine the existence of PK. The first and most obvious consisted in measuring whether the scores that were wished for occurred more often than might be expected by chance. A second effect, which was found by analyzing the data after the fact, was described as "decline." In this effect, as the trials progressed there was an orderly and steady decrease in the strength of PK ability.

The most adequate experimental model in PK studies is to use the subject as his own control by the alternate use of wishing and nonwishing series. In the latter case the subject simply throws the dice without wishing for a particular number. Unfortunately, this model usually has not been employed. The most typical procedure has been simply to compare the total score of the individual to the chance level of expectation. This approach requires absolute control on all other conditions, if the deviation between scores is to be properly interpreted. Any factor such as fatigue, peculiar dice, or the mood of the subject conceivably can confound the results when nonwishing controls are not employed. All such factors must be controlled adequately if the deviation obtained is to be attributed to PK.

Since there have been a vast number of PK studies, it is hopeless to try to describe them all in any detail. Fortunately, many of these studies tend to duplicate each other so that they can be grouped and condensed.

While the first published report of PK was in 1942, the data on which it was based were collected at a much earlier time, from 1934–1937. Thus the beginnings of PK research go back almost as far as those of ESP. Based on these data, some twenty-one different research reports were produced with generally very significant results. At the time these studies provided very convincing evidence that the ability of subjects to obtain dice scores that they wished for was well in excess of chance. The problem presented by these data was one of interpretation. Were these deviations from chance due to PK, as the authors claimed, or could they be attributed to some other aspect of the experimental conditions under which the tests were conducted?

It must first be said that the tests were performed in a rather haphazard manner, as was the early work in ESP. One subject would work by himself at home. Others would not. Different target scores were used and varied without prearrangement. Thus there is some difficulty in reproducing the procedure that was used in any particular case. This in itself does not nullify the results; it only confuses their interpretation, since the variations that occurred were not planned and may not have been recorded.

Another serious problem concerned the accuracy of scoring hits and misses. Since most of the subjects and experimenters were eager to establish the existence of PK, it would have been desirable to have some type of objective check on scoring, such as the use of two independent scorers or photographic records. In some cases subject and experimenter alternated roles, which might have introduced confusion into the scoring system. Certainly, where motivation is high to establish an effect, adequate control for accuracy is essential.

Another basic problem presented by these data involved statistical assumptions. In discussions of the results of these PK tests, Rhine and others have pooled the results in various fashions. Since tests using probability statistics assume that pooled data come from independent studies carried out under similar conditions, the pooling of the data was not correct or defensible. This is one of the unfortunate results of not controlling experimental conditions more carefully.

In general, most studies failed to use any control for the "wishing" experimental state. Those studies that did use controls were either unsatisfactory methodologically or obtained only negative findings. Perhaps the most interesting early attempt at control was found in the solo effort of a Mr. F. In one series he wished for the six faces to appear. In the second series he wished for ones, but not for sixes. However, the results were identical both times. Since both sets of scores deviated from chance, it appeared that other factors were producing the deviations, probably biased dice.

The evidence for PK in this early series was based on the results of studies that depended exclusively on the probability model for evaluating their findings. Further analysis of these studies showed that in most cases the six face was used as the target. In other words the target had not been varied systematically over all possible dice faces. This failure permits dice bias to influence the results. Since there was available, even before the PK material was published, an account of nonwishing series of dice throw, which showed that the higher numbers tended to occur more frequently than predicted by the probability model, the PK results could be due simply to the bias of the dice and have nothing to do with PK at all.[4]

In 1947 the American psychologist Joseph Pratt carried out a definitive systematic series of nonwishing control dice throws.[5] He was able to show that the deviations from chance that were obtained approximated the pattern of results obtained in the PK experiments in which psychic wishes were made.

Thus the PK effects apparently shown by this early series tended to evaporate in the cool light of scientific scrutiny and controlled study. It was at this time that interest developed in the decline hypothesis. Biased dice could not explain why PK should decline with time. While such a hypothesis was an indirect approach at best, it at least attempted to extract something positive from the huge accumulation of data that had been obtained.

Later investigations of PK in the period ranging from 1945 to the present were built on the remains of a decapitated structure. As a whole this later research benefited from the earlier mistakes in design, execution interpretation, and analysis. Controls were employed, independent observers recorded the results, all six faces of the dice were used as targets, and so forth. At first these studies attempted to replicate the earlier ones, but these attempts were fruitless when proper controls were employed. In addition to the repetitions a number of different conditions were used for the tests. In one study, Australian aborigines were employed as subjects. In another, subjects wished for certain targets before going to sleep.

Perhaps the most impressive series of this type was carried out by the magician John Scarne, who was a skeptic about psychic matters. He went to great pains to insure that his dice were perfectly formed, by the use of precise measurements and by discarding dice periodically after a certain number of throws. He carried on his tests over a period of 15 years, making a total of 6 million rolls of the dice, wishing for the number 7 each time. By chance it was to be expected that low scores (numbers 2 through 6) and high scores (numbers 8 through 12) would each have occurred 2,500,000 times whereas the number 7 would have occurred 1,000,000 times. In fact he obtained 2,499,998 lows and 2,500,001 highs and 1,000,001 sevens. These results are incredibly near those that would be predicted on a chance basis and of course, show no trace of a PK effect.

Beyond such direct attempts at simple accumulation of hits

and misses, various psychological refinements were introduced into the experimental procedure.

In one series of four studies believers in PK were compared with nonbelievers. Both groups scored significantly above chance but not differently from each other. Unfortunately, the latter three experiments in the series could not replicate the results, so that no over-all conclusion could be drawn. In these and other experiments of this type, patterns of PK decline and incline were sometimes noted. Subjects might tend systematically to decrease or increase in PK ability over time or trials. But these effects were vagrant and failed to appear predictably.

In another series the observer either wished along with the subject or wished against him. These studies are interesting but their design difficulties make the results ambiguous.

Other studies have attempted to relate PK performance to various personality measures, including those measured by projective and standard paper-and-pencil personality tests. No relations were found.

A variety of studies conducted by friends or by husbands and wives working in teams under relatively informal circumstances, sometimes have obtained remarkable results, but unfortunately these results vanished under more carefully controlled conditions. For example, in part of one session a subject obtained fifty-two hits in seventy-two runs. These results were checked by the wife of the experimenter and by the subject himself. But when results were recorded independently and targets were varied systematically, the same subject could do no better than chance.

While most experiments have used dice, other means for testing PK have been used with varying degrees of precision. In one instance plastic disks were released through a tube, in others, coins were tossed; a roulette wheel has been used. None of these methods has any particular advantage over dice throwing, and all are subject to bias. Sometimes, however, these studies introduced interesting variations by employing different types of subjects, such as college students and groups of children, or by studying the effects of experimenting during the night or in the dark. Occasionally, remarkable runs of accuracy were observed, but these tended to wash out when all the data were compared, or replications were attempted.

Another general method that has become popular in recent years is the specification of placement on a target. Objects are released to fall on an area marked off in some manner, such as with tiny wires, and the subject wishes for the objects to fall into specific areas. Generally, the results with this apparatus are the same as those found with dice, with an occasional exception occurring in uncontrolled circumstances. Most of these studies were carried out by nonscientific persons, such as retired businessmen whose knowledge of appropriate scientific procedure is questionable. Even in these instances, however, the results were usually negative.

In summary, the studies of dice throwing and other related apparatus have not shown any clear proof of the ability labeled PK. At best there appears to be evidence of an occasional individual run of accuracy. These findings are not unlike those found in relation to ESP.

For this reason there has been some effort to look for PK "stars" analogous to ESP stars, since the results obtained from the general run of the population were negative or inconclusive.

A number of known high-scoring ESP subjects were tested for PK without positive results. However, two other individuals have been studied extensively for evidence of PK ability.

The first series of studies was carried out in England, using a subject named Blundin. This series was plagued by incorrect design, illness on the part of the subject, and finally loss of some of the data. The investigations proceeded over a six-year period in five different series. The results were generally negative, though the result of pooling all the data was positive. Unfortunately, all these studies contained a number of the deficiencies previously described —namely, the targets were not randomized completely, the data were not recorded independently, and often there were no witnesses, so that positive findings would have to be questioned in any case.

The other individual to be studied over an appreciable period of time was a Swedish engineer named Forwald. From 1951 through 1961 this subject was studied more extensively than any other PK subject to date. In the earlier studies with him a placement type of apparatus was used. Dice were released electrically to roll down a runway onto a walled table that was divided into different target areas. The early results indicated that the subject was able to attain results greatly exceeding the level of chance. However, it was then found that the apparatus tended to favor one side of the table as against the other. This tendency was contaminating the results and complicating their interpretation. This technical problem raises some doubts about a number of subsequent studies of the same type that produced results in the same direction as might be produced by the bias, though exceeding it in absolute magnitude. In a further set of experiments two sets of materials were used; the willing was done for one set but not for the other, so that a control was present.

These studies continued to be conducted over the years, with different techniques and variations used, and with varying results. In general the studies were undermined by their freewheeling, unplanned character. Not one of them could be described as well designed or adequately controlled. Thus, while some positive findings were reported, the setting in which these findings were obtained renders them unacceptable in scientific terms. In general, it does not appear that "stars," as in ESP experiments, exist in relation to PK with the same degree of clarity and predictability.

When it became evident that a direct approach to PK was not likely to produce positive, unambiguous results, the concept of PK decline was introduced indirectly to demonstrate that some ability must be in operation. General sources of error would tend to remain constant so decline on PK in the data would provide a kind of evidence that it existed. Such identification is by itself unacceptable without replication, since any data can be searched for relationships; something is bound to be found if enough time is spent. In order to confirm the finding it is necessary to obtain it in an independent study in which relevant factors are controlled. The early series of studies, where testing for decline began, were not really appropriate. The conditions, as already mentioned, varied greatly from study to study, and many necessary controls were not incorporated.

In some of the early data it has been shown that decline was due to two factors. First, subjects tended to choose the number six as a target more in the early series than the later ones. Second, the dice were biased toward the six face. These two tendencies taken together would account for decline. A puzzling finding in these studies was that there appeared to be no relation between the number of hits and the rate of decline. If both measures were tapping PK ability they should have been related to each other.

In the one later experiment that clearly applies to the decline hypothesis, no PK accuracy was found. The results in regard to decline pattern were very slight, though statistically significant. However, once again certain questions arise as to experimental procedure. Differences in results were noted with different exprimenters, and the targets chosen were not equally distributed. In short the experiment, while positive, has a number of technical loopholes, and cannot by itself be taken to prove anything.

In reviewing the history of PK research, one sees a recapitulation of the cycle of events associated with the earlier work on ESP. The work on PK originated in the Rhine laboratories and was at first of poor methodological quality. The early results were largely or totally explained away in terms of dice bias and other sources of error inherent in the experimental conditions. Later attempts to replicate the earlier findings under more carefully controlled conditions met with partial or total failure. The main advance from one study to the next was in the realization of new sources of experimental error. Apparatus bias was common. The subjects were left free to choose their own targets; the shaker used to mix the dice was not foolproof. Recording errors rarely were insured against by the use of photographic records, multiple scorers, and the like. Few of the studies incorporated controls for wishing, believing, and other relevant personality and attitudinal variables that might influence PK. Studies that attempted to relate PK to personality characteristics indicated either that they were unrelated, or that PK did not exist, so there was nothing to which personality could relate. It is only reasonable to conclude that in a scientific sense PK has not been shown to exist. In passing, one may comment on the relatively crude apparatus that has been used to measure PK—an effect that is tenuous at best. It would seem more fitting to use some highly delicate apparatus such as a needle suspended on a thread to measure PK, since it could detect the slightest force acting upon it. In fact several tests have been made in Britain with such an apparatus. The findings have been uniformly negative.

PARAPSYCHOLOGY AND SCIENCE

One is forced, therefore, to conclude, in reviewing the results of the various parapsychological researches on PK, ESP, and prognostication, that no general phenomena of a psychic nature have been demonstrated. The most noteworthy psychic phenomenon has been the ESP "star" who performs at a high level of improbability over a long period of time.

At the present time these extraordinary individuals provide the best evidence for the existence of ESP since the probabilities associated with their performance are so astronomical as to defy refutation.

How, one may wonder, are psychologists able to ignore such evidence? There are several answers to this question. First, while there is no doubt that something is responsible for these unlikely probabilities, it might be something of a mundane nature of which no one is yet aware, just as in the past dice have been shown to be biased and observers unreliable.

Second, science is built upon the principle of repeatability. The whole concept of the experiment is that it represents a non-biased sample of possible demonstrations. In ESP research the sample is extremely biased. Only a very few persons seem to possess this psychic ability. The characteristics of such individuals defy description. While these individuals are themselves reasonably consistent, they do not represent a fair sample of the general population. Therefore no general conclusion can be drawn from them. At this point they represent a unique, unreproduceable event.

Thus it is understandable that ESP research has been viewed with indifference or disdain by scientists. It does not fit into the normal pattern of scientific discovery and demonstration.

Since the implications of ESP are of such a fundamental and revolutionary character, findings in this area are, of course, greeted with an especial skepticism. Nevertheless, when all is said and done, the test results of the high-scoring ESP subjects still stand. In the few instances described, no one has given a reasonable explanation, other than ESP, for the results, though one may be forthcoming in the future.

The unique case is a problem not only in parapsychology. A similar difficulty occurs in clinical psychology where the clinician is more interested in the individual personality than in the generalized description of individuals, such as the standardized test provides.

A number of technical and statistical procedures have been devised for studying the individual as a unique entity. His scores on standard tests have been compared, not only for their absolute value, but for their over-all pattern. Factor analysis has been applied in order to determine the most efficient terms in which to describe the individual, and also to study the consistency in his behavior in a number of different situations or on a number of different occasions. The latter measure approaches the ESP-testing situation, which also involves the repeated application of the same test on different occasions. But none of these methods is really applicable to ESP testing, since each involves a measure of different personality characteristics under approximately the same conditions. However, these other techniques do provide a precedent for the study of the single case as a legitimate enterprise in psychology.

As is customary in the development of science, advances in precision are usually made at the expense of relevance. In the old days the investigation of psychic phenomena was far more mysterious and interesting than it is today. Then the student of psychic research could visit strange houses, looking for ghosts, attend séances to communicate with the dead, and investigate interesting incidents of precognition, the location of hidden objects, or the telepathic reception of distant events. These activities, while interesting in themselves, belong in the category of case histories. They can demonstrate and illustrate, but by themselves they cannot prove, because they occur in uncontrolled circumstances and cannot be repeated at will. Therefore they do not fall within the province of scientific investigation. At best they can suggest hypotheses.

The attempt to make psychic investigation scientific and respectable has led its researchers into the strange detour of experimental methodology, which to a large degree has led to their downfall.

Due either to ignorance or indifference, the vast majority of experiments undertaken have not been worth the effort involved, since no clear interpretation could be made of the findings. The major findings that have accrued are not those originally hoped for, but rather they are of a methodological nature. It is much clearer now that the possible errors associated with parapsychological research are numerous, but generally of the character that must be dealt with in any psychological experimentation. The reason that they seem to have occurred with such profusion in parapsychological research is that the workers in this area do not have a proper technical background in psychological-research methodology. If there is one lesson to be drawn from the effort that has been made in this area in the last thirty-odd years, it is that one must either do such work with all the technical trimmings or not attempt it in the first place. Anything less than a first-class experiment always will be ambiguous and add nothing to human knowledge.

Unfortunately, researchers in parapsychology have belonged to a small, isolated minority. They have received almost no support from the psychological community or from other sciences. More to the point, practically no money has been made available for this work. Researchers have proceeded either at their own expense or on a shoestring budget. But research is expensive; it cannot be performed adequately unless proper funds are available. Such funds have not been provided for parapsychological research largely because of the prejudice against such research that exists among behavioral scientists. The prior studies in the area have given the area itself a bad name.

Beyond noting the amount and describing the methodological quality of studies that have accumulated, one must also weigh the fruitfulness of their findings. To date, their findings have been very slight for the effort involved. There is little evidence of a scientific character to shake the skeptic.

If one were to summarize the evidence at this date, in a sympathetic rather than hypercritical manner, one could only say that there seems to be little or no evidence for psychic ability among the normal run of subjects. However, in exceptional subjects ESP seems to occur to a relatively striking degree.

Are these "star" subjects throwbacks to a primitive condition or the advance guard of a new development in evolution? An examination of their personality and general behavior provides no support for either belief; generally these subjects seem average persons.

No one has really suggested a satisfying theory to account for ESP or any other paranormal phenomena. This is not serious, since the evidence to support the phenomena is so slight. However, it is a problem in the sense that beyond philosophical speculation or unsupported armchair theorizing we are at a loss to rationalize such phenomena if they occur. However, lack of an explanation has never slowed scientific progress. It is certainly possible to demonstrate an effect before being able to understand why it occurs.

If parapsychological research is to be pursued, the wisest strategy would seem to be the extensive and systematic exploration of the unusual case. Little or nothing is to be expected from the study of the average subject. The affects, if they exist, are too vague and too uncertain to be clearly measurable or manipulated in the average person.

Of course many psychologists may, and do, feel that the evidence to date does not merit further investigation in this area. While their stand may be justified in part, the weight of historical and anecdotal evidence testifying to psychic phenomena in every country and culture of which we have knowledge certainly suggests that behind the stories must be some validity. On the other hand, personal experience suggests that if these phenomena exist, they must be extremely uncommon. Otherwise each individual would have experienced them, just as almost every person has experienced the existence of different colors. It is precisely because of the uniqueness of psychic phenomena that their scientific study is so difficult.

Many psychic investigators, both sympathetic and skeptical, have been struck by the unpredictability of the effect of different conditions on the subject. They have further noted that whatever the conditions, there are definite maximum performance levels beyond which subjects do not appear to go. As has been suggested, persons act as if there were forces within their personalities that prevent the manifestation of psychic abilities.

This explanation is testable by the use of drugs and hypnosis to reduce the inhibition on these unconscious forces, but it is not to be anticipated that much information will be gathered since unconscious processes do not lend themselves to easy manipulation or measurement.

Another approach to the study of psychic phenomena, which has been almost totally ignored in modern times, is that which is described in many Eastern and some Western systems of self-development and liberation. From the viewpoint of many such systems, from yoga through Zen Buddhism, the occurrence of psychic phenomena is the fruit of self-development. Thus it is normal occurrence at certain stages of development, but an uncertain or nonexistent occurrence for most persons not engaged in such systems of self-development. This is certainly an interesting idea, but cannot serve as a guide either toward better subjects or clearer explanations, unless a developed subject, who is willing to lend himself to such research actually is found. If such people exist, their willingness to be investigated as scientific freaks is doubtful, since they would have other, and from their viewpoint more valuable, things to do with their time.

Thus we are faced with a difficult dilemma. Should paranormal research be abandoned at this juncture as a waste of time, or, on the contrary, should it receive added sympathy and support, now that so many of the methodological difficulties inherent in it have been clarified? The choice is a real one, but, in all likelihood, it will not be made. Rather, a few dedicated individuals will carry on, stumbling along, committing various errors in experimental design, proving little to the skeptical, but keeping alive the hope and the flame that has been burning since the British Society of Psychical Research was formed.

In an area where a number of the earlier psychologists have looked for a significant breakthrough, we are currently surrounded by error and vague inconclusive results. There is no reason to think that the situation will change dramatically unless assistance is forthcoming from the outside or an extraordinary subject or group of subjects is found.

In conclusion, one can say only that regardless of one's prejudice for, or against, this whole area, in science a field is considered guilty until proven innocent, or unproven until clearly demonstrated. On such grounds we can only conclude by saying for ESP, prognostication, PK, and related phenomena, the verdict is: not proven.

Chapter Seven

Multidimensional Analysis of Human Behavior

Modern psychology can be visualized as a solid geometrical figure similar to Guilford's three-dimensional model of intellect mentioned earlier. The figure's height symbolizes the content level, which varies from physiological function of the bodily mechanism to the behavior of individuals in groups. At any level, or at any given height in the solid, there is a field of psychological specialization that explores the relationship among variables in that area. Thus the area at the base of the solid may be considered to be physiological psychology, next might come the area of intellectual abilities, above that the area of personality, and at the top the behavior of the individual in the social context.

This figure then can be visualized as moving through time. As it moves the relationships at any given level may change. Thus intellectual ability may grow until the sixteenth year and later be impaired with age. Theoretically, the relation between levels also may vary systematically with time. These changes within and between levels of analysis can be due to normal social and physiological processes associated with increase in age. In that case they are studied under the heading of developmental psychology. If changes within and between dimensions are produced consciously rather than culturally and physiologically determined, we can refer the process to clinical, counseling, or educational psychology, all of which are concerned with the conscious improvement of various aspects of human performance.

As is natural in the development of any science, rapid advance is made at the price of specialization. Thus each of the aforementioned aspects of psychology tends to become more insulated from the other with the passage of time, having its own national organization, graduate program, and eventually its own language. This tendency is probably unfortunate, since each conceptual level can arrive at only a partial truth about human behavior. The situation may in the future approach that of the blind men feeling the different parts of the elephant.

For this reason it is particularly important to determine what is known about the relations among these different levels of psychology, since they must be related to each other in any complete description of human behavior. It is also possible that the relation that exists between different levels has a different character from either of the areas entering into the relationship. Indeed, it is an open question as to whether such a relation really does exist. Is there such a thing as psychology in a general sense, or are there rather separate levels, each more or less independent?

This problem has not been explored systematically by psychologists themselves, though occasionally some of their studies bear on the question indirectly. The issue strikes at the conceptual heart of the field and may influence its future development to a great degree. For these reasons an attempt will be made in the following pages to present some of the problems and possibilities surrounding the issue, as suggested by multidimensional studies of human behavior.

THE PSYCHOLOGICAL "SYSTEM"

Perhaps the most general similarity between different levels of psychology is that each of them can be described in "system" terms. Thus the bodily mechanism often has been described as a complex organic system designed to maintain a delicate chemical and physiological equilibrium.

Personality is often defined similarly. The components of this system will vary depending on the descriptive concepts of particular psychological outlooks. But the basic concept of a dynamic equilibrium between a complex network of forces always is clearly employed.

Finally, psychological ideas of behavior in social settings and as part of social systems long have been formulated in terms of interlocking statuses and roles that interact to perpetuate the social structure of which they form the fabric.

It seems reasonable to suppose that all levels could be taken together in a more comprehensive system involving physiological, psychological, and social forces, all in a continuous, complex interaction that seeks to attain a steady state in the midst of continual external and internal change.

Such a preliminary definition of the situation has been drawn. For example, the American psychologist Gardner Murphy has borrowed field theory from physics to formulate a systems theory of human behavior.[1] More recently, the American psychologist James Miller has attempted, and is attempting, to formulate a generalized systems theory that includes within its scope atoms, molecules, crystals, viruses, the cell, the organ, the individual, the small group, social institutions, societies, the planet, the solar system, the galaxy, and so forth.[2] These attempts are extremely interesting since they demonstrate that while the subject matter may be quite different, its organization tends to take the general form of a system.

This type of analysis has many advantages for descriptive purposes. All relevant components can be included and related. The systems model comes very close to the actual situation that it is intended to describe. But this very advantage is a disadvantage in another sense. Any model or theory that can include everything has difficulty in attributing specific effects to anything. In a system there is a tendency for everything to affect everything else in a hazy conglomeration of undifferentiated effects.

Thus the scientist often is puzzled when he has to use such a model for purposes of exploration, or for the determination of new knowledge, which is of necessity discrete. The systems approach is deficient in suggesting which areas in it should be studied and which can be ignored temporarily on the basis of some set of priorities. It does not guide; it integrates.

In our present discussion we can view the "system" in psychology as a convenient integrating concept, but one that does not, of itself, tell us much about relations among different levels of analysis, except that such relations ought to exist, since in any complex system everything affects everything else.

In order to approach the question in a more refined and differentiated manner, it is helpful to consider the basic problem involved in studying relationships within any one level, and then, on the basis of this knowledge, return to the problem of relating different levels to one another.

MULTIDIMENSIONAL MEASUREMENT

On the physiological level, one's first tendency is to study those variables that are measured easily, such as heartbeat, blood pressure, and breathing rate. As the research becomes more advanced, the measures that are attempted become more subtle. Nerve currents are recorded. Delicate surgery is used to alter or destroy specific tissue. Whether they are crude or subtle, physiological measurements are related directly to the physical body and its various organs and functions. In this respect the physiological psychologist has little trouble in defining his measures or his variables. They are dictated by the material nature of the body itself. His central problem is to refine his technique so that new sorts of measurements become possible.

In contrast to this situation, most areas of psychology do not have a simple means of defining variables. There are no material correlates of psychological conditions except the behavior with which they are loosely associated. The psychologist has, therefore, either to define a psychological concept in terms of some behavioral or physiological manifestation, or he has to create an instrument for measuring something that he believes ought to exist in every human being, whether or not it does in fact exist. In the former case the psychologist defining a psychological variable such as motivation may measure it in terms of the number of times an animal will cross an electrified grid to reach a given motivating goal such as food, water, a mate, and so forth. This then becomes an operational definition of the variables or concepts that are under study. The other approach is to create an instrument that is supposed to measure a variable that on theoretical or experimental grounds the psychologist assumes to be important. Thus tests of attitude or personality are designed to measure attributes that are considered conceptually important in explaining human behavior, but are not definable by any simple behavioral manifestation.

The success of either of these approaches is difficult to judge at the time they are applied. Only in retrospect can their relative advantages and drawbacks be perceived clearly. If measures defined either in terms of specific limited behavior in a carefully defined situation or as a test score on a test do not relate to other measures, then their usefulness is questionable. Whether or not they do relate to other measures, it is still necessary to show that they measure what they are supposed to. It is one thing to say that a given test measures a given characteristic or dimension; it is something else to prove it. The establishment of the validity of any measure involves the same general procedure for both behavioral and test examples. In a general sense a behavioral observation in a highly specified setting, such as crossing an electrified grid, does not differ from behavior on the highly specified setting of a standardized test. In both situations the subject behaves either by moving or writing or thinking. The measure is obtained in terms of his response.

There is no direct way to establish whether such measures are doing what the psychologists want them to do. In contrast to the pulse, which has a clear physiological correlate, personality characteristics, individual abilities, and the like do not have such simple specific correlates. The psychologist therefore employs a number of indirect means for determining, after the fact, what he actually is measuring. His general approach is to compare a given measure with other methods of measuring the same variable. If the given new instrument is performing satisfactorily, it should relate to other measures of that variable. There is some circularity involved in this reasoning, since the first measure of the variable may have been incorrect and so acted to perpetuate the error in each subsequent validation process. On the other hand, if a group of these instruments seems, as judged by impartial observers, to be measuring a given characteristic, and each is related to the other, it is reasonable to suppose that validity has been demonstrated.

Unfortunately, the very process of measurement contaminates the score or observation, and it is often difficult to decide whether similarity between supposedly similar measures is due to the fact that they measure the same variable or that they share the same type of error. This problem is not as unlikely as it may sound at first. For example, ratings of friendliness and curiosity may be highly correlated, not because the characteristics are similar, but because they both are measured by means of ratings. Most persons tend to use all rating criteria in the same manner, regardless of their specific content.

There are as many classes of tests and measurements as there are levels of behavior. The type is determined by the level of behavior that it measures. You cannot efficiently measure intellectual ability with a stethoscope or social behavior with an inkblot. At any given level there are certain characteristic types of errors that tend to occur as a function of the instruments that are used. Thus measurement of the behavior of an animal moving across an electric grid depends on constant accurate current flow, equal conditions of dryness, heat, and the like. There is quite a different set of errors associated with paper-and-pencil tests. The subject can lie about his response. He can answer in terms of the social desirability of his response rather than what he feels to be the absolute truth. He may have a positive or negative bias. He may be too varied in his responses or not varied enough. All of these sources of bias have nothing to do with the measurement of the variable that is being studied. They are imposed upon it.

Because of these imposed measurement errors, it is common to find that tests that have a similar form may give comparable results even if they do not measure the same thing. When such a relationship occurs it is strictly common error shared by the measures. This error obscures the intended measurement and clouds the interpretation of the result. This type of error becomes a source of confusion when one instrument is validated in terms of another.

The solution would seem to be to use an instrument of a different type or one drawn from a different level. Unfortunately, when this is done the results create another problem. What typically occurs is that the degree of similarity between measures of the same variable taken on different levels is quite small, or nonexistent. Does this mean that the instruments are not measuring the same thing? Not necessarily. It may simply represent a situation in which the types of errors incorporated in the first measurement work in a different direction from those in the second. In such a case the errors would act to mask any true relation.

Most of these problems recently have been resolved in the formulation of a new approach to the validation of tests called the multitrait, multimethod matrix analysis.[3] Its general principle is as follows: First, it is necessary to measure the same variable on different levels. Second, it is necessary to measure different variables using tests of the same general form. If under these conditions there is a greater relation between tests of the same variable made on different levels than there is between tests of different variables made on the same level, validity is demonstrated.

In order to clarify what is meant, let us imagine a hypothetical study in which the investigator is interested in the sociability and aggressiveness of his subjects. In order to be able to interpret his findings, he incorporates two different measures of each variable. He rates his subjects on both of these criteria. In addition he gives to each subject a standard personality test that provides measures of the same two variables. In this way the psychologist obtains four scores for each subject, two ratings and two personality-test scores. In order for him to determine the effect of the test instrument on the scores he need only relate the ratings to each other and/or the personality test scores to each other. Assuming that sociability and aggressiveness have little or no relation (as has been indicated by a number of studies of personality measures and small-group-member description), any relationship between the ratings or between the test scores can only be attributed to error imposed by the subject on the instrument.

The relationship between sociability and aggressiveness is measured by relating the appropriate ratings to the appropriate test scores. Presumably, different types of measures of the same variable eliminate sources of error due to the form of the test instrument. Thus the correlation between the rating of sociability and the score on sociability obtained on the personality test reflects a real relationship between these variables, since both measures are designed to tap the same content, but do not share the same type of measurement error.

The important question that remains is whether the relation between different test scores obtained on the same test is smaller than the relation between the same variable measured by different methods. One might expect that this would certainly be the case if psychological measurement has any meaning at all. Unfortunately, this is not necessarily so. If the original measures are not very reliable or are of limited validity, then the sources of error may exceed the similarity of measurement across different tests. In any case, the discrepancy between the measurement of test error and the measurement of a real relationship between two different measures of the same variable can be obtained.

Thus in this simple illustration of a multitrait, multimethod approach, we can see how method or test error can be separated from valid measurement of given variables, in order to determine whether, and to what extent, the test score actually measures what it is supposed to measure. But the multimethod, multitrait approach still cannot tell us whether we are studying the variables that we ought to be studying. It can only tell us whether we are studying the variables that we think we are studying.

The "ought" question usually is answered in a variety of ways. Psychologists may study variables that currently are popular because of various irrelevant historical circumstances. They may study them because they are paid to do so, or because a convenient instrument has been devised to measure a particular variable. They may study variables that have important social implications, ones that personally interest them, or that they feel have been ignored unjustly. A theoretical position may suggest the importance of studying a given variable. Previous work in the area may have shown that a given variable is potent in that it relates to other variables that are considered to be important.

All these motivations may exist in varying degrees in any given research project, though for obvious reasons some are given greater prominence in the description of the final report than others. Certainly, it is reasonable to study a given variable if it is known to relate to others of general interest and if it relates to theory in the area. These practical or systematic reasons serve as their own justification up to a point. But the theory may change or be abandoned. And a series of relationships between variables may be shown to be due to nothing more than common error in measurement, or to the fact that differently labeled tests are, in fact, measuring almost the same thing. For example, one well-known finding in social psychology was that authoritarian personalities tend to conform. However, it later was found that the measure of authoritarianism really was measuring conformity, so that the finding was invalid in one sense and redundant in another.

FACTOR ANALYSIS IN MULTIDIMENSIONAL STUDIES

For these reasons another approach to deciding which variables should be studied in any given area has been formulated and applied to a limited degree in recent years. This approach depends on the application of factor analysis to a large group of measures obtained from a given conceptual area. The general purpose of such a factor analysis is to determine the smallest number of dimensions in terms of which all the measures included in the analysis can be efficiently described.

Factor analysis previously has been described in relation to the isolation of intellectual abilities. While it was in this area that the technique was developed and refined, it subsequently has been applied to most areas of psychological investigation.

In all cases the objective is the same: to attempt to form underlying fundamental dimensions from a large variety of data drawn from numerous sources that are all on a given level of analysis, such as personality measures, measures of ability, or measures of behavior in group situations.

Perhaps the most thoroughly factor-analyzed area, beside that of intelligence ability, is the field of vocational aptitudes. One of the central applied functions of psychology is the selection of personnel for various types of jobs at different levels in corporate or business organizations. Rather than to design a completely new test for each job, it is far more economical to isolate the fundamental factors that are involved in any job performance and then, in a given instance, study the manner in which these factors relate to a particular job. In this way the elements are at hand, and need merely to be recombined for an appropriate prediction.

A great amount of work has been done on the factor analysis of abilities and aptitudes for purposes of job analysis and vocational counseling and prediction. The factors were recently brought together by the American psychologist John French, who reviewed a great number of independent studies of aptitude and achievement.[4] A large number of factors were identified in a number of different studies varying from such general characteristics as "deduction" and "induction" to such rather specific characteristics as "aiming" and "speed of symbol discrimination." These factors are certainly not of equal importance, but at this stage of the development of the field the problem of identification of independent content supersedes the organization of the contents in terms of priority and significance.

The second major area in psychology to which factor analysis has been applied extensively is that of personality. Here once again French recently has brought together the relevant material in a huge review of sixty-five different analyses covering clinical observation, interest inventories, attitude scales, personality questionnaires, behavioral ratings, and objective scores.[5] In the course of this analysis, over four hundred and fifty different factors were reduced, by comparison, to less than fifty widely replicated factors involved in personality description. These factors are currently being reduced in number by more carefully controlled factor-analytic investigations.

Another major contributor to the factor analysis of personality characteristics has been the American psychologist Raymond Cattell.[6] In one major study he compared the results of twelve different factor-analytic investigations. He was able to identify twelve clear and six relatively clear personality factors. An especially valuable aspect of this analysis was that objective measures were used to help to identify the personality factors. These objective measures, such as good two-hand coordination, high index of carefulness, and low ratio of emotional to nonemotional words recalled are extremely valuable in the standardization and specification of factors, since the individual cannot readily guess what they measure. Consequently, these variables are not subject to the many sources of testing errors that can contaminate self-reports on standard instruments such as the traditional personality test.

A further though more modest line of factor-analytic investigation involves the analysis of materials obtained from the description of small-group members in interaction. These descriptions are related to personality but are based directly on social interaction shared by the members rather than standard personality measures. The early work in this area was brought together by the American psychologist Launor Carter [7] and later replicated by the American social psychologist Edgar Borgatta and others. The surprising finding obtained by these investigators was that, despite a wide assortment of measurement procedures, ranging from group-member ratings and sociometric choices, to interaction analysis, it appears that there are only from three to five independent dimensions needed to describe group-member performance in the small-group situation.

To a lesser degree, factor analysis has been applied to many other areas in psychology. It has been used as a technique for deriving an objective set of psychiatric diagnoses. It has been used to determine what certain widely used psychological tests, such as the Rorschach, actually are measuring. Factor analysis has been used to test the validity of psychoanalytic theory of personality types and to compare the behavior of identical twins. However, in spite of these examples it must be emphasized that the factorial approach to the isolation of fundamental dimensions of psychological measurement has not been accepted widely among psychologists. This in part is due to ignorance of the method and its power. A cultural lag is partially responsible. Psychologists are trained to think in terms of a few variables at a time, and to emphasize the importance of theoretical constructs and variables that are related to popular or significant theories current at the time. The constructs of these theories are arbitrary, the product of the theorist. They may or may not represent fundamental dimensions in the factorial sense. No one knows until it is too late.

A further difficulty with factor analysis is that it requires a great deal of time and patience to perform when only a simple hand calculator is available. It was this difficulty more than any other that held back the use of the technique. With the advent of high-speed computers, factor analysis has been reduced to a routine procedure carried on almost completely by the computer. As a result, at the present time factor analysis is the most frequently performed statistical calculation on such computers.

The impact of this work is bound to be great as it accumulates. But at the present time most psychologists prefer to ignore these implications and proceed with their customary concepts and practices. The factor analysts are only a small, highly vocal minority among the larger group.

Nevertheless, it is hard to see how any other approach can provide what factor analysis can give: a description of the simplest and most general dimensions of description. If one of the laws of science is parsimony, it would seem that factor analysis provides the only satisfactory means toward such a goal in psychology.

If, as we predict, each area of psychology comes to be defined in terms of general factors, then any given individual or case will be described in terms of his scores on each of these factors. In such an instance all persons will be measurable in the same terms, and the number of measures will be the smallest number possible in keeping with generality of coverage.

The efficiency of such a development would be tremendous. Measurement procedures would be directed at obtaining specific measurements of factors. As they were provided, a standard set of dimensions and measurements would be used in all experimental work in a given area. From such a development research would truly become cumulative, since it would cover the domain, and could systematically explore all relevant relations between the dimensions whose generality and significance had been demonstrated. Science generally has been most successful in situations in which knowledge was accumulated in an orderly manner, so that each individual could take advantage of the work of those who had gone before. Such a logical unfolding is quite different from the arbitrary, chaotic, and unsystematic exploration of the many areas of psychology that has tended to occur in the past.

At present there can be little accumulation of knowledge in an efficient manner since no one is certain of what is being measured or what ought to be measured. There is thus a great and chronic need for the organization and simplification of the relation between measures that factor analysis is equipped to produce.

Factor analysis is based upon a mathematical model that in itself is purely abstract. If the data to which this analysis is applied happens to fit the mathematical model, the results should be excellent. However, there is no preordained guarantee that this should be the case. There therefore has been interest in studying exactly how factor analysis behaves in various empirical situations, in order to judge its actual, as distinguished from its theoretical, success in reducing data to their most parsimonious and general form.

The problem recently has been investigated by Cattell.[8] He used several different experimental situations involving tomato plants, coffee cups, and solid balls suspended on strings to test the effectiveness of factor analysis in natural situations that involve experimental error and in which a definite factor structure is known to exist before the analysis is undertaken. For example, in the study of solid balls a series of thirty-two different tests was performed in order to generate the data that could be used for the factor analysis. The experiments included the following operations. The ball was dropped from a height of eighteen inches into a salad bowl filled to the brim with water. The water that splashed out was collected and measured. The ball was hooked by a string behind a roller toy that was pulled forward, causing the string to wind around the toy; the distance the ball traveled before reaching the toy was measured. From thirty little experiments of this type independent measures of the behavior of the ball were obtained. These were factor analyzed in order to determine the fundamental dimensions in terms of which balls ought to be described. Four factors were obtained—size, weight, elasticity, and string length—that exactly matched the four known factors related to the physical description of the ball on the string, thus validating the analysis.

While all the technical problems surrounding factor analysis are not fully solved, it seems clear that this procedure has, can, and should make an important contribution to the ordering of psychological data, eventually reducing the chaos of information that is currently available into some more basic form. If this development occurs, it is reasonable to expect that on each level of analysis the dimensions in terms of which data analysis can most reasonably be carried out will slowly emerge.

ANALYSIS OF INTERLEVEL RELATIONSHIPS

As we have seen, analysis and the description of different levels of analysis appear to be approaching a solution on their own levels. This will result in a more orderly and systematic development of each of these levels. What effect will it have on the understanding of interlevel relationships?

This question can be examined from two viewpoints. First, present interlevel studies can be examined to see what is known about such relationships. Second, a general model can be given showing how such relationships might be explored as the levels themselves become more clearly organized.

Psychologists usually are not interested in the space between adjacent levels for several reasons. First, psychology itself is a relatively new science, and must establish specialized areas as its prime focus, so that each accumulates enough specific information to allow it to function on its own. Second, specialists in adjacent areas usually build up various defenses to avoid looking at others who are doing similar work. This maneuver helps to maintain their own specialty. Third, attempts to pass from one level to another are rather rare unless a practical problem demands it, or knowledge within areas has progressed to a certain stage. While there are relatively few studies of this type, there are a sufficient number to suggest certain preliminary conclusions.

For purposes of clarity let us distinguish among a number of specific levels representing traditional divisions in psychology. It is simplest to visualize a solid that can be cut at various points producing a plane, as described at the beginning of this chapter. Each plane literally is an area of subject matter in psychology. The height of the solid represents the level of generality of the subject matter; the length of the area cut out represents the extensiveness of the subject matter; and the width or depth represents the level of understanding that is current in the area. If such a scheme were adopted, the shape of the solid would vary with the height, since the amount of knowledge and depth of understanding varies considerably as one passes from one level of psychology to another.

For purposes of clarity we shall assume that all areas are equally developed, an assumption that is incorrect. Thus the solid takes a regular shape. The important dimension for our present discussion is height. At the bottom of the solid is physiological psychology, concerned with the relations of physiology to behavior. Next is found the study of intellectual and other abilities. Above that comes the study of personality, involving the description of the whole person as a set of consistent determinants. Finally, above personality comes social behavior.

This structural model is only partially satisfactory. Intellectual ability is nearer to personality than to physiology, and personality is nearer to ability than to social behavior. Further, the differences in methods of measurement used on these levels have been ignored. Since, in the last analysis, any attempt to compare measures obtained from different areas must be reduced to the comparison of scores, the nature of measurement is important. Here we can distinguish three types of measurement, though many others could be added. First, there is behavior observed by another individual. This may be behavior in a test situation or an interpersonal setting. Second, there is the self-report, an instrument filled out by the subject in which he describes his own assessment of himself. Third, there are various projective measures designed to see beneath the self-report to the basic organization of the individual. These three types of measures can be compared in their own right, regardless of the level of the subject matter to which they are applied.

If, for the sake of simplicity, we reduce our model of the areas of psychology from a plane to a point we can redraw our mental diagram to emphasize the relation between content and measurement. Thus on all levels variables can be observed objectively, and the subject can observe them from within. In addition, in the personality area unconscious motivation can be inferred from various projective measures such as the Rorschach, TAT, or sentence-completion tests.

In theory, the best way to study interlevel effects would be to obtain measures on all levels for the same group of subjects. Since the most efficient measures on each level are not really known, and because of practical difficulties in administering great numbers of tests, such a direct approach has not been attempted to any great extent.

There have, however, been selected attempts to test several possible combinations of levels and methods that may supply some general hint to what may be found when more of the combinations have been tested.

In order to facilitate the presentation of these studies it is helpful briefly to describe the various combinations of subject matter taken two at a time.

The first major grouping involves the relation of physiological psychology to the other levels of psychology. When these categories are analyzed it becomes evident that what is called physiological psychology is just such an interlevel application between physiology and variables on other levels. The physiological psychologist is not interested in physiology itself. He is concerned with the impact of physiology on intellect, personality, and behavior.

There are, for example, numerous studies of the relation between the nervous system and intellectual ability. These studies concern the attempt to localize intelligence, to relate brain description to intelligence, and to describe the physiological basis for intelligence.

Further, a number of attempts have been made to relate physiological bodily needs to personality development either in psychoanalytic terms of oral, anal, and genital satisfaction or in the more common-sense terms of drives and motivations. Other attempts have been made to relate body type to general personality characteristics.

Relatively little has been done to relate the physiological level to social behavior. Physiological drives appear to direct social behavior mainly in times of emergency or stress. Under normal conditions of civilized living physiological emergencies virtually are eliminated, though these drives may continue to influence behavior in various socialized forms such as the cultivation of taste in food or drink, and the subtle ramifications of sexual behavior.

It is hard to generalize about the relation of physiology to psychology because the subject matter of physiology is concrete, whereas psychology deals with variables that are reduced to behavioral operations only with difficulty. On the whole, one is not impressed with the degree of relationship between the two. At best the physiological substratum provides a parallel for psychological phenomena, but does not explain them. For example, one of the more interesting effects of physiology is produced by the stimulation of the cerebral cortex with an electrode. When this is done the individual may have certain specific sensory experiences—music, flashing lights —or he may relive a very specific memory, such as the sound of a mother calling a boy which he heard many years before.

However, it is impossible to tell from a study of physiology exactly what effect will be produced, except that it will have certain very general characteristics. These characteristics are known not from a study of physiology but from past observation of the psychological effects of such stimulation.

A further example of this problem is provided by studies of brain waves. When the EEG machine for the electrical amplification of brain waves was first developed, hopes were high that science had found the way to study thought by the amplification of brain currents. Such a hope has not been fulfilled. After extensive investigation on normal and abnormal subjects, it is clear that brain waves tell most about their own level of analysis—that is, they relate to other physiological conditions such as epilepsy, sleep, general activity, and so forth. No one has related specific thoughts to specific variations in brain waves.

Without further example, we shall pass on from the study of physiology to describe the relation between method and level in the study of abilities, personality, and social behavior.

Perhaps the nearest approach to a general study of this sort is provided by the long-term research of the American psychologist Lewis Terman on persons of superior intelligence. Terman studied a group of a thousand intellectually gifted children over a period of almost forty years.[9] His findings clearly showed that a high IQ is associated with better-than-average adjustment. The individuals in his sample received a better education, achieved higher professional status, and attained generally better personal adjustment than the average. Thus high IQ is not a personal hindrance, as is sometimes believed. It should also be mentioned that even the physical status of this group was above average. Also, the early measure of IQ remained relatively constant over the years, indicating its stability. These results are not terribly surprising. They suggest that persons with superior ability are able to function more effectively and therefore make relatively satisfactory adjustments. However, no hint is given of the relation of particular abilities to particular kinds of personality adjustment or formation.

The case is quite different if we relate tests of ability to measures of social behavior. Here we find a wealth of material that has been generated by the standardization of aptitude tests. These tests are standardized by relating the test score to external criteria of performance. Generally the most satisfactory criteria are the ratings of an expert observer, or objective productivity measures, position attained, or similarity of test performance to those who are already successful in the given area.

There are a tremendous number of such tests, good, bad, and indifferent. Their effectiveness varies with their purpose and the carefulness with which they were standardized. There are, for example, tests that have been made for a specific and limited purpose such as selecting persons for a new type of job in a factory. The test is used once in a single location. On the other hand there are many tests that are standardized on a number of groups and used in many different types of vocational predictions. It is hard to generalize from these tests since they differ somewhat in purpose and greatly in methodological quality.

The clearest use of intelligence or aptitude tests for the prediction of complex social behavior has been made in relation to general unfactored intelligence tests measuring IQ rather than the more specialized aptitude tests. The reason for this is largely practical. The IQ is a widely used measure that is readily determined without special effort on the part of the researcher for correlation with predictors of social success such as job attained, or school marks. Tests of aptitude require special administration outside the normal current of the testing program.

The strongest relation between intelligence and any practical work criterion is that of school marks. The correlation here is approximately .50 to .60. If the correlation is squared, an estimate of common variance is obtained. "Common variance" describes the extent to which two variables vary in the same manner, as measured on a scale ranging from 1 to 100 per cent.

In the present instance, the common variance is about 30 per cent, indicating that 30 per cent of the variation in school marks from person to person is due to differences in intelligence. The remaining 70 per cent of the variation is due to other causes, such as personality, the nature of the teachers, the school system, parental prodding, and the like. Generally, as one passes from elementary school through high school and to college the degree of association between the IQ and grades decreases slowly but perceptibly. This indicates either that the measure of IQ is less accurate as one gets older, or that other, nonintellectual factors determine school grades to a greater extent in college than they do in elementary school. It is also interesting to note that the best measure of school marks is not intelligence, but previous achievement. This illustrates the central predictive principle that the best prediction about future performance is that it will be the same as past performance. Human behavior tends to be consistent over time.

It is also interesting to note that intelligence tests relate more closely to achievement tests than to marks. This is somewhat surprising, since marks are intended to reflect achievement. However, marks are less reliable than achievement tests, and it is possible that both intelligence and achievement tests share the same kinds of measurement error since they are both paper-and-pencil tests—that is, when IQ is measured by group intelligence tests.

A final interesting but obvious point about the relation between intelligence and grades is that its absolute magnitude depends, to some extent, on the course content in which the grades were obtained. The correlation between English grades and IQ may be .50, whereas the correlation between shopwork and intelligence may be only .30. While this is what one would predict, it does illustrate why aptitude tests are required if a higher degree of selectivity is needed in a given instance.

Intelligence is less clearly related to performance out of school.

In general, different occupations require different levels of education. These are in turn, related to actual intelligence. Thus IQ may set a broad limit to the type of occupation or profession that is attained. However, within any occupational group there is a great deal of variation in IQ, so that 10 per cent of coal miners do as well as 50 per cent of lawyers on an IQ test. This variation is even more impressive when one notes that IQ reflects social conditions, since a coal miner would probably have an impoverished educational environment, his IQ on such a test really would represent an underestimate of his true potential.

When IQ is related to success in various types of jobs, the results are generally positive, but low. The highest relation to IQ is in the supervisor category, in which the correlation may be .40, or 16 per cent, of the variance. On the other hand for semiskilled workers the relation may be .20, or only 4 per cent, of the variance. For these reasons intelligence measurement is not sufficient as a basis for the prediction of vocational success.

There are an almost endless number of aptitude tests varying in length, quality, and focus. The general tendency over the years has been to refine the elements that go into these tests and recombine them in different proportions as the need arises to meet a new situation in an old area. Thus there are well-established tests of mechanical ability, clerical aptitude, and the like. Because of the relatively simple functions associated with such work, it is possible to simulate many aspects of the job performance in a paper-and-pencil test with a minimum of supplementary equipment. However, most jobs are more complex and require a more sophisticated approach. For this reason there has been a tendency to design general aptitude tests that measure a number of important aptitude factors, such as mechanical reasoning, numerical ability, or spelling. Norms on these factors are then obtained for various professional groups, so that the individual profile on these batteries can be compared with known groups. In general the discrimination provided for the individual case is low for these tests, since the range within any given occupational group is large. Thus for a single person the test adds little to the accuracy of any prediction of future success. However, if a large number of persons are available for a few positions the tests enable a better selection than might otherwise be possible. They also aid the individual in ruling out for himself certain professions or jobs for which he is clearly unsuited.

The central problem with all aptitude tests is not so much the test itself as the criteria used to validate it. It is hard to obtain an adequate measure of job success. For the most part ratings must be used, even though they may be biased or unreliable. However, where the relation between specific test scores and job success is tested, the results are rather poor. In general the correlations run about .25, accounting for only 6 per cent of the variance involved in the relationship. While 6 per cent is better than 0 per cent, it is very low in terms of any general prediction between the levels of test and job performance.

PERSONALITY AND GROUP MEASURES

The last remaining category concerns the relation between personality and social or group measures.

Studies of this type were reviewed recently by the American social psychologist Richard Mann.[10] All these studies involved the relation between scores on personality tests and various measures of behavior in a small group, including objective interaction, inferences drawn by observers watching the group, and the descriptions made by members engaged in the interaction. Presumably, the personality of group members is of major importance in determining the way in which they behave in social situations.

The main personality variables that have been studied in the small-group context include intelligence, adjustment, extroversion-introversion, dominance, masculinity-femininity, conservatism, and interpersonal sensitivity. In the over one hundred seventy-five studies that were reviewed by Mann approximately five hundred personality variables were found. Three hundred and fifty of these were classified under the headings just mentioned. The remaining hundred and fifty variables were drawn mainly from projective tests of uncertain reliability and validity. They were eliminated in order to avoid contaminating the analysis with data whose meaning was unclear.

In terms of small-group measurement six major small-group performance variables were isolated: leadership, popularity, total interaction rate, task activity, social-emotional activity, and conformity. These six variables were then related to the seven personality variables in terms of the evidence presented by the one hundred and seventy-five independent studies that were included in the review. For purposes of clarity, the relation of each behavioral group variable to all the personality variables will be described separately.

The most carefully studied relation of a small-group variable to various personality measures involved the relation between personality and leadership. The reason for this relative density of findings is the practical importance of leadership as a social-psychological phenomenon relating to problems of social organization and social control. In general, it was found that a strong positive relation exists between leadership behavior and intelligence, adjustment, and extroversion. Smaller relations also exist with dominance, masculinity, and social sensitivity. Finally, a negative relation exists between conservatism and leadership. These relationships are generally not surprising, since it is mainly the personality characteristics of the leader that determine his selection by the group.

The relations associated with leadership are replicated largely by those associated with social popularity. The latter is related to the personality characteristics of extroversion, intelligence, and adjustment; but, unlike leadership, it is related positively to conservatism. The remaining personality characteristics have not been covered sufficiently in the existing literature to permit comparison.

The total amount of activity of the individual in the group bears the most direct relation to his intelligence. Some relation to extroversion and adjustment also exists.

In contrast to the total amount of activity of the individual in the group, the amount of task-directed activity appears to be associated with a different cluster of personality characteristics. Unfortunately, the amount of task activity is related to the amount of total activity, so that the general measure of activity may contaminate the more specific task measure. When no effort is made to control over-all activity rate, then relations are found to adjustment, extroversion, masculinity, intelligence, dominance, and conservatism. However, when the absolute amount of activity is controlled, intelligence, adjustment, and masculinity are negatively related to task activity. This is extremely interesting, since it relates task activity to maladjustment, stupidity, and femininity, but the number of studies in which such control was possible are very few, so that the finding cannot be accepted fully at this time.

There is relatively little known about the relations between social-emotional activity and personality characteristics. What is known suggests that this type of activity is associated with intelligence and adjustment, but it is hard to separate the total rate from social-emotional activity in measuring these relationships.

Interpersonal sensitivity seems to be related to both leadership and popularity, but for reasons discussed previously in relation to the study of social perception, the measure of interpersonal sensitivity is open to suspicion, so that the meaning of these correlations is not clear.

Finally, conformity in group situations is related to adjustment and extroversion when the individual describes his own personality. However, when personality is measured by objective or standard measures, conformity is found to be negatively related to adjustment and extroversion, indicating that the viewpoint of the observer determines the result. As one might expect, the conservative individual tends to conform in the group setting.

A review of the findings just described indicates that they are not as independent as their presentation might suggest. Most interaction characteristics relate positively to intelligence adjustment and, usually, to extroversion. We must assume either that different group behaviors can be related to the same personality characteristics or that the group behaviors are not so different as they seem.

Regardless of the particular relations between the interaction and personality variables, the most interesting question concerns the magnitude rather than the sheer existence of these relations. Here the results are fairly clear and somewhat shocking. The highest correlations between behavior and personality in these studies were about .25, which accounts for only 6 per cent of the variance. The majority of the correlations were somewhat smaller. Thus the relation between the personality of the individual and the way he is observed to behave in group situations seems rather slim.

While the preceding review clarified the general nature of the relation between personality and social-behavior measures to the extent that this currently is known, it was not designed to illustrate or separate the type of measurement from the level of measurement. Rather, the levels were related and the types of measures pooled.

In order to supplement this approach it is useful to describe a series of studies in which the level is varied but the type of measurement is controlled. These studies bear some similarity to the multitrait, multimethod matrix previously described. In general, such an approach can be applied only to personality characteristics that are general for the population, rather than to social behavior or individual abilities. While social behavior can be observed and self-observed, it cannot be tested. Only personality allows all three types of measurements in a natural manner—that is, only personality characteristics can be measured as paper-and-pencil variables, as behavior observed by others, and as observed by the individual himself. Further personality variables can be inferred from projective materials. Thus a given personality variable can be measured from as many as four different levels. Each such study constitutes a sample of one variable measured on a number of different levels. The relation between levels can be estimated by relating the measures so obtained.

Perhaps the clearest example of this type of study has been supplied by Borgatta.[11] In an early pioneering study of this general type he compared a projective test, role playing, and normal social behavior, each measuring reaction to frustration. In this study normal behavior and role-playing were found to be much more clearly related to each other than to the projective-test behavior. Unfortunately, the great number of scoring categories used led to unreliable scores, so that the results were not as clear as they might otherwise have been.

Several years later a modified repetition of the general design was undertaken. A large number of three-man groups were observed while planning the spontaneous performance of a chosen scene, and when actually enacting it. They were also given a Conversation Study Projective Test in which they were asked to say what the three men who were pictured in the test material were talking about. The responses in all three situations were analyzed and compared. A very close correspondence was found between role-playing and actual behavior, indicating that persons used the same patterns of behavior in both levels of measurement. Some parallelism also was noted between the projective measure and the behavioral measures. Specifically, the projective measure of emotional-assertive and task-ability factors related directly to measures of the same factors in the behavioral situations.

In a further, more ambitious study, almost two hundred subjects were examined in group situations and by means of standardized tests. Four different levels of measurement were employed: interaction, as measured by an external observer, rankings by other group members, self-rankings, and scores on standard personality tests. The results of this study, as one might expect, were fairly complex. In general, it was concluded that there is a fairly close relationship between the interaction scores and the rankings of peers. Also the self-rankings and the personality-test measures seem to be closely related to each other. Self-rankings and personality-test measures are both obtained from the individual, whereas interaction and behavior ranking are both obtained from objective observers. The study indicates that measures of the same general form and character are the ones that are most closely related.

These findings are not surprising. The nearer one level is to another, the closer is the relationship—as one would expect. On the other hand, these studies are but spots of light in the darkness separating different levels. While the results may be reasonable, they represent only the first harvest and the preliminary estimate of what lies between social and psychological levels of measurement.

Another interesting attempt to formulate the relation between levels of measurement has been undertaken by the Kaiser group under the general direction of the American psychologist Timothy Leary.[12] Here the effort has been more theoretical than research-oriented, though some preliminary research has been reported. In this system each conceptual level is viewed as a circle that is divided into eight sections, representing eight descriptive dimensions. These characteristics were arrived at by analysis of various

behavior mechanisms. They are called: managerial-autocratic, re-
sponsible-hypernormal, cooperative-overconventional, docile-depend-
ent, self-effacing–masochistic, rebellious-distrustful, aggressive-sadistic, and competitive-narcissistic. The first word in each pair is
intended to represent relatively normal behavior, whereas the second represents a pathological extension of the tendency. These eight
types of behavior are measured on five different levels of personality: the level of public communication as seen in group behavior; conscious communication, such as one individual's talking
to another or simply talking to himself or writing; private symbolic communication, as in dreams and fantasies; unconscious motivation; and aspiration. With the exception of the unconscious area,
measures have been devised to tap the different levels. Unfortunately, little data have yet been produced to clarify the relation
between these levels on the given variables.

The Kaiser system certainly is interesting as a prototype of
interlevel analysis. Unfortunately, it partly overdetermines the
problem by assuming artificially that each level should be measured
in the same terms. It seems quite probable, in view of the research
we have discussed, that each level should be described in its own
terms rather than strait-jacketed, forcing them all to speak the
same language.

A final question can be asked about multilevel research by ex-
panding the upper level of social behavior into a more complex
configuration. When we speak of social behavior we assume a generalized social setting in which behavior is manifest. This generalization is overly broad. In fact, any typical behavior is performed
in a specific set of situations. When we refer behavior to a class
of situations it is customary to speak of role performance. Any
role consists of a complex series of behaviors that are associated
with the occupancy of a given status in a certain class of situations.

Virtually nothing is known about the relation between different
social situations in a rigorous scientific sense, though a vast amount
of observational material is available.

From one viewpoint, role performances can be seen as parallel
to each other, rather than interlevel. However, the relation of one
role performance to another depends on their relative position in
the social framework of which they both form a part.

Since all psychological statements ultimately refer to behavior, it is extremely important to clarify the possible contexts of behavior, regardless of the level from which it derives.

Consistency of behavior is partly dependent on strictly psychological processes. However, this consistency is also created by the cultural and social influences that enforce various patterns of normative behavior. In order to understand the relation between the two, it is necessary to examine the relationship between individual behavior in different situations.

The simplest approach to this fundamental problem is to ignore all personality variables and focus on the situation or social setting as a determinant of behavior. From this view each distinguishable social situation is a case. All such situations taken together make up a population of all possible social situations. The crucial question is whether there are a vast, or even infinite, number of such situations, or whether they can be divided into a relatively small number of classes. This question is of vital theoretical importance in the development of social psychology, and, indeed, of all psychology. The assumption is usually made by psychological researchers that one situation is pretty much like another, so that a finding obtained in one situation will tend to hold in another. However, social psychologists know, in fact, that changes in social situations produce changes in human behavior directly, or through the mediation of a status system within which social situations are imbedded. But neither the psychologist nor the social psychologist knows whether this influence can be simplified into an orderly typology of social situations or whether each situation is unique. If the latter holds true, then there are reasonable grounds for stating that a general science of psychology is impossible, since no general statements could be made to cover all situations. If, on the other hand, a limited number of general situations exist, then any finding could be related to some or all of them, depending on its nature. The social situation is the framework for all psychological investigation and must itself be analyzed and systematically classified if the setting of psychological research is to be properly understood and evaluated.

To date no one appears to have examined the problem of describing social situations in a systematic manner. Sociologists have described types of social situations, but their approach has been intuitive and theoretical. They have not tested whether, in fact, their typologies describe independent events and cover the existing social situations. Psychologists have tactfully ignored the problem.

The sole exception to this tacit avoidance of the problem is presented by a small series of factor-analytic studies designed to determine the dimensions of group description.[13] These investigations take the group rather than the individual as their unit of analysis. At this time, three such studies are available. They were planned in different contexts and utilized different designs and instruments. The results are therefore scarcely definitive.

Some parallel dimensions were found in these studies, such as purposefulness, polarization, task interest, control, and involvement activity. However, the replications were not perfect, and, for many factors, nonexistent. If these studies are pursued they should aid in the formulation of small-group theory, since they will indicate the dimensions of small-group experience. More important in the present context, these dimensions might be used to describe various social situations. However, we are concerned not with the dimensions but with the social situations themselves. Regardless of the terms in which any given situation is described, the relation between situations remains unsolved and uninvestigated.

There are several avenues, of varying difficulty and validity, that may lead to a better understanding of the relation between social situations. The most difficult approach is to attempt to observe them directly. This involves extensive natural observations with no assurance that the results could be interpreted, since natural situations inherently are uncontrollable and open to a variety of errors.

A more practical approach might be to attempt to create a vast number of different social situations in the laboratory, using some type of role-playing procedure to create a microcosm of society. This approach would have the advantage of greater controllability, and would still involve the observation of real behavior. However, the problem of standardizing a great number of social situations so that they could be repeated in role playing is a vast undertaking in itself, but one well worth the effort.

Perhaps the most realistic, though not necessarily the best, method of approaching the problem is through some standard paper-and-pencil test that would be designed to measure how individuals behave in a variety of social situations. Certain interaction category systems such as Interaction Process Analysis attempt to perform such a feat, but a trained observer must be employed with these methods. What is needed is an instrument that the individual can administer to himself. Given the instrument, one could then be provided with a fairly large series of standard social situations involving such typical settings as the family, friends, job, military, political, and social situations. The individual might be asked to describe his reactions and typical behavior in each such situation. By comparing the item profiles across situations for a number of individuals, relations among situations could be determined. If groups of individuals agreed in attributing certain patterns of reaction to certain groups of situations then evidence would be provided for a typology of situations. It is rather astonishing that in view of the importance of the issue no one seems to have investigated the relation between situations. Using the pencil-and-paper approach, this would not constitute an unduly large undertaking.

Closely related to the problem of classifying social situations is the problem of defining and classifying social roles objectively. While there is considerable disagreement about the precise definition of role performance and role behavior, or even just the term "role," there is general agreement that any social situation, in as much as it has any formal characteristics, is defined in terms of certain status positions, with which are associated certain role-performance expectations and actions. Thus the teacher in the classroom, whatever his personality, is expected to teach, and the student is expected to learn. The policeman is expected to enforce the law, and the fireman to put out fire. The group leader is expected to aid the group in achieving its goal, and the mother to take care of her child. If we stick to the rather simple roles defined by society, there is little operational difficulty in naming different social roles. However, the problem is not so simple if we seek to make a generalization encompassing all roles in all situations. Any given situation or set of situations can be broken down into a number of interlocking roles, or in the limiting case to one role, such as a writer at work. Generally, most situations involve two or more persons.

The description of situations is at one higher level of abstraction than the description of role performance. But a similar approach can be used in investigating their properties. Recently, the author attempted just this type of analysis.[14] The central problem facing the investigation was the development of an instrument for measuring role behavior. There is no standard instrument for this purpose at the present time that provides a quantitative measure of various aspects of role performance in a standardized and efficient manner. To evolve such an instrument various studies of role description and personality and group-behavior description were examined in order to derive a relatively inclusive list of role-description terms. Through pretesting, a preliminary list of sixty-eight terms was reduced to forty that were designed to cover as much of the descriptive domain of role performance as was possible. A group of a hundred and twenty-five undergraduates were then asked to describe their relationships with their father, mother, college professor, boy friend, and girl friend, using in each instance these forty items. Thus there were five parallel sets of data filled out by each subject. These data were used to investigate a number of basic questions relating to role performance and situation typologies.

The first general question concerned the issues of the idiographic versus nomothetic approaches to personality and role description. An idiographic approach assumes that each person is unique in his viewpoint and actions, and must be studied as a clinical entity rather than as an experimental subject. The nomothetic viewpoint approaches the individual as a sample of general law or principle. Generally, the research scientist takes the nomothetic viewpoint. If, in the present instance, each person reacted to the given other (father, mother, friend) in a unique manner, it would not be possible to derive any general descriptive dimensions for the sample as a whole. However, factor analysis revealed that common dimensions of description were employed by all subjects to describe the given role situation, indicating that common frames of reference do exist for the description of a given role performance and thus substantiating the nomothetic viewpoint.

The next question to be evaluated concerned the issue of whether different role performances could be measured in terms of the same dimensions. In other words, could there be such an instrument as a "general role-performance questionnaire"? This problem is usually ignored, or the answer assumed, in practice. The very nature of the role concept implies that all roles are in some basic sense similar. This similarity should be in their fundamental components, just as all forms of matter are similar in the sense that they are built from a limited group of elements.

Unfortunately, this particular investigation did not tend to support the assumption that different role performances could be measured in terms of the same components. While certain dimensions such as "affection" and "manipulation" occurred in the description of more than one role performance, for the most part there was little replication of dimensions from one role-performance situation to another. This finding suggests that different roles cannot be measured in terms of the same set of elements or basic dimensions. If this finding is replicated by others, it will deal a serious blow to the problem of social description, since the difficulties involved in systematically describing different social roles would be endless. Each role might need its own dimensions for descriptive purposes, or there may turn out to be clusters of roles that employ similar dimensions. We can fervently hope that the latter possibility is correct. At this point, however, the prospect is rather gloomy. It is analogous to the situation produced in physics by the finding of even more subatomic particles, particles that do not appear to fall into a neat pattern.

A final question of general significance investigated in this research study was whether, and to what extent, performance in one situation was related to performance in other situations. To study this problem all scores in different situations were intercorrelated. Approximately one in five of these correlations proved significant. In almost 50 per cent of these instances the relationship appeared to be due to similarity in content in the two situations. Thus having a lack of involvement in one situation was related to having detached pity in another. The amount of direct relation between situations was in itself encouraging, but it is not surprising, since the same person was involved in the two situations. Consistency is a function of the influence of personality across situations rather than the effect of the situations themselves, since the personality remains constant.

Of greater interest, therefore, is the other 50 per cent of the one-in-five significant relations, which were not parallel in content. For example, persons who adopted a passive analytic manner toward their mothers tended not to be passive and uncritically accepting of their male friends. While the reactions in the two situations are not opposites they are certainly not equivalent, and would not have been predicted before the fact. These nonparallel reactions are interesting because they demonstrate the way in which social and personality factors combine to produce unlikely behavioral consistencies among situations. If all consistencies across situations were parallel in content, there would be little reason to study them. It is just because half of them are not that the problem of relating personality to role performance is intriguing and important.

SUMMARY AND CONCLUSIONS

It is difficult to draw together the material presented in this chapter into a simple summary. This material was not systematically executed. Often it was carried out for entirely different reasons than those that have motivated us here. For example, persons interested in aptitude testing were both unaware and generally disinterested in the implications their work held for the relation between conceptually different psychological levels.

However, a number of general conclusions are suggested by the preceding material. First, it appears that the analysis of given levels and the relationship between them represents a vast unexplored territory, whose existence is not suspected by most psychologists. With the growth of psychology there has been a parallel increase in specialization. This development, in turn, has led to a tendency for insulation between conceptually adjacent areas, so that persons become ever more intimately acquainted with a smaller and smaller area. One can be a specialist in projective tests, or vision, or principles of learning, and ignore other aspects of psychology more or less completely.

This specialization produces certain rewards both for the specialist and for the science that he represents. But at some point the tide must turn, and the separate subareas must be brought together within a common conceptual whole. This is necessary both for the sake of an organized approach to the general field and because many problems involve more than one subarea for their complete solution.

As we have indicated, there are two major areas to be investigated: the description of a given level, and the relationship between one level and others to which it is related. It is easier to study a given level in a systematic manner than to pass between levels. The areas of intelligence, aptitudes, and personality each provide material to show how an area can be explored systematically and its underlying dimensions isolated and replicated. In principle, this kind of investigation can be carried out on virtually any psychological level in order to determine what, in fact, are the basic psychological dimensions in terms of which the area ought to be described and measured. While the procedures for the analysis are at hand, and have been made practical since the advent of computers, they are currently being applied by relatively few investigators. Either the need is not recognized, or most researchers prefer to remain within the more comfortable domain of their immediate specialty. But if psychology is to develop in an orderly manner on any given level it is essential for such fundamental work to be undertaken.

As has been previously indicated virtually no one has undertaken a large-scale comparison of the relations among levels of psychology. Such comparisons as have been made are generally the product of accident and other interests. In part, the study of between-level relations must wait on the clarification of relationships within one given level. However, to a limited degree, differences among levels can be investigated at the present time. Fundamentally, the relation among the conceptual levels in psychology represents the underlying skeleton of the subject. Psychology as an entity exists only to the extent that such interlevel relationships exist. A brain, muscles, blood vessels, and bones do not constitute a body. They each must be related to the other in a complex system. Similarly, the various areas and levels in psychology considered separately do not make a subject. It is only as the relations between them are studied that the true nature of the human system will be clarified.

It is sobering, therefore, that almost all of the studies that have been performed in this no-man's land between levels have been uniformly discouraging. The correlations obtained are small, whether aptitude or intelligence measures are related to job performance, or personality is related to group behavior. But regardless of the size of the relationships, they must be studied in order to gain some vague approximation of the total structure of psychology, and to be able to formulate a grand strategy for future development of this field as a science. The fact that the interlevel analysis has been so generally overlooked is a dramatic testimony both to the newness of psychology as a science and to the effects of premature specialization.

Chapter Eight

Changing
Human Behavior

The final test of the maturity of any science is its ability to predict and control. In psychology this test is defined in terms of the ability of psychologists to determine and alter human behavior by the systematic variation of psychological relationships.

In one sense all the applied areas in psychology are and have been concerned with the problem of changing human behavior in one way or another. The industrial psychologist seeks to make behavior more productive and task oriented. The engineering psychologist seeks ways of adapting behavioral tendencies and limitations to man-machine interactions. Clinical and counseling psychologists are interested in altering personality dynamics and producing relatively important and fundamental changes in personal behavior. The educational psychologist is interested in increasing the utilization of innate capacity for learning and understanding new intellectual and motor relationships.

This applied interest does not mean that psychologists actually can change human behavior in any dramatic fashion. It means merely that they are interested in the attempt. It is only rarely that workers in these fields derive new facts of fundamental importance related to producing human change. Usually, they adapt facts obtained from the basic areas in psychology and attempt to relate them to their own particular fields of interest.

This process of translation of basic materials into applied areas often tends to be slightly devious. The applied psychologist often wishes to enhance the prestige of his specialty, and would like to have it appear that a new idea originated with him rather than with an academic psychologist. But the nature of application tends to preclude the search for new knowledge and the understanding of new relationships. The applied psychologist constantly must face a practical situation of such complexity as to defy ordered study. He is required to supply a variety of answers to situations that extend far beyond the boundaries of present psychological knowledge. Consequently, it is rare that he is able to find time or conditions that are favorable to a precise and carefully controlled investigation of variables related to the production of human change.

On the other hand the applied psychologist does generate all manner of ideas, theories, and methods to meet his own particular problems. But these constructions are usually untested, overly generalized; and they do not contribute to knowledge to any great degree. Applied psychologists might disagree with this statement, but evidence to substantiate it will be provided later in this chapter.

While the knowledge on which the applied psychologist depends is generated by other psychologists working in the basic areas of physiological, experimental, social, and personality psychology, it is ironic that the basic-research psychologists have little interest in the problem of changing human beings as such. As scientists they place the greatest weight on the systematic accumulation of knowledge aimed at deriving general laws of behavior that apply to all persons. Their emphasis is upon those aspects of human behavior that are invariant. From their point of view the change of human behavior is a source of variation and error that must be controlled or eliminated in their experiments.

Nevertheless, all scientific experiments really are studies in behavior change, though they are not usually viewed in that light. The classic psychological experiment involves the examination of the effect that variations in Y produce on X when all other conditions are either held constant or randomized. If the experiment is successful X will vary in some orderly manner as Y is varied. What is such a procedure but the study of artificially induced behavior change of a very circumscribed type?

In modern experimental methods the arrangements among variables are more complex, but the same general principle is true. All such experiments are designed to study the systematic variation of dependent variables that occurs when the independent variables are altered according to the experimental plan.

While it is true that all experiments in psychology study alteration in human behavior, the nature of this alteration is usually so limited as to have little practical significance for applied psychologists. Thus findings related to the conditioning of an eye-blink reflex or the learning of nonsense symbols do not lend themselves to easy transference into applied areas where large and socially significant aspects of human behavior may be examined and altered.

Nevertheless, there are a number of cases where the work of the basic psychologist has contributed either intentionally, indirectly, or virtually by accident to the work of the applied psychologist. Sometimes the basic psychologist demonstrates how certain fundamental knowledge might be applied. Thus Burrhus Skinner, who is a strict research psychologist, was among the first to point out the implications of teaching machines for educational psychology.

In other instances the work of basic psychologists is assimilated by applied psychologists who, for example, may attempt to model a method of therapy on certain principles of learning theory developed by experimental psychologists.

By various indirect avenues of approach the basic psychologists have provided a slow but perceptible supply of useful knowledge, which has been developed by the applied psychologists and used to alter or in attempts to alter human behavior.

Some of these developments such as subliminal perception in advertising and brainwashing in prison camps are widely known and looked upon with suspicion. Other developments such as the scheduling of rewards or reinforcement and the alteration of interaction patterns are less widely known or understood.

It is as yet premature to say that psychologists or behavioral scientists can change human behavior in any complete or systematic manner. It would be unreasonable to suppose that such could be the case. Nevertheless, some significant inroads in the problem of behavior change have been made and are worth discussing and analyzing.

THE GOALS OF BEHAVIOR CHANGE

The production of behavior change can be viewed in two ways. First, one can seek to aid, help, or improve an individual's adjustment to his environment. This approach is used in one form or another by counselors and psychotherapists who attempt to bring mentally ill persons back into the normal community. Some therapists emphasize the normalizing function of psychotherapy, whereas others emphasize the releasing of the unique creative potential of each patient. In practice, however, most therapists are content if the patient is able to make a relatively satisfactory adjustment to his family, friends, and work.

In the second major approach change is viewed as a procedure for *manipulating* human behavior. In particular, advertising, certain techniques of industrial and educational psychology, and the application of learning-theory principles to human behavior seem to involve such impersonal manipulation.

Generally speaking, the activity of therapists causes little general concern except to their patients. Psychotherapy is accepted as a necessary function in a society that generates and recognizes mental illness. By definition, psychotherapists focus their activities on sick people. They do not directly affect the larger segment of society that is relatively healthy.

The other manipulative procedures are designed to change behavior of all persons, sick or well. They *do* constitute a threat for the average person. He does not like the idea of being manipulated. It violates his image of himself as a free man in a democratic society. Of course, he overlooks the fact that the social life of any individual is essentially a series of subtle and complex attempts of other people to influence his behavior or his attempts to influence theirs. Such influence attempts are so woven into the social fabric as to be virtually invisible, unless special attention is focused upon them. But they exist from the moment the average man gets out of bed to the moment he returns to it at night. Every medium of communication that he comes in contact with—from the newspaper, radio, and television, to books, magazines, and bill-boards—tries to convince him to do something and not do other things, to believe in this but not that.

The whole structure of social interaction is built upon conscious and unconscious attempts to influence other people. However, for moralistic and tactical reasons such influence attempts are under-played or even denied. As individuals living in a democracy we are obligated, not to force other people to do what we want, but rather to attempt to persuade them. However, the goal is the same even if the methods and ground rules vary.

It may be said truthfully that the only persons we do not attempt to influence are those with whom we already agree or in whom we have no interest. If people were not constantly in need of affecting and influencing others, there would be little motivation for social interaction, beyond the basic need for social contact that is common to all. It is the subtle interplay of influence attempts that lends to interaction its peculiar interest and character.

In spite of these obvious facts, there is still widespread concern about the use of psychology as a scientific means for manipulating and controlling people. This concern is an indirect compliment to the progress of psychology, but it is a premature fear at the present time. On the other hand, if psychology continues at its present rate of progress, the issues involved will have to be faced.

The conscious manipulation and control of human behavior is no better or worse than the people behind the manipulation. A scientific or technological advance can lead inevitably to either progress or destruction. This is very clear in the present age, and has been true since the invention of gunpowder. In this context the alteration of human behavior and personality must be seen as another example of scientific progress that can be applied with destructive or constructive results, depending on the purposes of those who possess the knowledge.

This fact alone necessitates the advance of psychology in this area. If we do not obtain the necessary knowledge, others will. And the purpose to which they might put it will certainly not be to our advantage. Thus we and all countries are pushed into research and progress, in self-defense, if for no other motive. Psychologists dealing with the problem of changing behavior are not concerned with whether it ought to be done, but who will do it first and for what purpose. That it will be done, and is being done in a clumsy manner at the present time, is undoubtedly a fact.

However the necessary psychological knowledge for precisely controlling behavior is not available at the present time. Since it will not become so in the very near future, an extended opportunity may present itself for the gradual examination and application of tentative solutions to the problems inherent in control and alteration of human conduct and behavior. This is a great advantage that must be utilized by examining the situation realistically. The one attitude that cannot be allowed to gain dominance is a reactionary wish to avoid any further contact with principles of human control because of their threat to individual independence. The problem is rather how to integrate these discoveries with our social institutions and personal beliefs and to discover ways in which these principles can be used for the general benefit rather than exploited for a privileged few.

Psychotherapy can present a model for such an integration. No one questions the psychotherapist's attempt to alter his patient's personality and behavior. His activity is viewed as socially desirable. He threatens only those immediately related to the sick person, and he attempts to reduce such threat to a minimum, if he is able. The main reason that psychotherapy is accepted widely is that it can help people perform more effectively and feel happier about themselves and others. These ends are clearly advantageous both for the individual and the society at large. There is no reason why other principles of behavior change cannot perform a similar function if they are wisely applied. The various perceptual and motivational principles of advertising can be used to make life richer for all, rather than to exploit an economic decision. But this can only happen if individuals with power are motivated toward the general good or are regulated by some source of control that helps to insure that they do not exploit unduly the society of which they are members.

This task is neither obvious nor easy. Government has long sought to guide and control the excesses of private industry and the corporate tendencies of organized labor. The danger of any special power group grows as the techniques and methods at its disposal become more powerful. On the other hand such techniques aggravate and necessitate the need for a successful system of social controls.

The advance of psychology will not of itself provide social solutions to the problems that it will create. These are the concern of sociologists, anthropologists, economists, historians, and politicians, as well as the general public, who must in the last analysis choose where to place their mandates. But if the problems are ignored, as they usually are, until the last possible moment, then severe misuse and exploitation for limited benefit are inevitable. Thus it is essential that the difficulties attendant on the perfection of such methods be studied as the methods themselves are evolved, so that men shall be prepared for them when they come.

The problem of human control is related to that of automation, of which it is an expression. As science reduces personal experience to impersonal principle, the necessity for reconciling human performance with mechanical and impersonal action becomes more necessary and pressing. It is part of the general readjustment necessitated by the rapid scientific progress of the last decades.

As mentioned earlier, basic research scientists have not been interested in the production of change for its own sake. On the other hand applied psychologists lack the opportunity and interest in carrying out basic research on the production of change. Therefore most of the present-day work of importance was created almost accidentally in the course of investigations that had quite different objectives. Nevertheless, the validity of such studies is no less than if the investigations had been designed originally to study the production of change as their central focus. In other cases the measurement or production of fundamental personality and behavior changes *was* the central focus, but these cases form the minority of relevant research reports.

CHANGING BEHAVIOR AS A FORM OF MATURITY

As a starting point it will be helpful to consider the process of behavior change as a problem of maturation and socialization. Looking at the subject this way one inevitably asks the question: What are the normal changes that tend to occur over a number of years in typical individuals living in the society at large? Such change, if it occurs, would provide a base line for judging the effectiveness of conscious attempts to produce additional changes, which would not occur over time as a function of conditions within the society.

There have been relatively few projects of this kind because of the technical difficulties of studying the same group of people over an extended period of time. However, several studies are available that suggest a preliminary picture of the extent and nature of such change.

One of the first and most thorough, though limited in focus, was carried out using the Strong Vocational Interest Blank. Retests of the same subjects after one, two, five, six, nine, ten, and twenty-two years result in a relatively high test-retest correlation of approximately .75. Similar studies have been carried out using other specific instruments. Since the motivation for such research lay in establishing the reliability and stability of the measure over a long time period, relatively little attention was paid to systematic changes which did occur and which are, in their way, more interesting and significant than those aspects of adult behavior, personality, and attitudes that remained constant.

Other studies have pointed up interesting changes due to the passage of time. In a study of the Army Alpha intelligence test scores, using a thirty-year follow-up, it was found that scores on five of the eight subtests measuring different aspects of intelligence showed significant improvement. However, these shifts were all systematic so that the correlation between the early and late tests was relatively high—.77.

Similar results have been obtained in a follow-up of Terman's group of gifted subjects, referred to earlier. A twelve-year repeat of an intelligence test on these subjects indicated that all subjects increased significantly in intellectual performance, but the group members maintained their relative positions with regard to each other as indicated by the test-retest correlation of .90.

Perhaps the most ambitious investigation of the consistency of the personality of adults over a substantial time period was undertaken by the American psychologist Everett Kelly.[1] In this study, over three hundred engaged couples were tested and followed up sixteen to eighteen years later. At both points they were given five tests and an extensive mail questionnaire. In addition a thirty-six-trait graphic scale was used to rate each individual. In each instance he was rated by his marriage partner, five acquaintances, and by himself.

The first test to be compared was the Allport-Vernon Study of Values, designed to measure relative interest and motives in six areas: the theoretical, esthetic, social, political, economic, and religious. In this, as in all cases, the tests for the men were treated separately from those of the women, on the theory that sex might be related to the type of change that takes place. While five of the twelve possible measures changed significantly for the men and women the most significant was in the religious area. Religious interest increased sharply for both men and women. At the same time women's esthetic values tended to decrease, while men's esthetic *and* theoretical interests also decreased. Whether these shifts reflect changing cultural standards or the effects of maturity cannot be determined from the study itself.

The second major instrument for measuring change was the Generalized Attitudes Scales, investigating attitudes toward marriage, church, rearing children, housekeeping, entertaining, and gardening. Significantly attitudes toward marriage, church, rearing children, and gardening grew more favorable. Only attitudes toward housekeeping decreased in favorability. Eleven of the fourteen possible changes were significant.

The Strong Vocational Interest Blank was also administered. In general scores on this instrument remained constant, indicating that patterns of interest are quite stable over time.

Analysis of the personality variables of self-confidence, sociability, masculinity, and interest maturity indicated little change except for a decrease in self-confidence among women and a slight tendency toward increased masculinity among both men and women.

Finally on a comparison of self-ratings on ten personality variables, 40 per cent of the comparisons were significant. In general they indicated a decrease in energy and neatness, and an increase in breadth of interests and irritability.

In summary, the various measures suggest a number of conclusions. First, significant changes were found in about half of the variables measured. Second, these changes were relatively small, though they were statistically significant. The changes tended to occur in parallel fashion for both sexes. Thus sex does not seem an important determinant of either consistency or change in adult personality.

In order to aid in the interpretation of these findings, as well as producing others, a variety of additional analyses were undertaken. In the first, the relative amount of consistency found in different measures was determined. Within the limitation of the instruments studied, it was clear that the most consistent variables were values and vocational interests. Self-ratings and personality variables were only three-fifths as stable, and the attitude measures were only one-fifth as stable as the values. These findings are certainly interesting for anyone planning a strategy of behavior change, since they suggest the relative variability of these different aspects of the individual.

Another striking finding of general significance was a trend toward maturational regression toward the mean. Persons who had been either high or low in a given characteristic tended on retest to fall nearer the group average. This effect should not be confused with statistical regression toward the mean, which was controlled for. Whether this regression was due to social pressures acting on extreme deviates or the simple wearing effects of time on the individual cannot be determined.

A further interesting finding was that the change scores on different variables did not tend to relate to each other. Change in one variable did not tend to be associated with change in other variables. Persons appeared to change in a piecemeal manner rather than in clusters or as a whole. This finding has widespread and disturbing implications for psychotherapy, in which the general assumption is made that the whole individual or at least large segments of his personality can be altered simultaneously.

Another analysis of some interest was carried out to try to determine what type of person from among the sample tended to change the most over time. Preliminary findings appeared to suggest that, among men, persons who at an early time appeared to be greatly interested in helping other people through profession, service, and training later became somewhat disillusioned and preferred to work with ideas and things rather than people. Also, persons whose professional interests changed from service fields toward those of architecture, mathematics, or business tended to show a parallel lowering in the maturity of their interests. These findings are suggestive, but must be taken as illustrative of the analysis, rather than particularly significant in themselves.

A final analysis was performed to determine whether the changes in both partners of married couples tended to be mutually related. No evidence was found to indicate that wives or husbands changed toward each other's original position. Further, it was found that while their interests and personalities tended to be initially similar, this similarity was not increased over the eighteen-year interval. This in itself must be taken as eloquent testimony to the stability of adult personality over time, or the relatively small impact that the personalities of marriage partners have on each other, despite the length and intimacy of the relationship.

Thus it appears that, while over-all change due to the passage of time may not be great, the change that does occur contains many interesting implications and requires further and more intensive investigation. Such study is required in order to supply a firm basis for the study of planned change, since these normative changes form the base line for any measurement of change produced by conscious intent.

EVALUATIVE STUDIES OF BEHAVIOR CHANGE

The simplest and most direct approach to the study of behavior change is to evaluate procedures that currently are believed to produce change. There are literally thousands of research projects undertaken in such varied applied fields as advertising and psychotherapy. Many of these studies have not been published, since the information was for specific administrative purposes, or the results were unsatisfactory. But the volume of published evaluative material is huge. We do not usually comprehend the magnitude of the literature because it has accumulated in different areas. Professionals in one area rarely venture into other areas. Thus teachers would be unlikely to read extensively in the literature of psychotherapy research, and vice versa.

The very overabundance of evidence has acted as a deterrent to systematic organization and assessment. However, it seemed reasonable to assume and hope that this large volume of material contained a wealth of information about the process of behavior change itself, as well as its specific evidence about the effectiveness of the methods tested.

For these reasons the author undertook a preliminary attempt to organize some of the literature in evaluative research in order to determine what general information it might contain, and to assess its general quality.[2] In order to reduce the task to manageable proportions it was decided to deal only with studies of evaluative methods whose goal was to produce personality or behavior change of a fairly fundamental and lasting character. Further, it was required that these studies employ a control group. (As will be made abundantly clear, an evaluative study made without a control group is not worth the effort.) Finally, it was required that the study be of a reasonably elegant and methodologically sophisticated character. In order to limit the selection further, four content areas were selected for investigation: psychotherapy, counseling, human-relations training, and attempts within the educational setting to change personality and behavior.

By the application of these criteria to the existing literature, some five hundred studies were chosen. Further examinations of these reduced their number to slightly under two hundred. These investigations represented a relatively adequate sample of the evaluations of methods used in the four content areas that attempted to produce important behavioral and personality changes. In their areas these investigations constituted the cream of the crop. It was reasonable to assume that, if there was anything of significance to be found, it would be in this material.

Each of the studies was analyzed by the use of a general coding system that described such characteristics as the subjects used, the number of practitioners employed, the setting, the type of experimental design, the nature of the method, the change criteria, and the amount of change found.

All this information was pooled and subjected to a general analysis. It is not our present purpose to describe the detailed results. However, two general conclusions of importance emerged. The first was concerned with the problems inherent in the design and execution of evaluative research; the second with the productivity of such research regardless of its design.

As the various studies were reviewed it became evident that they were contaminated by a number of different types of technical error. These errors will be described below, in order to enable the reader to judge such research for himself, and to give him some insight into the kinds of pitfalls that await the researcher in each stage of this type of psychological experimentation.

POSSIBLE ERRORS IN EVALUATIVE RESEARCH

The basic design of evaluative research is of classic simplicity. Two groups of equivalent subjects are employed. Both are measured before and after the experiment by the same instruments. The first group receives the change-inducing experience. The second does not. If the first group changes more than the second as measured on the criteria of change, the effectiveness of the experience is demonstrated.

Since the design of evaluative research is apparently so simple, it is strange that most, if not all, experimental evaluations contain basic errors in experimental design and execution.

Some of these errors uniquely are associated with evaluative research. Others are associated with all experimental studies. First, we shall describe some of the latter errors, since they are more general than the former.

One of the first steps in any research project is the assignment of subjects to the experimental and control groups. In a surprising number of cases, researchers have assigned subjects to one or another group on the basis of convenience, or have simply taken two existing groups and called one experimental and one control. However, the experimental model of evaluation research requires that the experimental and control groups be equivalent if the study is to be meaningfully interpreted. This equivalence can be attained only by the systematic assignment of subjects either by a matching and/or a randomization procedure. Nothing else is satisfactory.

Another problem that haunts all psychological research in general, and evaluative research in particular, is the use of appropriate measures of change. What is appropriate is determined in part by the goals of the method tested, and in part by the practical limitations of the measurement situation. Further, the experimenter is limited by the actual availability of tests that are standardized adequately.

Unfortunately, almost all tests are subject to a variety of distortions, errors, and contaminations. If the subject is honest, the test usually is reasonably accurate. However, in those situations in which the individual is under pressure of one kind or another to appear better, healthier, and more productive and efficient than is actually the case he can often fake the test results to some extent by answering the way he thinks the tester might desire, rather than the way that he, the subject, really thinks and feels. Some tests, such as intelligence tests, are based on the assumption that the subject will try to outdo himself. However, most of the tests used in evaluative research are not. They may, therefore, provide misleading results. For example, if the subject believes that the method to which he has been exposed should change him, he is likely to respond as if it had. Particularly at the end of any experiment, there is likely to be a positive halo of general good feeling that may be reflected in the final measurement. This "good-by effect" has nothing to do with permanent change and therefore can produce misleading results.

It is for this reason that a postexperimental follow-up is so important in studies of change. It is less important how the person behaves immediately after the experience. The crucial question is whether the change persists over time. If it does not, the method has little use. A six-month or one-year follow-up can answer this question, but it is rarely undertaken, because of the practical difficulties involved.

One of the central points in any experiment is a clear description of the experimental procedure. Most evaluative research is exceedingly vague on this point. While the method that is tested may have a name, and consist of certain general features, no one ever has reduced method to a mechanical series of operations that could be repeated by any person if he wished to reproduce the experiment. In fact, most of the better change procedures are exceedingly complex combinations of different components. For this reason it is hard to know either beforehand or afterward precisely what happened during the experiment. This clearly can lead to problems of interpretation, whatever the results.

These are the kinds of general difficulties that beset all experimentation, including evaluative research. There are a number of additional problems uniquely associated with evaluation that require some clarification.

In all studies of behavior change we find a practitioner applying a particular method. The practitioner may be a counselor, or a therapist, but whatever his training and profession, he never appears without his method. Unfortunately, the evaluation is intended to assess the method, not the practitioner. If the classic evaluation design is applied, no distinction can be made between the two. Positive findings may be due to the unique quality and character of the practitioner, the method he uses, or to some combination of the two. In the vast majority of evaluative studies reviewed it was not possible to distinguish between the effects of the practitioner and his method, and unless such a distinction can be made, the findings of any study must be ambiguous.

Just as the practitioner must be separated from the method he uses, so the subject and his own beliefs must be controlled. Specifically, subjects differ markedly in the degree of faith that they may bring to different methods. This faith largely is independent of the method itself and must be controlled if the method and not the faith is to be measured. The power of faith is hard to over-estimate, as will be documented later in this chapter. However, virtually none of the studies reviewed provided any control for this form of contamination of experimental findings.

Another related problem involves the effect of the special atten-tion devoted to the subjects during the experiment. In any innova-tion such as that associated with the application of new behavior change methods, there is, at first, a disproportionate amount of atten-tion and interest generated. Most methods when they first appear are greeted with great enthusiasm and interest, and the methods are used with greater energy than at a later time and the subjects are followed with greater care. While this may be beneficial for the subjects, it confuses the interpretation of the results. So often, the first evalua-tion of a new method is extremely promising, but the initial results are never replicated elsewhere. The reason for this pattern is that the initial testing of the method generally was accompanied by a unique amount of interest and attention devoted to the experimental subjects. Everyone waited to see what was going to happen. Hopes were high. No subject is immune from such attention or expectation. Unfortunately both these factors may cause the subject to change—independent of the method. When the method is no longer a novelty, a subsequent evaluation consequently may reveal either much less change than in the original study or simply none at all.

A quite different problem involves the effect of measurement on the production of change. When the subject is measured at the beginning of the experiment he is made aware indirectly—by the nature of the measuring instruments that are employed—of the kinds of variables in regard to which the experimenter hopes to de-tect change. This experience may sensitize the subject in one direc-tion or another, since it serves him as a guide in an otherwise am-biguous situation. It is therefore necessary to eliminate any effect that the testing itself may have on the final results. Particularly where the subjects are fairly intelligent, it is not unreasonable to suppose that they will figure out the purpose of the experiment from the nature of the tests given, and change in the desired or expected direction, or in the opposite direction if they are contrary. It is necessary to guard against such a possibility, but virtually none of the studies reviewed had attempted to do so.

There are also certain statistical problems involved in the analysis of evaluative research. It is not enough to show that the experimental group has changed more than the control group. It is also essential to demonstrate that they began from the same place. If they did not, the change may be due to a statistical artifact that is completely unrelated to the effectiveness of the method.

The foregoing discussion describes some of the technical errors that creep into evaluation research, despite its deceptively simple design. Others could be discussed, but these are sufficient to demonstrate the difficulties involved.

There are other problems of a pracitical rather than technical character. Any evaluative study is a threat to the practitioner being evaluated and an upsetting influence on the organization within which the evaluation is conducted.

Under most conditions the practitioner has little to gain, personally or professionally, from an evaluation. If his work is shown to be effective, it will constitute no more than an objective confirmation of what he already believes to be the case. If the evaluation finds that there actually has been no change in the subjects, his job may be jeopardized and his technique questioned. It is natural, therefore, that in many instances the practitioner does not welcome evaluation, and acts in such a way as to distort its outcome.

Similarly, most organizations that are functioning reasonably well do not welcome any objective assessment. It may lead to the need for change, which is inherently undesirable to the higher echelon that has a stake in preserving the status quo. When evaluation is undertaken it is usually due to strong outer pressures or the particular interest of a key individual. But it is hard to control the evaluative process once it is instituted. Findings may come to light that are embarrassing to the organization as a whole, even though the original study is limited in focus.

On the other hand, most evaluations are undertaken by interested parties to prove the effectiveness of particular methods. The persons doing the testing generally believe in the method being tested.

This bias tends to have a self-fulfilling character, whether it originates in the investigator himself, or from the persons within the organization sponsoring the research. In many such studies it is the unspoken expectation that positive results should be obtained. If they are not, heads may roll.

It is clear that these situational and organizational pressures influence evaluative research in an adverse manner. Unfortunately, the distortions that they introduce are impossible to detect after the fact, and only the independent investigator is immune from them.

All the preceding factors contribute to the difficulty of executing correctly evaluative research with respect to behavior-change procedures. But they do not indicate what the better studies in the areas have found. To obtain this information the two hundred studies under investigation were coded and the resulting information was analyzed to determine the general relationships involved.

This analysis suggested a number of specific conclusions of little general importance. In addition, however, it did demonstrate several important trends.

Generally speaking, the studies tended to be simply designed. Less than 40 per cent of them used more than two types of change criteria; few of them took advantage of modern developments in factorial-experimental design.

When all studies are combined and the amount of change that was found on different instruments examined, a very clear finding emerges; in about 45 per cent of the studies reviewed, change was found. This tendency seemed extremely general and was independent of the precise type of measurement used in any given study.

An analysis of experimental error contained within these studies, which were, as a group, of a fairly select character, indicated some fairly alarming tendencies. For example, in about 90 per cent of the studies there was no control for the effect of the subject's belief in the method being tested on the test itself. In 60 per cent of the studies there was no way to distinguish between the effect of the practitioner and the method that he was using on the results. In 50 per cent of the cases no control was used for the effect on scores of exposing the experimental subjects to the special attention associated with the application of any new method. Thus it is fair to conclude that even the best evaluative studies currently available contain serious sources of experimental error that cast general doubt on whatever conclusions they may contain.

When the data were reanalyzed for separate content areas the results were conspicuous by their absence. With one or two minor exceptions no differences were found between the studies conducted in the different areas of psychotherapy, counseling, human-relations training, and education. The design of the study, the types of errors, the amount of change—all were similar in all the different professional areas. Since the types of criteria that were used to measure change did not differ either, it is reasonable to conclude that the methods used in each of the four areas produced the same kinds and amounts of change.

Since these four content areas usually are treated as being conceptually separate, utilize different training procedures for the education of practitioners, serve different populations, and are derived from different historical and social conditions, it is certainly surprising that the evaluative studies show no demonstrable difference among them.

In view of this fact, a further tabulation was made in order to determine whether certain methods, regardless of the content area in which they were applied, showed differential change patterns. For this purpose four methods were compared: the nondirective supportive approach, role playing, psychoanalytic therapy, and eclectic therapy drawn from various sources. Sufficient studies of each of these approaches were available to make the comparison meaningful. The results clearly indicated that all methods produced change about 45 per cent of the time, which indicated that there was no differential superiority among them, and that, in the amount of change produced, they did not differ from all other methods tested in the remaining studies.

One possible explanation for this state of affairs is that experimental error was masking positive findings that otherwise might have appeared. To check against this possibility, the relation between the degree of error in the study and amount of change obtained was tested. There was none. Change was found as often in studies poorly conceived as in those in which the design was carefully wrought and executed.

Thus it appeared that only one positive conclusion could be

drawn from the cumulative examination of evaluative research. Change is produced in about 45 per cent of the instances in which it is tested. Other differences between method, subjects, content area, or errors do not seem to exist.

These conclusions raise serious doubts as to the scientific value of such research. If no general conclusions can be drawn further to differentiate methods, practitioners, or subjects, what is the use of the effort? This question deserves serious consideration from those who sponsor such research. Beyond the immediate validation that it may provide for a particular method in a particular situation, evaluative research would appear to have little general interest or significance.

The main reason for this dismal condition appears to be the fact that the methods that are tested in evaluative research are so complex as to defy any orderly or exact description. If results are found, it is impossible to know to what they are to be attributed—is it the whole method, some part of it, the practitioner, the subject, the setting, and so forth? In a situation in which the method itself cannot be described precisely, and in which many other sources of error are rampant, the tendency is for every study to look like every other study, since error spreads in all directions and settles at a common level. For this reason all studies find about the same amount of change, and individual differences among them are lost in the general fog of inexactness and error.

THE COMPONENTS OF "BRAINWASHING"

Scientific experimentation depends on precisely defined and measured variables. If methods of producing change are too complex for such description, the most reasonable solution would appear to be to break down these methods into their components, which can be more exactly described. The components can then be tested separately and in combination in a systematic and cumulative fashion. This already has been done to some extent. The clearest example of such an approach is in the area of the effect of communications procedures on attitude change. Other less focused studies have examined certain components, such as "faith," "operant conditioning," and "feedback" which are incorporated into many behavior-change procedures. Some of the results of these studies will be described in the concluding sections of this chapter. Before discussing this material, however, it may be profitable to show how an actual behavior-change procedure can be broken down into its components.

One of the more sensational and sinister methods for dramatically altering human behavior that has recently come to the public's attention is described popularly as "brainwashing" or "thought control." Studies of the effects of brainwashing carried out by interviewing returned prisoners of war generally have indicated that the process was less mysterious and terrible than it seemed at first. In large part the impact of "thought reform" on American prisoners in the Korean War was a testimony to their lack of preparation to meet it more than to any unknown feature of the method itself.

As a procedure designed to change human behavior in a drastic and permanent fashion, brainwashing utilizes a complex series of interpersonal maneuvers that can be broken down into a relatively familiar set of components. The two major social influences on the prisoner are the group and the interrogator. The group consisted of a number of persons who believed in an alien system, were hostile to prisoners, and who assumed them to be guilty of great crimes. All means of identification of the prisoner with his former life were removed. He had no contact with the outside world; his military status was unrecognized; and his only position was that of a deviant in the group. In addition, the prisoner had to face real physical punishments, tortures, and humiliations. These were administered not to obtain secrets but as punishments for his misdeeds and the erroneousness of his beliefs. The group approved of all such punishments as well deserved. Thus the prisoner literally had nothing to support him. Physical threats were ever present, social support was removed, and cultural connections with his own society were suddenly cut off.

These conditions were, in their time, unexpected, since the typical prisoner of war might expect torture but was unprepared for conversion attempts. It was this pressure toward political and ideological conversion that caught the American soldiers off guard.

In addition to these physical and public pressures, the prisoner was subjected to the almost diabolical influence of the interrogator. The use of interrogation itself is not new. Military-intelligence agents have long used it, as have all police forces and other groups habitually dealing with hostile adversaries. In particular, the use of politically oriented interrogation is an integral part of the Communist system, which has been used extensively to extract confessions from deviant Communists. It is in the combined effect of group pressure, physical punishment, and the impact of interrogation that brainwashing achieves its potency.

The interrogator bears a certain superficial resemblance to a psychotherapist or a priest. He is interested in the prisoner's experience and wants to help the prisoner to see the light and change his ways. The interrogator differs from other practitioners mainly with respect to his ends. He wants to change the ideology of the prisoner whether the prisoner wants it changed or not.

The interrogator employs several powerful approaches. First, he assumes that the prisoner is guilty. Second, he takes as his task the need for bringing the prisoner to the point where he freely confesses his crimes; the actual confession is viewed as an important aspect of the experience. Third, the interrogator encourages the prisoner to talk freely about himself and his experiences. However, no matter what the prisoner says, the interrogator is never satisfied. Thus the prisoner is placed in a hopelessly ambiguous situation. In a limited sense, the interrogator is an interested party in a hostile environment. On the other hand, like an indifferent or implacable parent, the interrogator can never be pleased. The prisoner cannot tell what really is wanted since the interrogator gives him hardly any clues. The situation is surprisingly like the one pictured by Kafka in *The Trial*. The prisoner is accused, but of what he does not know. Whatever he does or does not do seems to make no difference. All his supports are slowly removed. His standards are dissolved and his motives frustrated, creating an intolerable situation physically, socially, and psychologically.

In addition to the preceding, the prisoner is required not just passively to accept, but to participate actively in his own reformation.

He always must make an active response, openly proclaim his new beliefs and his old guilt.

Finally, by the sheer power of repetition, the will and resistance of the prisoner slowly is worn away. The captors, by virtue of their environment and their own patience, can repeat and repeat an incident or a point, beyond endurance and beyond reason, slowly to overpower the will, memory, and motivation of the captive.

With nothing to support him, the prisoner must either abandon himself completely to his fate, exepecting nothing better than torture and perhaps death, or he must make successive attempts to please the interrogator by confessing more and more, in the hope of pardon, release, or better treatment.

Some may wonder whether it is worth all this trouble to convert enemies just for the purpose of using their statements for propaganda purposes. Probably it is not, if this were the only goal. But for the militant Communist there could be no more challenging task than converting his own enemy, thereby proving directly and indirectly the superiority of his own system.

While brainwashing may be an overwhelming experience to those unfortunate enough to be subjected to it, the elements that collectively constitute the procedure are in common though less sinister use in our own society.

Certainly, the influence of group norms on individual behavior is a characteristic of all social groups. The hostility of the group toward the deviant is also universal. Isolation of the individual from his normal social and cultural ties is a situation that is *used* by psychotherapists and human-relations specialists: the psychotherapist sees the patient in the isolation of his office and in an atmosphere in which freedom of reaction and expression is encouraged, unlike most social situations; the human-relations specialist makes frequent use of workshops specially organized in cultural islands, away from mass urban centers and everyday personal contacts, in order to remove these sources of stability from the individual, so that he may be freer to experiment with new behavior.

As has been pointed out, the interrogator resembles the therapist as he listens to the individual recount his life; and his emphasis on the participation of the individual in the process of change is similar. However, most therapists are not as rigid in their definition of what is to be learned and done as interrogators are. Some therapists have specific objectives; others attempt to get the subject to define his own objectives.

However, both the interrogator and the psychotherapist use ambiguity as a weapon. Since the captive, or the patient, is never sure just what the interrogator or psychotherapist really wants, he must keep producing new material in order finally to be able to please the former.

In both the captive and therapeutic situations, the assumption is made that something is wrong with the individual. In the one case he is assumed to be guilty of various crimes of a practical and ideological nature. In the other he is assumed to be physically or mentally ill. However, whatever is wrong, it is clearly the responsibilty of the interrogator or the psychotherapist to correct the condition.

Finally, the extensive use of sheer repetition is a familiar advertising technique. Perhaps the central feature of most advertising, particularly of the hard-sell variety, is the ceaseless repetition of a simple message. While it is desirable that the message itself have a certain intrinsic appeal, it is the repetition of the message that serves to stamp it in and enables it to eliminate competing messages from other sources of information.

Thus the anatomy of brainwashing reveals that it is not a new and diabolical discovery of advanced Communist technology, parallel to a trip to the moon, but rather the combination of a number of widely used behavior-change principles combined for military and ideological purposes.

In some respects brainwashing represents a nightmarish version of the manipulation of human behavior. It is the sort of thing that makes the average person shudder, when he hears about such things as the use of perception without awareness to sell popcorn in movie lobbies. Brainwashing is certainly an extreme form of such a direct and all-encompassing influence attempt. But it is not the way in which brainwashing is done that is to be feared, since its principles are known and widely used. It is rather the use to which these principles are put. A direct analogy exists in the use of atomic physics in the building of hydrogen bombs. If men wish to put knowledge to use for destructive purposes, they cannot be stopped. But it is not the knowledge that is to blame.

Brainwashing is an important illustration of the fact that the manipulation of human behavior, for whatever ends, is one of the crucial problems of our time. It cannot be ignored, since our ideological enemies will use the opportunity to perfect what they know and use this knowledge for their own purposes. The only protection is greater knowledge, though this in turn leads to greater danger. But the danger produced by knowledge is less great than the danger inherent in ignorance. Thus human progress is literally forced upon us, not so much out of selfless dedication to the truth, but for the purposes of survival in a hostile and swiftly changing environment.

STUDIES OF BEHAVIOR-CHANGE COMPONENTS

If the world were quieter, the need for change would not be so evident. However, technological development independent of political events would cause a great increase in our need for understanding the production and guidance of change. New machines and new interaction patterns between machines have displaced individuals and recast the meaning and significance of their lives. In such instances, large-scale change is inevitable. If it is understood it can be guided in a gradual manner. If it is not, the results are bound to be destructive and disruptive.

The best hope for attaining such knowledge is by studying behavior-change components. Perhaps the most systematic and carefully conceived set of studies of behavior-change components are those that have been carried out over the past ten years at Yale University under the general guidance and direction of the late American psychologist Carl Hovland.[3] These studies of changes in attitude, taken as a group, represent almost the only large-scale attempt to study aspects of the behavior-change process in a systematic and cumulative manner.

It is to be noted, however, that attitude change is a fairly pallid form of alteration in comparison with the type of personality and behavior changes sought by many professional practitioners. Thus the results of these studies do not provide answers to some of the more searching problems facing the practitioners. This is due not to any deficiency in the research, but simply to the fact that it was not intended to perform this function.

Fundamentally, the Hovland group has been concerned with the impact of communications upon attitudes. This interest is related on the one hand to recognition of the importance of communication as a fundamental human activity, and on the other to the study of attitudes as a fundamental social-psychological characteristic of the individual to whom the communication is directed. Under ordinary circumstances people are interested in changing only the attitudes and superficial behavior of other persons. Serious attempts to change personality and basic behavior patterns are left to the specialist. In this sense communication as a normal social function is to be associated with attitudes, one the logical target of the other.

At the same time that Hovland and his group were studying the effects of different communciation patterns and procedures on the stability and alteration of attitudes in controlled laboratory situations, other researchers were examining attitude changes as they occurred in the uncontrolled society.

These studies attempted to assess the effects of mass-media communications, such as newspapers, radio, and television, on the attitudes of average persons interviewed in the course of survey research.

In many cases the same relationships were examined by the two quite different procedures: the laboratory-controlled investigation, and the survey research, studying persons in a normal uncontrolled situation. What was especially interesting in this unusual parallelism of such divergent techniques was that the results did not agree. The findings in the laboratory were not replicated in the normal social situation.

Thus there are two different and interesting problems presented. First, what is the relation between communications and attitude change? Second, why do different types of studies of the same questions fail to replicate one another?

One of the most widely tested propositions in survey research is that mass media have relatively little influence on public opinion. For example, in one study of voting behavior only 5 per cent of the individuals interviewed changed their opinion as the result of exposure to mass-media communications. In contrast to this striking and well-authenticated finding is the equally striking and no-less-well-authenticated one that, under normal laboratory conditions, and regardless of the precise experimental procedure, attitude change is produced in from one-third to one-half of the studies.

In order to be able to interpret these discrepancies it is necessary to reconsider the nature of laboratory and survey research, and, in this light, review some of the findings produced by these methods in relation to attitude change.

Perhaps the major difference in the two research conditions is that in a survey-research design the subjects choose whether they wish to be exposed to a given communications procedure. The subject decides whether to buy a newspaper or listen to a particular television program. However, the subject in an experiment has no such choice. His exposure is at the discretion of the experimenter. Since it is well known that people do not normally tend to expose themselves to opinions with which they disagree, the experimental situation forces exposure to a much greater extent than the natural situation, thus making a greater opportunity for change, while persons at large may not change, simply because they ignore statements of the opposition, or do not expose themselves to them.

Further typical differences between the two research approaches are easily noted. For example, survey research evaluates the results of complex communications, whereas laboratory investigations may study the effect of a single communication from one source of a very limited character. In addition, the typical survey study measures long-term changes occurring over weeks, months, and years. The change in the laboratory is usually of a short-term duration, involving hours rather than days, and is thus more easily detected.

Studies in the laboratory associate a certain authority with the communication that is offered. The very fact that a scientist or researcher makes a statement during the course of an experiment lends it a certain weight in the subject's mind. However, in naturalistic circumstances the individual has little idea from where the statement comes or to whom it is to be attributed; thus he is liable to give it less weight.

Another interesting difference involves the conditions associated with the reception of communication. In the naturalistic situation individuals often are free to discuss the communication with family and friends, whereas in an experiment such interchange is controlled or eliminated. It is known that discussion with an intimate reference group, such as a family, makes an individual more resistant to the attempts of outside influence.

Another possible difference between the procedures involves the populations that they sample. Survey research, by its very nature, attempts to sample the total population in a fairly representative manner. Experimental research generally is performed on the most available subjects, namely, college students. Findings obtained from a study of college students may not apply to other groups. Certainly the subjects represent a fairly select group.

Finally, one of the most crucial differences involves the type of attitude change that is studied. The typical experiment is designed to demonstrate a relationship under controlled conditions. For this reason an effort usually is made to select an easily changeable attitude, so that the experiment has a reasonable chance of success. On the other hand survey research examines attitudes that are fairly deeply rooted in the individual, such as voting behavior and political attitudes, which are less amenable to change.

Thus it appears that the difference in absolute amount of change found in laboratory and survey studies can be explained in terms of the nature of the exposure; the amount of time that passes between the measurement of change, the influence and prestige of the communicator; the effect of reference groups; the types of samples used; and the nature of the change criteria that are employed.

However, the difference in extent of attitude change that is found is not the only area of discrepancy between these two types of studies. For example, one of the well-established relations involving communciations and influence concerns the distance between the attitude of the communicator and the person with whom he is communicating. Laboratory studies have shown that the greater the discrepancy involved, the *greater* the change in attitude that is produced. However, when a similar study was carried out under naturalistic conditions, quite different results were obtained. In this instance it was found that the greater the discrepancy between the attitudes of communicator and the person receiving the communication, the *less* the change. Further analysis of the results suggested that under naturalistic conditions, when the source of the communication is usually ambiguous, and the subject is deeply concerned with the issue or attitude, he tends strongly to resist any attempt to change his attitude. This resistance seems to manifest itself in a number of ways. First, he may see the communicator as unfair or biased. Second, the content of the communication itself can be distorted. The greater the initial discrepancy in opinion between the recipient and the communicator, the greater the distortion is likely to be.

Most interesting in the naturalistic situation is the fact that subjects with small discrepancies between their opinions and those of the communicator changed most, and those with large discrepancies changed least. These results are of course contradictory to those achieved in the laboratory, when the amount of discrepancy was directly proportional to the amount of attitude change. The crucial conditions determining these different outcomes seem to be the credibility of the communicator and the depth of personal involvement in the issue.

Another example of different results in laboratory and survey investigations involves the varying effects of different orders of presentation of communications for and against given issues. In general, survey research clearly has indicated that primacy is of great importance in changing attitudes, especially in the area of propaganda. Whichever side gets its message across first, tends to be the most convincing.

In the laboratory this primacy effect tends to vanish. It is rather whether an individual receives both sides of an argument, than the order of the arguments, that seems to be important in changing his mind. In much survey research individuals receive only one side of the argument because of the way in which they choose to expose themselves to mass media. This artifact would tend to increase any apparent primacy effect that might be present. In the laboratory all sides of the issue are presented systematically to all subjects under controlled conditions.

Other factors also influence the relative effects of primacy—the setting in which the communication is received and the nature of the communicator. When the setting is unambiguous and the audience is aware that differences of opinion exist, then primacy has little effect. Further, when two persons present different points of view, one after the other, no primacy effects are noted. However, when the same individual presents contradictory material, the material presented first has the greatest effect.

These results suggest that concern over primacy in law trials or political debates is probably not warranted, since it usually is clear that different communicators are representing different sides of the issue, and the issue itself is controversial.

These findings are of interest in themselves. However, the problem they demonstrate has implications beyond the immediate area of attitude-change experimentation. One of the central difficulties that haunts all psychological research is the gap between the laboratory, in which experiments are conducted, and the natural social world to which these results must eventually be applied. The findings in attitude research clearly indicate the ways in which laboratory results may be misleading when applied directly to social situations.

It is therefore of particular interest to examine the discrepant results between survey research in the natural condition and attitude-change studies in the laboratory situation, in order to determine the ways in which these diverse approaches can be successfully integrated.

In general, these methods differ in their definition of the basic communications situation, the issues studied, the subjects used, and the type of communicator involved. The differences in their findings have been attributed to one or another of these factors. These differences are not arbitrary, but rather are the direct outcome of the different experimental designs employed in the two approaches to the problem.

The experimental approach to attitude change is relatively straightforward. A certain attitude of the subject is measured by an appropriate test. He is then subjected to a specific type of experience designed to change his attitude. His initial attitude is then reassessed in order to measure whether and how much attitude change has occurred. Parallel with this basic procedure a control group of similar or identical subjects also is measured before and after, but undergoes no attitude-change experience. If the experimental subjects change more than the "controls," the influence of the attitude-changing method is demonstrated.

This design is essentially a one-way analysis from premeasure through intermediate experience and ending in postmeasure. Such an experimental limitation of direction is permissible in terms of simplifying the acquisition of knowledge, but it tends to be misleading, since real communication does not take place in such a one-way direction. In natural situations communicator and recipient interact to some extent, and a variety of feedback opportunities are present. These interactions may be as important as the direct influence process of one person on another. Further, certain characteristics of the individual, such as his original attitude, predispose him to be interested in certain types of information. The more he learns, the greater his interest becomes. Thus attitude change in this instance tends to accelerate itself when the initial predisposition is favorable. This kind of effect usually is ignored or lost in the simple attitude-change experiment.

The survey-research design, particularly when it takes the form of a panel study, has much greater flexibility. In the panel design a selected group of persons are interviewed repeatedly at different times. No attempt is made to control the forces and communications influencing them. The main tool in such research is the relation between variables either at a given moment or over time. This approach helps us understand how a complex network of measures varies with respect to each other and themselves over a reasonably long period. Unfortunately, since no controls exist, it is difficult or impossible ever to be able to state that one event causes another, since the measures of the two events both occur in uncontrolled conditions. For this reason survey and panel research generally are used to suggest hypotheses that may be tested precisely in an experiment. In this way the two kinds of research can interact in a fruitful manner.

There are, however, certain practical issues that no experiment can handle directly. One cannot, for example, study a real voting campaign in a controlled manner since neither political party would lend itself to such venture. Neither can experiments last over long periods of time, because of the attrition of subjects and other problems, such as the expense of maintaining the research staff, or necessary space and equipment.

There are, however, a surprising number of instances in which an experimental approach can be adapted to the domain currently covered by survey research. There is no reason, in principle, why experimental studies of attitude change cannot use issues that have deep social involvement rather than such peripheral questions as "When do you believe we will find a cure for the common cold?" There is no irrevocable reason why most experiments must be done with college students; or why the number of viewpoints presented should be limited artificially; and no reason to force the subject to listen to a communication if he prefers not to do so. The very act of information selection can become an important experimental variable.

Unfortunately, such extensions and improvements in experimental design must be paid for in terms of time, effort, and cost. The reason that trivial change criteria, college students, and forced participation have been used is that it was simpler and cheaper to do so. The more complex the design, the greater the expense. It is more difficult to run a series of experiments than a single study. For this very practical reason the experimental manipulation of one or two variables under highly controlled conditions is likely to continue. It is, however, a relatively inefficient approach in the long run. Much more, and much more relevant, information can be uncovered by complex designs employing a variety of issues, communciations procedures, subjects, and types of exposure. But this development must await a more general realization of the importance of such research, and the availability of large sums for investment in it.

The nearest approach to a complex long-term analysis of the effects of communications procedures on attitude change has been conducted at Yale. Generally each separate study has been of the limited experimental type. However, by careful planning, one study has built upon another so that the results have been more cumulative and fruitful than might otherwise have been the case.

A number of general issues have been examined in these studies, many of which have been already touched upon. The effect of varying the communicator's attractiveness and expertness has been determined. The influence of reference groups on attempts to induce attitude changes has been examined. A "sleeper" effect has been isolated, indicating that when the communicator is credible, change tends to occur long after the communication has terminated.

Another topic of broad concern has been the analysis of individual differences in degree of persuasibility. This characteristic has been related to other personality characteristics, in order to clarify the relation between attitude change and personality structure.

Relatively little has been done on the important issue of the relation of the type of attitude to the amount of change that occurs. Beyond the previously noted finding that ego involvement in the area decreases the likelihood of change, little is currently known.

THE SIGNIFICANCE OF BEHAVIOR-CHANGE TESTS

The study of attitude change has thus accumulated some well-authenticated information about the way in which such change occurs, as well as clarifying the effects of different experimental designs on the results obtained. But a great deal more remains to be done, if the findings are to be more than merely interesting, but of general practical significance. While these studies present a worthy model for the investigation of behavior-change procedures, many of the findings are not directly relevant, since they focus on the relatively superficial aspects of persuasion, rather than structural personality change. But it is only by such study of the components of attitude and behavior-change procedures that we can hope slowly to learn how to change behavior in a systematic and predictable fashion. A number of independent studies of various components of aspects of behavior-change procedures have been carried out in various psychological areas for a variety of purposes. A superficial inspection of some of them indicates that there is substantial evidence that certain behavior-change components do produce demonstrable effects in different situations. In order to clarify the significance of such studies three different components of many change procedures will be examined in terms of existing evidence. These three components have been chosen purposely from different areas in psychology in order to sample the full range of components that are involved in any actual change procedure.

The first component is feedback. Studies of feedback are derived from the areas of communications theory, group interaction, or the influence of knowledge of test results on individual performance. Second, we shall consider operant conditioning, a concept drawn directly from the work of learning theorists. Third, we shall examine the effect of faith, which is primarily the province of the clinical and personality psychologist.

In its most general sense "feedback" refers to the interaction of communications processes. Thus when one person responds to another his response may provide a feedback of the original communication. But feedback is more specific than reaction or interaction. In the group situation feedback may consist of the observations made by a group observer on the progress and functioning of the group. On the neural level, feedback refers to the re-entry of nerve currents into previously traversed paths. The provision for adequate and continuous feedback is an important feature of any systems network. By means of feedback a system is constantly in touch with its own behavior.

On the human level feedback usually is maintained by an outer agency that provides reactions to given behavior at stated intervals. This outer agency usually is another human being, but it may also be a machine or a simple test result. The nature of the agency is immaterial as long as it represents an ordered reaction to the continuing behavior of the individual.

The studies of human and mechanical feedback are remarkably uniform in outcome. Regardless of the nature of the subject or the feedback, virtually all studies indicate that feedback does influence the subject's behavior. This degree of unanimity in experimental findings is extremely noteworthy and without many counterparts among examinations of other behavior-change components.

Beyond the general demonstration of effect, studies of feedback have tended to differentiate types of feedback and compare their relative influence on behavior. For example, in one study of Air

Force personnel the relative effects of objective, highly structured feedback and personal group-member mutual feedback were compared. In this case the effects of objective feedback were clearly superior.

In other studies positive feedback, emphasizing the desirable aspects of behavior, has been compared with negative feedback of an exclusively critical nature. The findings have generally favored positive feedback. The comparison of different levels of feedback also has been made. In this case feedback varied from a relatively superficial account of what was said to a psychological depth interpretation of the "real" meaning of the behavior. Moreover, the relative effects of interpreting results versus the cold presentation of the bare facts have been compared.

The evidence that has accumulated at the present time is insufficient to establish clearly the superiority of one type of feedback over another. Realistically it is probable that different types work most effectively in different situations. It is, however, clear that any kind of feedback is better than none at all, in terms of the individual's satisfaction and the accuracy and adequacy of his performance.

The second component, operant conditioning, is associated primarily with the early studies performed by Burrhus Skinner.[4] The general model for such conditioning is very simple. When an individual performs a given act by chance, such as saying a certain word, he is rewarded. Under this regime he very quickly learns to perform the given act with increasing frequency. If he is rewarded intermittently rather than every time he performs the act the learning will be more resistant to obliteration.

It may seem that such an obvious procedure does not merit the imposing title of "operant conditioning"; however, the applications and implications of this simple procedure are numerous.

Most of the work on operant conditioning has been done with animals. However, a series of studies recently has been performed to demonstrate that operant condition occurs in human beings with and without their conscious awareness. Thus one individual can influence another simply by reinforcing, or rewarding those aspects of the other's behavior that he wishes to encourage. In one early study the experimenter asked the subjects to name as many words as they could. After each plural word he muttered, "Mmm-hmm." He shortly found that the number of plural words rapidly increased. This result is noteworthy in view of the vagueness of the reward involved. Apparently the ambiguity of the situation maximized the influence of such transient verbal reward responses as "mmm-hmm."

In another study, involving mental patients, the researcher systematically varied his behavior during control- and experimental-interview periods. During the experimental period the experimenter reinforced any emotionally toned statement made by the patient with a look or a grunt of some kind. During the control periods he did nothing. The number of such statements rapidly increased during the experimental period.

A great number of similar experiments have demonstrated beyond doubt that human behavior is subject to rapid conditioning with and without awareness on the part of the subject and/or the experimenter. Generally, the experimenter is aware of what he wants to condition. But in ordinary situations the individual undoubtedly reinforces others without understanding what he is doing.

These studies have led many behavior-change specialists to reconsider the effect and nature of their technique of influence. In particular, psychotherapists, who have long viewed themselves as nondirective or patient-directed, have become aware increasingly that even the most innocent acknowledgment of a response has a reinforcing action. It now appears that a great deal of patient behavior in psychotherapy may be caused by operant conditioning. The patient's language, the things he talks about, even his dreams may be influenced subtly by the way in which the therapist rewards what he says. The ambiguity inherent in therapy sessions only magnifies any reward that occurs out of ordinary proportion.

This realization has led to isolated attempts at reformulating psychotherapy as a process of operant conditioning in which the desired response is rewarded systematically. Where the symptoms are clearly defined, some success has been reported. What is equally interesting is the resemblance between operant condition of human behavior and the operant condition built into teaching machines. A good teaching-machine program is built on the principle that the subject generally should be able to answer the item. Thus he is rewarded quickly for the correct response and the answer is learned through operant conditioning.

Whatever its practical importance, the application of operant conditioning to behavior change is interesting as a rapprochement of learning theory and personality change, two areas long widely separated.

The third component to be described is "faith." This psychological variable generally has religious overtones, but in the present context we will ignore these.

Most practitioners long have recognized that the belief of the subject in the method that was applied was an important factor in changing his behavior. The most striking evidence of the power of faith as an agent of change is provided by the various studies of placebos. As part of many pharmacological studies inert organic compounds called placebos are administered routinely to act as controls for the active substance whose effect is being tested. It has long been recognized that the placebo produced effects in such instances, even though it was nothing more than a sugar tablet. This observation has led to the direct study of placebos themselves. In one instance, for example, a sterile water solution was given to groups of bleeding-ulcer patients under two conditions. In the first the patients were told that the injection consisted of a new drug that would produce results. In the second the patients were told that the experimental medicine was of undetermined effectiveness. A follow-up after one year indicated remission of symptoms in 70 per cent of the first group but only 25 per cent in the second group. Similar results have been reported in the treatment of warts. Other studies have indicated that a placebo can produce as much symptomatic improvement as psychotherapy, at least for a limited period. All these findings provide strong evidence of the power of faith as an agent of change independent of any particular method.

Perhaps the most striking study of this series, though by no means the most methodologically elegant, was performed with only three chronically ill, bedridden patients.[5] One of the patients had a fatal cancer, one had chronic inflammation of the gall bladder, while the third suffered from pancreatitis. All were considered hopeless. Since the patients appeared to have nothing to lose, their doctor enlisted the aid of a local faith healer in their treatment. At first the doctor had the faith healer work without the patients' knowledge. Nothing whatever happened. He next told the patients about the faith healer and built up their expectations about his power. He then told them that at a certain time the faith healer would begin to work on them. At that time the faith healer actually had stopped his work, so that any effect was strictly in the minds of the patients. The results were remarkable. The patient with pancreatitis was cured permanently. The others showed remarkable improvement, though permanent cures were not effected. However, the results illustrate how faith in the absence of any external agency can produce remarkable results.

Faith, operant conditioning, and feedback are by no means the only components of behavior-change procedures that have been validated experimentally. A variety of others could be described. These include the impact of participation, the force of social norms, and the effects of practice on the learning of new behavior. Along with operant conditioning, the effects of negative conditioning and deconditioning procedures have been demonstrated. In addition to the effects of faith, the degree of involvement of the change agent in the procedure and the comprehensiveness of the method that he uses have been shown to effect the amount of change produced. Finally, the creation of therapeutic stress, the opportunity for catharsis (the bringing of an attitude, behavior pattern, and so forth to one's conscious attention, thereby eliminating it), and the focus of the subject's attention on himself have each been shown to influence subsequent behavior and lead to certain types of behavior change.

As these components of behavior-change procedures are studied separately, the elements of behavior change should become clearer. Once the elements are identified, then various combinations can be explored, in order to determine which combination of components has the greatest effect in a given instance. This work has scarcely begun at the present time. It is here, however, that the future of behavior-change research must lie, if the area is ever to shift from an art applied by professional personnel to an understood and predictable science of human development and change.

Conclusion

The Future of
Psychology

If one extrapolates trends and developments from this century into the next one, there can be no doubt that psychology has an important future. Its growth has been phenomenal, certainly out of all importance to its discoveries to date. Presumably, this growth and concentration of effort will begin to pay off huge dividends at a certain point in time. It must be remembered, however, that the number of persons in the field is misleading, since most psychologists are involved in applied activities, rather than in basic research. The scientifically active psychologist is in the minority. The knowledge that is to be expected from psychology must be limited to the number of psychologists actively engaged in research. This number will largely depend on the amount of money that is made available for such research. At the present time most of this money is supplied by various government agencies, including the Armed Forces, the National Science Foundation, and the National Institutes of Health. Private foundations also contribute, but to a far lesser extent than the government.

The trend has been for government to spend increasing amounts of money in support of scientific research. Presumably, psychology will continue to receive its proportionate share in the future. Beyond that, special conditions will be required to increase the percentage of the investment made in psychology and research. In general, the necessary condition is that some gradual discovery or dramatic breakthrough clearly shows, to officials and the public alike, that the national defense and safety are affected by progress in psychological research. In such an event there is no limit to the amount of money that might be poured into certain areas of psychological research. The current space effort is eloquent testimony to the fact that money literally is no object to such a national effort.

What psychological development could produce a crash program in psychological research? One likely candidate might be a breakthrough in the extension of the limits of human performance. Such an extension could involve the elimination of fatigue effects, improvement of muscular coordination, reduction of psychic and emotional tensions, and improvement of intellectual performance. If any of these extensions could be effected dramatically without permanent harm to the individual, it might make a crucial difference in establishing national superiority, particularly in specialized man-machine relations, where man is usually the weaker link. Such extensions can be effected in a number of areas even today through various pharmacological means, and through hypnotic suggestion without permanent damage. If methods are found that can produce lasting extensions of human limitations they would certainly attract wide public interest. Each man could apply the finding to himself, at least in his imagination. The value of such research would be obvious to all. It would threaten no one. It could contribute to the national defense and welfare. Thus it might be the avenue for a huge research development in psychology generously supported by the government, and perhaps by private corporate sources as well.

It seems almost inevitable that some development of this character must occur sooner or later, and lead to a rather dramatic increase in support for basic psychological research. The only factor that might prevent such an increase is the general suspicion of psychological research that is prevalent throughout the community. Psychologists are viewed as impersonalizing and controlling other persons. Both these tendencies are viewed by many nonpsychologists as threatening. This alarm is premature, since at the present time most psychological tools are rather crude, most test instruments are open to various known sources of error, and the methods for controlling and changing people are relatively unsophisticated or, if sophisticated, then unvalidated. Thus the public fear of psychologists is based on an image of psychology that is not realistic at present. It may, however, become more realistic with time. In many nondemocratic countries the development of psychology has been hampered seriously and crippled because the government feared the result of freely conceived and executed research. The direction of research by the state, out of fear, or as the outcome of a dictatorial form of government, certainly can limit the development of any science, and particularly psychology. Presumably in a democracy it is to the advantage of the society to have all the sciences develop freely. These developments, such as the hydrogen bomb and automation, do produce severe problems in their time. But they also supply the best insurance for the survival of the society as a whole. The same freedom of investigation that produces the problems can generally solve them, if unhampered by external restraint.

As with the individual patient in psychotherapy, it is necessary for the positive curative forces in the society at large to exceed the anxiety-ridden, destructive forces in order for the therapy to continue. Similarly, if psychology appears to be more threatening than beneficent, it certainly will proceed more slowly in its development, since it will have to do so in the face of public suspicion. Even under such conditions, however, special historical circumstances could force rapid research advances. No one, for example, felt that the hydrogen bomb would benefit him personally, but its development was carried out quickly because of national purposes that demanded it.

It appears, therefore, that in the future psychology is assured as a thriving discipline unless psychologists themselves go out of their way to destroy or deteriorate their public image.

The shape of the future will be limited in the long run more by psychologists themselves than by any outside group. This has been the case since the inception of modern psychology in the last century and continues to be so at the present time. As latecomers to the scientific community, psychologists have felt the need to be overly scientific in the formal sense. They have insisted on precision and care at the expense of imagination and creativity. Generally, the two are inversely related. The ability to measure a given variable accurately is usually inversely proportional to its general importance. Thus psychologists have tended to get better and better at studying less and less.

If this tendency to restrict the field of their operations is a symptom of immaturity, it is reasonable to assume that as psychology passes through its adolescence it may abandon certain aspects of its rigid definition of scientific procedures in both a technical and substantive sense.

When psychology was separating from philosophy in the last half of the nineteenth century, psychologists were highly conscious of the need to distinguish their efforts from those of philosophers. Great emphasis was placed on an operational, experimental, nonspeculative approach. With the passing of time, philosophy itself has changed its character and becomes far more operationally oriented, so that the relation between the two is not so distant as it was at the turn of the century. However, the heritage of the early days of modern psychology still influences both the choice of research procedures and, more particularly, the subject matter that is investigated.

There are signs that the climate in psychology may be changing, due to the increasing respect for the field held by scientists working in other areas. This tolerance takes the form of fragmentation rather than any new integrative approaches. Little subsocieties are formed to investigate topics or conduct seminars on subjects that psychologists of the previous decade would have found of little interest. This in itself is probably a good thing, but it is not a substitute for the expansion of the base line of psychology.

It must be remembered that modern psychology is essentially an American development. Most psychological research is done in the United States. Whether or not it is qualitatively superior to that done elsewhere, it is certainly quantitatively overwhelming.

In view of this condition it is natural that psychology contains certain tendencies inherent in the American culture that characterize it and to some extent limit its development. Many of its pragmatic and eclectic tendencies reflect predominant values of the American culture. These may be good, but all values have their limitation. From this viewpoint it would seem that psychologists ought to begin to re-examine what the cultural influences are, and have been, on psychological research and to reconsider the contributions to psychology that have been made by other cultures in the present and in the past as a means of seeing their own work in a new light. These contributions may, and should, alert them to areas of psychological experience that currently are underrated and ignored. However, such an expansion of outlook is difficult to achieve and requires considerable inner security on the part of the individual undertaking it. Thus the re-evaluation of the content and relative priorities in the development of the various specialties in psychology would require a relatively normal and mature field for its execution.

A comparison of other Western and ancient Eastern psychologies with American psychology suggests several preliminary conclusions that may be relevant to any general re-evaluation.

The European psychologists, with the possible exception of their British brothers, often place greater emphasis on the use of theory and systems and less on experimental demonstration. However, the topics that they investigate are no more broad than those of American psychology. If anything, some of the specialties that have developed here do not have a European counterpart. There is, for example, relatively little engineering psychology actively under investigation in Europe, and the use of high-speed computers is far less widespread. European psychology differs from American psychology in the older traditions that it represents rather than in the development of new areas of specialization.

If we pass to the many Eastern systems for personal development from yoga through Zen, one is impressed by much material that is psychological in nature. Regardless of its merit, which is difficult to judge before the fact, these materials suggest that from early times men have studied psychology as a way to develop themselves beyond the point normally required by everyday life. Western psychology has shown interest in the problem of bringing persons who were sick back into the fold of normality, through physiological and psychological therapy. It has, however, almost ignored the problem of developing men *beyond* the point of social normality. As described earlier in this chapter, such information would have great social importance, in addition to the benefit that it might confer on the individual. It is strange, therefore, that the topic has been ignored so generally, particularly since the problem was raised during the early development of modern psychology. For example, in an interesting paper directed toward this problem, William James, the founder of American psychology, discussed the energies of men, and how they might be increased beyond normal levels.[1]

At that relatively early time in the development of modern psychology James discussed the contributions of techniques of yoga and religious and mystic exercises designed for this purpose. He analyzed certain remarkable cases in which emergency situations, such as war, had led to an incredible increase in the expenditure of energy. One officer, for example, was able to carry on for a number of sleepless days under unremitting battle conditions with serious wounds that under any more normal conditions would have immobilized him from the start.

If at this time in the development of modern psychology these examples were known and discussed by a leading figure, why were these avenues ignored in later development?

There are various answers. Psychology became ultra-experimental and scientific in the most limited sense of the word. Only behavior observable by the impartial witness was considered proper material for psychological investigation. Any phenomenon not easily reducible to this form was regarded with suspicion and discarded as inappropriate for scientific investigation.

In addition, many of the systems and records of man's attempts to extend his own limitations were mixed with religious material of various kinds. Religion was the last thing with which the empirical psychologist wished to concern himself. Such generalized theological discussions were just what he wanted to avoid, since they reminded him of his philosophical parent, and seemed scientifically meaningless.

Further, most attempts at improving men's abilities, talents, morality, or spirituality had a strong moral or idealistic bias. The scientist, as scientist, was not supposed to be interested in such suppositions. They were a source of embarrassment to him. His goal was only the maximization of the truth and the minimization of error. Thus the moral tone of these accounts and attempts repelled him. He was not interested professionally in improving people but only in understanding why they were what they were.

Finally, the American culture itself may have played a part in limiting psychological investigations. Since this culture is so new, it lacks a deep sense of historical and cultural continuity, on which many of these systems of development and ideas are based. There is, therefore, something that is inescapably alien to the Western psychologist about Eastern psychologies, which prevents him from approaching them directly.

As a consequence of these and other factors, modern psychology has largely sidestepped the crucial question of the possibility of man's development.

Some relevant knowledge has been gained indirectly in the course of exploring other lines of investigation, such as the information-processing limits of human senses, or the effect of hypnosis on the restoration of memory. However, systematic attempts to explore the problems involved in developing human ability, personality, and behavior have not been even formulated, much less investigated.

Perhaps the pressures of our age will force psychology to turn to the problem of human improvement as a necessity of survival, but such a tendency is not yet in evidence. For example, a current attempt to study the development of such a characteristic as altruism generally has met with indifference, hostility, or ridicule.[2] A similar reaction is often directed at the study of ESP, which is certainly concerned with the development of unusual human functions. This attitude is independent of the facts, whatever they may be.

Thus in assessing the future of psychology, the crucial question appears to be whether psychologists will accept and investigate the potentialities of individuals as a central focus or whether they will continue to investigate normal human functions with additional attention devoted to various pathological states, including mental illness and other less permanent conditions.

The one emphasis does not preclude the other, but if psychology is to be free to expand, it must feel secure to experiment with new approaches and with new materials. This enhancement of its function has important implications not only for psychology but for the public at large. It becomes increasingly evident that whatever the personal motives of given individuals, modern technical progress is creating, and has created, a situation in which men must learn how to be better in all senses of the word if they are to hold their own, or even survive. In such a situation psychology cannot afford the historical luxury of a rigorous and rigid limitation of its field of operations. There is no other scientific discipline equipped to undertake the task of extending human limitations. The future of psychology in the next hundred years may be determined largely by the extent to which psychology is able to extend itself in this direction. Not only the knowledge that could be obtained, but also the change in its public image that would result, could have widespread effects on the productive vigor of the whole field.

It is not enough for the psychology of the future to describe, predict, and control human behavior. It must learn to develop and extend the behavior that it studies, if the results of its efforts are to fertilize and enrich human experience rather than reduce it to a formula whose significance is lost by the process of its derivation.

APPENDIXES

Appendix A

Automated Instruction

The diagram on page 277 is a highly simplified segment of a teaching-machine program. It is designed to demonstrate certain fundamental principles rather than illustrate any special elegance in the writing of programs. However, even such a simple program sequence is sufficient to demonstrate the following principles that are employed in the programming of teaching machines: (a) the presentation of new material to the student; (b) testing of the acquisition of this knowledge; (c) varying the sequence of the program in terms of the errors made by the student; (d) allowing the student to determine whether he wishes to review a part or all of the lesson, or go on to new material.

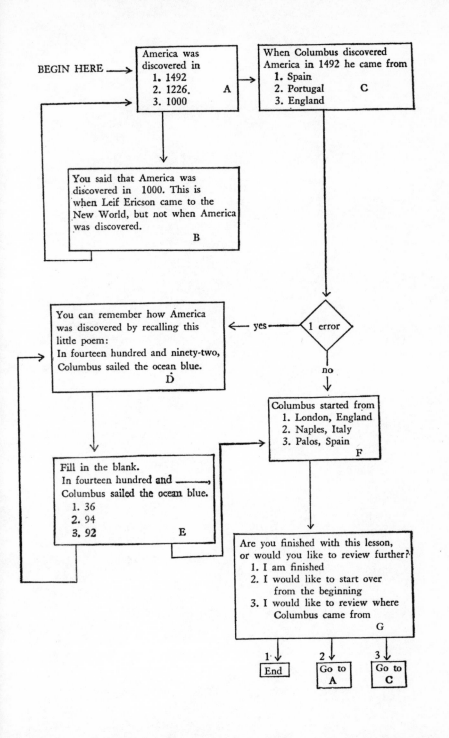

Appendix B

Factor Analysis

Factor analysis is a statistical technique for the organization of correlation data. As such, it simplifies the interpretation of these data and facilitates the identification of fundamental dimensions being tapped by the experimental measures.

The correlations to which factor analysis is applied represent the measures of common content between any two of the variables that are included within a given study. When all variables are correlated with each other, these correlations can be presented in a tabular form called a "matrix."

When the number of variables becomes large, it is almost impossible to read such a matrix, because of the number of relationships involved. For example, in a relatively modest instance involving thirty variables over four hundred and twenty different correlations are contained in the matrix. In order to understand this matrix each of these separate relationships must be kept in mind simultaneously. Such a task is vast and escapes the capabilities of the researcher.

To deal with this situation a number of techniques are available. While they differ in form and complexity, they share the common function of simplifying the matrix. They vary from a relatively crude restructuring of the matrix in order to bring together highly correlated groups of variables, to the full application of factor analytic technique, complete with such esoteric aspects as extraction, residuals, and rotation.

In some instances the degree of precision and the quality of the data may not justify full factor-analytic investigation. However, when it is feasible factor analysis is usually the preferred technique because of its precision and completeness.

The basic principle of factor analysis is that the correlation matrix is an estimate of an underlying order that is much simpler than the welter of correlations seems to suggest. However this order is not given.

It must be uncovered. In order to uncover it factor analysts engage in a series of statistical maneuvers designed to determine the nature and number of dimensions that are needed to account for the relationships described by the correlation matrix. Like any model builder, the factor analyst creates an imaginary model to which he fits his data. By a series of approximations the best fit to the model is obtained.

The first step in any factor analysis is the extraction of the first or "zero order" factor. The choice of this first factor in relation to the particular arrangements of correlations in the matrix is arbitrary.

After the first extraction has been performed, the nature of the matrix is changed quantitatively. This changed matrix appropriately is called the "residual" matrix. It represents the degree of relationship that is left among the variables when the amount of their relation to the first factor has been subtracted. In other words, the extraction of a factor determines how much each variable is related to this given factor. All the information that is not accounted for by this factor remains in the residual matrix.

In this general manner factors are extracted until the amount of information remaining in the residual matrix represents, or almost represents, random variation, experimental and sampling error, and the like. When this condition has been achieved, all of the useful information has been attributed to one or another of the factors, and the process of extraction is complete.

The next problem to be faced by the factor analyst is what to do with these factors now that they have been uncovered. In order to answer this question, it is necessary to realize that the arrangement of the factors in relation to each other, and the scores that they represent, is arbitrary, though the matrix of relations which they describe is fixed. The original zero-order factor was chosen arbitrarily as a convenient starting point. Its location determines the relative location of all other factors. These locations are not likely to be correct in terms of identifying underlying dimensions, since they were arbitrarily selected. For this reason a second major phase in the factor-analytic process is instituted. It is called "rotation" and involves the reorientation of the factors in relation to each other in order to satisfy certain criteria. The major criterion is that factors shall be located so that each factor is associated with a different cluster of test scores. When this criterion is satisfied the factor represents the content that is common to the particular cluster of relationships. When the location of factors in terms of test density is the sole criterion for rotation, the process is called "oblique" rotation. Often an additional criterion of factor independence is imposed. In this instance the process is called "orthogonal" rotation. When factors are independent, it means that they are uncorrelated. Scores on one factor are unrelated to scores on any other factor. In terms of obtaining pure underlying dimensions, orthogonal factors are intrinsically appealing. However, because of the interrelatedness of most human behavior, it is often more realistic to settle for oblique factors that are easier to obtain, and usually account for more of the information in the matrix because they are not hampered by the additional requirement of independence.

The execution of a factor analysis involves many mathematical and statistical problems that we have not touched upon, as well as a vast amount of simple computation. But the rationale and the basic procedure is as described, though the particular techniques used may vary with the investigator, the nature of the data, and the computational aids that are available.

REFERENCES

GLOSSARY

*SUGGESTIONS
FOR FURTHER READING*

References

CHAPTER ONE

1. Hebb, D.O. The effects of early experience on problem solving at maturity. *American Psychologist,* 1947, 2, 306–07.
2. Bexton, W.H., Heron, W., and Scott, T.H. Effects of decreased variation in the sensory environment. *Canadian Journal of Psychology,* 1954, 8, 70–76.
3. Skinner, B.F. Pigeons in a Pelican. *American Psychologist,* 1960, 15, 28–37.
4. Asch, S.E. *Social Psychology.* Englewood Cliffs, N.J.: Prentice-Hall, 1952.
5. Lewin, K., Lippitt, R., and White, R. K. Patterns of aggressive behavior in experimentally created social climates. *Journal of Social Psychology,* 1939, 10, 271–99.

CHAPTER THREE

1. Pressey, S.L. A simple apparatus which gives tests and scores— and teaches. *School and Society,* 1926, 23, 373–76.
2. Thorndike, E.L. The Psychology of Learning. (*Educational Psychology* 11) New York: Teachers College, Columbia University, 1913.

CHAPTER FOUR

1. Shannon, C.E. A mathematical theory of communication. *Bell System Technical Journal,* 1948, 27, 379–423, 623–56.
2. Cronbach, L.J. Processes affecting scores on "understanding of others" and "assumed similarity." *Psychological Bulletin,* 1955, 52, 177–93.

CHAPTER FIVE

1. Binet, A., and Simon, T. Le développement de l'intelligence chez les enfants. *L'Année Psychologique,* 1908, 14, 1–94.
2. Thurstone, L.L., and Thurstone, T.G. Factorial studies of intelligence. Psychological Monographs, No. 2, 1941.

3. Guilford, J.P. The structure of intellect. *Psychological Bulletin,* 1956, 53, 267–93.

4. Humphreys, L.G. The organization of human abilities. *American Psychologist,* 1962, 17, 475–83.

5. Drevdahl, J.E., and Cattell, R.B. Personality and creativity in artists and writers. *Journal of Clinical Psychology,* 1958, 14, 107–11.

6. Eiduson, B. Artist and nonartist: a comparative study. *Journal of Personality,* 1958, 26, 12–28.

7. Guilford, J.P. Creative abilities in the arts. *Psychological Review,* 1957, 64, 110–18.

8. Barron, F. Originality in relation to personality and intellect. *Journal of Personality,* 1957, 25, 730–42.

9. MacKinnon, D.W. The nature and nurture of creative talent. *American Psychologist,* 1962, 17, 484–95.

10. Getzels, J.W., and Jackson, P.W. *Creativity and Intelligence.* New York: Wiley, 1962.

CHAPTER SIX

1. Rhine, J.B. *Extra-sensory Perception.* Boston: Bruce Humphries, 1934.

2. Kahn, S.D. Studies in extrasensory perception. *Proceedings of the American Society for Psychical Research,* 1952, 25, 1–48.

3. Guirden, E. A review of psychokinesis, *Psychological Bulletin,* 1962, 59, 353–88.

4. Fisher, R.A. *Statistical Methods for Research Workers* (seventh ed.). Edinburgh: Oliver and Boyd, 1938.

5. Pratt, J.G. Dice bias and manner of throwing. *Journal of Parapsychology,* 1947, 11, 53–63.

CHAPTER SEVEN

1. Murphy, G. *Personality: a Biosocial Approach to Origins and Structure.* New York: Harper, 1947.

2. Miller, J.G. Toward a general theory for the behavioral sciences. *American Psychologist,* 1955, 10, 513–31.

3. Campbell, D.T., and Fiske, D.W. Convergent and discriminant validation by the Multitrait-Multimethod Matrix. *Psychological Bulletin,* 1959, 56, 81–105.

4. French, J.W. The description of aptitude and achievement tests in terms of rotated factors. Psychometric Monographs, No. 5, 1951.

5. French, J.W. The description of personality measurement in terms of rotated factors. Princeton, New Jersey, Educational Testing Service, 1953.

6. Cattell, R.B. *Description and Measurement of Personality*. New York: World Book Company, 1946.

7. Carter, L.F. Recording and evaluating the performance of individuals as members of small groups. *Personnel Psychology,* 1954, 7, 477–84.

8. Cattell, R.B., and Dickman, K. A dynamic model of physical influences demonstrating the necessity of oblique simple structure. *Psychological Bulletin,* 1962, 59.

9. Terman, L.M., and Oden, M.H. *The Gifted Group at Mid-Life: Thirty Five Years' Follow-up of the Superior Child*. Stanford, California: Stanford University Press, 1959.

10. Mann, R.D. A review of the relationships between personality and performance in small groups. *Psychological Bulletin,* 1959, 56, 241–70.

11. Borgatta, E.F. Analysis of social interaction: actual, role playing, projective. *Journal of Abnormal and Social Psychology,* 1955, 51, 394–405.

12. Leary, T. *The Interpersonal Diagnosis of Personality*. New York: Ronald Press, 1957.

13. Borgatta, E.F., Cottrell, L.S., Jr., and Meyer, H.J. On the dimensions of group behavior. *Sociometry,* 1956, 19, 223–40.

14. Mann, J.H. Studies of role performance. Genetic Psychological Monographs, 1961, 64, 213–307.

CHAPTER EIGHT

1. Kelly, E.L. Consistency of the adult personality. *American Psychologist,* 1955, 10, 659–81.

2. Mann, J.H. The assessment of efforts to change adult personality, Russell Sage Project No. 8-8548-131.

3. Hovland, C.I. Reconciling results from experimental and survey studies. *American Psychologist,* 1959, 14, 8–17.

4. Skinner, B.F. *The Behavior of Organisms.* New York: Appleton-Century-Crofts, 1938.
5. Rehder, H. Wunderheilungen, Ein Experiment. *Hippokrates,* 1955, 26, 577–80.

CONCLUSION

1. James W. *Selected Papers on Philosophy.* New York: Dutton, 1947.
2. Sorokin, P.A. *Forms and Techniques of Altruistic and Spiritual Growth: A Symposium.* Boston, Beacon Press, 1954.

Glossary

ACHIEVEMENT TEST. *A test that measures what has been accomplished in a specified area.*

APPLIED PSYCHOLOGY. *The use of psychological knowledge to solve practical problems, such as the improvement of mental health or the increase of worker productivity.*

APTITUDE. *The capacity to reach a high level of achievement in a specific area, such as art, music, or engineering.*

ASSESSMENT. *The evaluation of an individual in regard to a number of his traits.*

AUTHORITARIAN. *One who acts in a dictatorial way or prefers a dictatorial approach to leadership.*

AUTOKINETIC EFFECT. *The apparent motion of a small fixed light in a dark room.*

AUTOMATION. *The use of machines to take the place of men in industrial operations.*

BEHAVIORISM. *The school of psychology that stresses the use of objectivity in the measurement of all psychological entities.*

BINARY NUMBER. *A number selected from only two possible choices, such as the numbers zero and one.*

BIT. *A contraction of "binary digit." A "bit" of information reduces the amount of uncertainty about equally likely alternatives by one-half.*

BRAINSTORMING. *The rapid verbalization of ideas and problem-solving suggestions in a group situation. Primary emphasis is placed on the expression of new ideas at the expense of critical appraisal.*

BRAINWASHING.

The use of extreme psychological, social, and physiological pressures to effect ideological conversion.

CHANNEL CAPACITY.

The number of "bits" of information that can be distinguished by a given sense.

CLIENT-CENTERED THERAPY.

That kind of therapy in which the therapist helps the client to formulate his own problems and arrive at his own solutions with a minimum of direct influence. See *Nondirective therapy.*

COMMUNICATION.

Interaction between two individuals or between men and machines, one of whom acts as the stimulus for another.

COMMUNICATIONS THEORY.

The theory that analyzes how messages are transmitted from a sender to a receiver over a communications channel.

COMPLETION TEST.

A test consisting of unfinished items, such as incomplete sentences, that the subject is asked to complete.

COMPLEX.

A specific set of psychological symptoms, such as an inferiority complex.

CONDITIONED RESPONSE.

A response aroused by some stimulus other than that which naturally produces it, such as salivation, when it occurs in response to a tone rather than exposure to food.

CONTROL GROUP.

Identical in every respect to the experimental group in a study, except that it does not receive the experimental treatment. See *Experimental group.*

CORRELATION.

A statistical measure of the degree of association between two variables.

CREATIVITY.

The ability to arrive at a new solution to an old problem, or to perceive and solve problems that were not previously recognized as such.

CRITICAL CUT-OFF POINT.
The smallest acceptable point or score for classification of the individual in a given group or for a given position.

CULTURE.
The traits, beliefs, and products that characterize a people.

CYBERNETICS.
The study of the impact of machines upon human behavior and the analysis of human behavior in terms of principles derived from the study of complex machines.

DATA PROCESSING.
The organization and analysis of research data.

DEPENDENT VARIABLE.
The variable in an experiment that is changed as a result of the experimental treatment.

DISTRIBUTION.
The arrangement that is produced when a set of scores are ordered in terms of their relative magnitudes.

DRIVE.
The physiological state that causes the individual to become active in order to reduce the physiological need.

DYNAMICS.
The underlying bases of behavior.

EGO.
In psychoanalysis, the reality-oriented aspect of the individual.

ELECTOENCEPHALO-GRAM (EEG).
A record of the electrical impulses associated with brain activity.

EMOTION.
A type of behavior associated with various strong physiological reactions that may disrupt everyday activities.

ENCODING.
Changing a message into code.

ENVIRONMENT.
The physical stimuli surrounding the units of inheritance.

EXPERIMENTAL DESIGN.
The specific procedures constituting a given experiment.

EXPERIMENTAL GROUP. *The group that receives the experimental treatment that is being investigated.*

EXTRASENSORY PERCEPTION. *The study of thought transference and mental telepathy.*

FACE VALIDITY. *Validity that is established on an intuitive basis.*

FACTOR. *A statistically derived measure of the degree to which different kinds of scores actually are measuring the same characteristic.*

FACTOR ANALYSIS. *A statistical procedure for ordering the correlation matrix. See Matrix, Correlation.*

FEEDBACK. *The channeling of impulses or communications to a control center, from which future output can be regulated.*

FIGURE AND GROUND. *The contrast between the center of attention and the background against which it is projected.*

FREQUENCY CURVE. *A curve that describes how frequently different scores occur in a given distribution. See Distribution.*

FRUSTRATION. *The state occurring when an individual cannot achieve a goal or reduce tension.*

GESTALT PSYCHOLOGY. *The school of psychology that emphasizes the study of wholeness and principles of organization.*

GROUP BEHAVIOR. *The activities that are characteristic of human collectivities.*

GUIDANCE COUNSELING. *The giving of advice to the individual about the vocations for which he is best suited.*

HIERARCHY. *The arrangement of psychological characteristics in terms of an organization of ascending complexity.*

HOMEOSTASIS.
The maintenance of a system within narrow limits of toleration by an appropriate system of controls.

HYPOTHESIS.
A set of tentative relationships that is tested by experimental methods.

ID.
The unconscious aspect of the individual containing primitive, unexpressed desires and motivations.

INDEPENDENT VARIABLE.
The variable that is manipulated directly by the experimenter.

INFORMATION THEORY.
The theory that describes the influence of noise on the transmission of information. See *Noise.*

INGROUP.
The group to which the individual belongs and with which he identifies.

INPUT.
The information fed into a communication channel.

INTELLIGENCE QUOTIENT (IQ).
The relation between the individual's mental and chronological age.

INTERACTION PROCESS ANALYSIS.
A method of analyzing the interaction in group situations in terms of twelve general categories.

JOB ANALYSIS.
A study determining the components or elements that describe a job.

LEARNING.
A relatively permanent modification of behavior produced by training, activity, or observation.

LIFE SPACE.
The individual's perception of himself in his environment at any given moment.

MATRIX.
An orderly arrangement of numbers made in such a way that all possible pairs of numbers are compared.

MATRIX, CORRELATION.
A table that shows all possible correlations between a given set of scores.

MULTIDIMENSIONAL ANALYSIS.
An analysis that studies the effects that a number of different variables have on each other.

MULTIPLE-CHOICE TEST.
A test consisting of items that require the individual to select the correct answer from a number of alternate responses that are presented.

NATURALISTIC OBSERVATION.
Observation of behavior occurring under normal, nonexperimental conditions.

NEGATIVE CONDITIONING.
Conditioning of the avoidance of a response that the individual is used to making.

NEURAL CIRCUIT.
An arrangement of nerve fibers or cells that forms a completed pattern.

NOISE.
In communications theory, noise is taken to be any distracting or irrelevant sound or source of distortion in the communications channel.

NONDIRECTIVE THERAPY.
That kind of therapy in which the therapist helps the client to formulate his own problems and arrive at his own solutions with a minimum of direct influence.

OBJECTIVE TESTS.
Tests that are scored by a fixed set of rules.

OPERANT CONDITIONING.
A certain response of the individual is rewarded according to a fixed schedule of reinforcement.

PARAPSYCHOLOGY.
That branch of psychology concerned with psychic phenomena.

PARSIMONY, PRINCIPLE OF.
The use of the simplest possible explanation for a given scientific phenomenon.

PHENOMENOLOGY.
The study and analysis of direct perceptual experience as an end in itself.

PLACEBO.
A control that is used in studies of the effect on experimental subjects of nonactive solutions or pills (such as sugar pills) of similar appearance to the drug being studied.

PROBABILITY. *The likelihood that a given event will occur simply by chance.*

PROGRAM. *A set of discrete logical steps that guide the operations of a machine such as an electronic computer.*

PROGRAMMING. *Writing a program that tells a machine how to perform a given procedure.*

PROJECTIVE TEST. *A standard set of ambiguous stimuli to which the subject is asked to react.*

PSYCHOANALYSIS. *A method for the treatment of mentally disturbed patients originated by Freud. Particular emphasis is placed upon free association, the analysis of dreams, and the re-creation of earlier childhood patterns within the therapeutic situation.*

PSYCHODYNAMICS. *The underlying psychological causes of behavior.*

PSYCHOKINESIS. *The study of the influence of psychic processes on physical events, such as the effect of wishing for a certain die face to appear.*

PSYCHOLOGY. *The science dealing with behavior.*

PSYCHOPHYSICS. *The relation between the physical stimulus and the psychological sensation as reported by the individual perceiver.*

PSYCHOTHERAPY. *Any method used to treat mentally ill persons by psychological means.*

RANDOM GROUP. *A group whose composition has been determined by only chance factors.*

RANGE. *The difference between the highest and lowest score on any test.*

REINFORCEMENT. *A reward that is provided for particular behavior.*

ROLE.

The behavior of a person occupying a certain social status.

ROLE PLAYING.

A method of teaching and therapy involving the acting of assigned roles in order to diagnose and correct faulty role behavior.

RORSCHACH INK BLOT TEST.

A set of standard inkblots that are used as a projective test. See *Projective Test.*

SENSORY DEPRIVATION.

The experimental elimination of various sensory channels.

STATISTICS.

Mathematical procedures based on probability analysis that are used to aid in the analysis of research data.

STATISTICAL REGRESSION.

The likelihood that a given extreme score will be nearer the average value of the group if it is measured again.

THEMATIC APPER-CEPTION TEST (TAT).

A projective test consisting of a set of ambiguous pictures of people in various situations. The subject is asked to tell a story about each of the pictures.

THEORETICAL PSYCHOLOGY.

Psychology that is concerned primarily with the formulation of general theoretical principles.

TYPOLOGY.

The classification of a given domain into a limited number of systematically derived classes.

VALIDITY.

The extent to which a given test actually is measuring the variables that it is supposed to measure.

VARIABLES.

The special characteristics that are studied in a given experiment.

Suggestions for Further Reading

CHAPTER ONE

Flaherty, B.E. (ed.), *Psychophysiological Aspects of Space Flight.* New York: Columbia University Press, 1961.

Sells, S.D., and Berry, C.A. (eds.), *Human Factors in Jet and Space Travel—A Medical-Psychological Analysis.* New York: Ronald Press, 1961.

CHAPTER TWO

Berkeley, E.C., *The Computer Revolution.* New York: Doubleday, 1962.

Borko, H. (ed.), *Computer Applications in the Behavioral Sciences.* Englewood, New Jersey: Prentice-Hall, 1962.

CHAPTER THREE

Coulson, J.E. (ed.), *Programmed Learning and Computer Based Instruction.* New York: Wiley, 1962.

Fry, E., *Teaching Machines and Programming.* New York: McGraw-Hill, 1963.

Green, E.J., *The Learning Process and Programmed Instruction.* New York: Holt, Rinehart, and Winston, 1962.

CHAPTER FOUR

Attneave, Fred, *Applications of Information Theory to Psychology.* New York: Holt, Rinehart, and Winston, 1959.

Gagné, R.M. (ed.), *Psychological Principles in Systems Development.* New York: Holt, Rinehart, and Winston, 1962.

CHAPTER FIVE

Anderson, H.H. (ed.), *Creativity and Its Cultivation.* New York: Harper, 1959.

Getzels, J.W., and Jackson, P.W., *Creativity and Intelligence.* New York: Wiley, 1962.

CHAPTER SIX

Heywood, R., *Beyond the Reach of Sense: An Inquiry into Extra-Sensory Perception.* New York: E.P. Dutton, 1961.

West, D.J., *Psychic Research Today.* London: Camelot Press Ltd., 1954.

CHAPTER SEVEN

Leary, T., *Interpersonal Diagnosis of Personality.* New York: Ronald Press, 1957.

CHAPTER EIGHT

Biderman, A.D., and Zimmer, H., *The Manipulation of Human Behavior.* New York: Wiley, 1961.

Frank, J.D., *Persuasion and Healing.* Baltimore: Johns Hopkins Press, 1961.

Schein, E.H., Schneier, I., and Barker, C.H., *Coercive Persuasion.* New York: Norton, 1961.

INDEX

Index

abilities, 195, 203, 209, 211, 212, 218, 273
absolute magnitude, 213
achievement, 204, 213
adaptive flexibility, 159
adjustment, 211–212, 215, 216–217
advertising, 234–235, 240, 252
affection, 225
aggressive-sadistic behavior, 220
Allport-Vernon Study of Values, 237
altruism, 273
American Psychological Association, 102
analogue computers, 59, 73–74
animals, 45–46
Annual Review of Psychology, 23
applied psychology, 14–15, 17, 153, 231, 235, 267
aptitude, 204, 227, 228
aptitude tests, 152, 212, 214–215, 226
architects, 160–162
Armed Forces, 267
Army Alpha intelligence test, 236
Asch, Solomon, 49–50
aspiration, 220
astronauts, 233 ff.
attitudes, 236, 238, 248–249, 253–261
audio-visual display, 109
automation, 235, 271

Barrow, Frank, 159
basic psychology, 14–15, 17, 153, 230, 231, 235, 267
behavior, 199, 203, 209, 210, 217, 218, 219, 221, 229, 273; *see also* social behavior
behavior change, 229 ff.
behavior simulation, 72–82
behavioral content, 145, 146
biased dice, 184, 185, 189, 190
binary digits (bits), 114, 115, 125, 126, 130

Binet, Alfred, 141, 152
Blundin (PK subject), 187
body type, 210
Borgatta, Edgar, 205, 218
brain waves, 211
brainstorming, 158
brainwashing, 51, 231, 248–253
branching program, 92
British Society of Psychical Research, 168–169, 194
business psychology, 4, 10

Carrington, Whately, 178
Carter, Launor, 205
catharsis, 266
Cattell, Raymond, 204, 207
cerebral cortex, 211
channel capacity, 115
checker-playing machine, 78
chimpanzee, Ham, the, 45
clairvoyance, 173
CLASS, 108, 109
class products, 146
clinical interview, 32, 33
clinical psychology, 32–35, 39, 195–196, 229
cognition, 145, 147, 148, 149, 158, 163
common variance, 213
communication, 30, 57, 80–81, 111 ff., 120–125, 126 ff., 134–139, 220, 233, 248–249, 254, 255–261, 262
Communists, 250, 251, 252
competitive-narcissistic behavior, 220
Computer-based Laboratory for Automated School Systems, *see* CLASS
computers, 55 ff., 113, 133, 206, 227, 271
concept formation, 79–80
conceptual fluency, 158
confession, 250
conformity, 216, 217
conscious communication, 220

About the Author

JOHN MANN is an Associate Professor in the Graduate School of Arts and Sciences, New York University. His area of specialization is social psychology. Interested not only in the theoretical but also in the applied aspects of modern psychology, Dr. Mann has, during the past four years, acted as principal investigator for projects sponsored by the National Institute of Mental Health, the Russell Sage Foundation, and the Cerebral Palsy Association.

An active contributor to psychological literature, Dr. Mann has written many articles published in the technical journals of his field.

Dr. Mann now lives with his family in Pomona, New York.